"*The Generative Church* is a must-read for everyone who is involved in faith formation. The team of contributors that Cory Seibel has assembled for this book share detailed insights that each church needs to know for a time such as this."

—Ron deVries

Youth Ministry Catalyzer for the Christian Reformed Church in North America, Commissioned Pastor and Ambassador for Youth Unlimited (YU)

"As a former youth pastor, adult ministry pastor, lead pastor, and now denominational leader, I am convinced *The Generative Church* provides a clarion call to and rich theoretical frameworks for intergenerational ministry. These global scholars, practitioners, and authors articulate a hope for adults in the church to nurture, mentor, and empower rising generations. *The Generative Church* guides readers into constructs that will transform faith communities not only today, but also literally for generations to come."

—Daniel J. Hamil

Executive Director/CEO, North American Baptist Conference

"Dr. Seibel and the contributors to *The Generative Church* have given the church, particularly the Western church, a gift. This gift is not found only in the wisdom offered us by the authors, but by their vision of a church that promotes life and flourishing for all who will recognize God's kingdom at work in and through intergenerational community. *The Generative Church* offers an essential guide to embracing the intergenerational opportunity before us."

—Quentin P. Kinnison

Associate Professor of Christian Ministry, Chair of the Biblical & Religious Studies Division, Fresno Pacific University

"Nothing short of the future of the church. As a university president, I am invested in seeing the next generation flourish, find belonging and significance within their church communities. Accessible, well-written, and thought-provoking, *The Generative Church* is an important read for those of us in leadership who seek to empower future generations for the gospel of Christ."

—Melanie Humphreys

President, The King's University, Edmonton, Canada

"This rousing book is a collection of conversations that invite further conversation. Seibel opens with a call to intentionally invest in intergenerational interactions and each subsequent chapter offers stories, experience, and ideas that draw the reader ever deeper into that conversation. It will surely become a must-have addition to the bookshelves of all those exploring how to invest in the future generations of their worshipping communities. I certainly would like to talk some more."

—Murray Wilkinson

Growing Faith Enabler for the Church of England, UK

The Generative Church

The Generative Church

Global Conversations about Investing in Emerging Generations

edited by Cory Seibel

foreword by Malan Nel

WIPF & STOCK · Eugene, Oregon

THE GENERATIVE CHURCH
Global Conversations about Investing in Emerging Generations

Wipf & Stock
An Imprint of Wipf and Stock Publishers
199 W. 8th Ave., Suite 3
Eugene, OR 97401

www.wipfandstock.com

PAPERBACK ISBN: 978-1-5326-8180-6
HARDCOVER ISBN: 978-1-5326-8181-3
EBOOK ISBN: 978-1-5326-8182-0

Manufactured in the U.S.A. SEPTEMBER 13, 2019

This book is dedicated to the honor of all those who took an interest in us and guided us in the faith.

Contents

Contributors

Garth Aziz (PhD in practical theology, University of Pretoria) is senior lecturer in practical theology at the University of South Africa (UNISA). Ordained in the Baptist Church in Cape Town and serving currently at Waterkloof Baptist Church in Pretoria, Garth has served for more than two decades in some form of youth ministry in the Western Cape, South Africa.

Joseph Azzopardi (PhD candidate, Avondale College of Higher Education in New South Wales, Australia; masters in youth and young adult ministry, Andrews University, Berrien Springs, Michigan), a native of Canada, has served as a classroom teacher, school chaplain, and pastor of both rural senior congregations and an urban young adult congregation.

Anita Cloete (DDiac, University of South Africa) is an associate professor at the faculty of theology, Stellenbosch University in South Africa. She has teaching experience of sixteen years and her research focuses on media and religion, youth culture and spirituality. She has supervised sixteen masters and three doctoral students within the field of youth work.

Gareth Crispin (PhD candidate, Cliff College / University of Manchester) is lecturer in evangelism, mission and ministry at Cliff College, UK. He is a member of the Executive Committee of the International Association for the Study of Youth Ministry.

Kayle de Waal (PhD, University of Auckland) is head of the School of Ministry and Theology and senior lecturer in New Testament at Avondale College of Higher Education in New South Wales, Australia. He has published five books in the areas of first-century media culture, discipleship, and the book of Revelation. He also has twenty publications including book chapters and journal articles. His current research is focused on Paul's theology and the impact of globalization on the local church. He remains active in evangelism and leading mission trips with his family.

Darren Cronshaw (DTheol, University of Divinity) is pastor at Auburn Life Baptist Church in suburban Melbourne, head of research and professor of missional leadership with the Australian College of Ministries (Sydney College of Divinity), honorary chaplain at Swinburne University, and a chaplain in the Australian Army (Reserve).

Michael William Droege (PhD candidate, University of Pretoria; MA in theology, Drew Theological Seminary) is associate pastor at Wilson Memorial Church in Watchung, New Jersey, and a trainer-coach with Vibrant Faith.

Jan Grobbelaar (DTh in practical theology, Stellenbosch University) is affiliated with the Dutch Reformed Church in South Africa. He currently serves as facilitator of research and academic development at the Petra Institute for Children's Ministry; extraordinary researcher in the Unit for Reformed Theology and Development of the SA Society, North West University; research fellow in practical and missional theology for the University of the Free State, Bloemfontein; and researcher with the University of Pretoria's Centre for Contextual Ministry.

Wendell Loewen (DMin, Fuller Theological Seminary) is professor of youth, church, and culture and director of FaithFront at Tabor College in Kansas.

Ed Mackenzie (PhD in New Testament studies, University of Edinburgh) serves as a discipleship development officer in the Methodist Church of Great Britain and associate lecturer at Cliff College.

Malan Nel (DD, University of Pretoria) is currently extraordinary professor and a senior research fellow in practical theology at the University of Pretoria, South Africa. In 2012 he retired as director of the Centre for Contextual Ministry, which is housed within the university's Faculty of Theology and Religion. This ecumenical center, founded by Nel in 1992, still offers continuing theological training for pastors from a wide range of denominations and other Christian groups.

Cory Seibel (PhD, University of Pretoria) is a pastor at Central Baptist Church and affiliate professor at Taylor Seminary, both in Edmonton, Alberta, Canada. He previously served churches in Virginia and North Dakota and spent eight years as a full-time seminary professor.

Foreword

Malan Nel

I WANT to congratulate Dr. Cory Seibel and all the other authors who contributed to this vitally important publication. May his vision to get such a group of authors involved in this publication serve the purpose it was planned and prepared for in the near future. The generative church and intergenerativity is on so many agendas.[1] This is a timely and excellent contribution to this agenda.

When churches are doing well, one of the vital signs evident in such churches is an inclusive understanding of being the body of Christ on earth. This inclusivity is understood as encompassing all who are covenantally in Christ—who confess him to be Lord (cf. 1 Cor 12:3); but it also is inclusive as to gender and age. In practice, however, this vision is often not the case within the body of Christ. To argue that we have "lost the youth" is so often not true: we never had them. This is especially so when we see youth ministry chiefly as an investment in the future of a denomination.

It is a vital sign of healthy congregations that they have learned to say "we": "'We' is the word spoken most frequently in vital congregations," wrote Dick after his research among 719 congregations in the United Methodist Church.[2] This is a critical remark: for the church to become an inclusive body, the *M* of the *Me* must be converted (i.e., deeply changed) to the *W* of the *We*. This is a change that I have found in my research to be especially needed among the so-called "adult members" of the body. If Erikson—to whom Seibel refers in the introduction of this volume—is correct, then

1. While I use the concept *intergenerativity* in this foreword, it is not in any way meant to be construed in opposition to what is called *generative* in this publication. It is an attempt to sensitize and remind of a central truth in developing inclusive missional faith communities.

2. Cf. Dick, *Vital Signs*, 92.

developing *trust* is kind of normal for those who experience inclusive care by their basic caregivers in year one of life. Developing intergenerative sensitivity puts parental care and training central in developing such inclusive missional congregations. The developmental search in human beings is for acceptance; children and other young people want to be included. In a sense, only a sickly individualistic society prepares *me*-people who so easily exclude the *not-me*. This is even more troublesome in adult-minded societies where paternalism is still alive and well. And parents or other basic caregivers can do much to develop a different attitude—one where I am becoming a *we-person*.

This volume is a contribution toward becoming an inclusive intergenerative faith community. The volume as such does not focus on what I have tried elsewhere—to explore how we develop such faith communities. Or to say it differently: how do we facilitate the transformation to become an inclusive, missional, and intergenerative congregation? I tried to motivate such an attempt in my research on *Identity Driven Churches*.[3] This volume on the *Generative Church* provides excellent material to motivate well-informed intergenerative ministry. Without such good theological motivation any attempt to develop sustainable inclusive intergenerational ministry might prove to be short-lived. The leadership of any faith community would be wise to think through the Theoretical Conversations, the Contextual Conversations, and the Pastoral Conversations—to name the three parts of this book. This will benefit the development of what Seibel calls "the generative church."

What then is necessary to even start this transformation from what one sometimes might call adult-minded exclusivity to an inclusive and intergenerational philosophy of ministry? More than a foreword allows me to cover. A few remarks however might prompt further research among the scholars who participated in this volume. Let me immediately admit that nothing but a holistic understanding of "who we are as church of the Christ" will save the day for the process of developing intergenerative faith communities. This change lies on an attitudinal and perspectival level. It is indeed true that "Perception yields Behavior, yields Destiny."[4] And exactly this makes it so challenging. Osmer, referencing Quinn, wrote that "leading an organization through a process of 'deep change' in its identity, mission, culture and operating procedures" is critical for transformation.[5] In this volume, the authors of the different sections and chapters look at the many

3. Nel, *Identity Driven Churches*.

4. Cf. Callahan, *Twelve Keys Leaders' Guide*, 150.

5. Osmer, *Practical Theology*, 178; Quinn, *Deep Change*, 201.

angles implied in this deep transformation. My intention is not to discuss the content of their great contributions in any way but to prioritize a few critical starting points in furthering such transformation—in full appreciation for the six "core commitments" as quoted by Seibel in the introduction.[6]

Parents

In my doctoral work on Youth Evangelism, I already wrote that, if I could go back into congregational ministry, I would put 80 percent of my prime time into ministry with parents. The research and publication by Freudenburg and Lawrence was just a follow-up reminder that "parents are the primary Christian educators in the church, and the family is the God-ordained institution for faith-building in children and youth and for the passing of faith from one generation to the next."[7] We will be wise to empower parents as to our understanding of inclusivity and intergenerativity and equip them to develop people who understand the *we-ness* of being the body of Christ. In my book *Youth Ministry: An Inclusive Missional Approach*, I have argued for a Trinitarian understanding of ourselves as the body of Christ in our theological approach to youth ministry.[8] I quoted the remarkable reminder by Osmer (with reference to Moltmann): "He [*Moltmann*] grounds this ecclesiology in his social doctrine of the Trinity, which portrays the divine person perichoretically as existing in *centered openness*. They do not merely have their relationships; they *are* their relationships."[9]

Leadership

Getting the leadership together—bearing in mind the need for gender diversity and for including a balance of age groups—is essential. So too is helping them think through "what is going on and why is it going on."[10] An empirical approach may have more success in helping leadership change in attitude and perception—especially regarding the absence of youth in congregations and the reasons why! I once called it "registering their absence."

6. Powell et al., *Growing Young*, 25–27.

7. Freudenburg and Lawrence, *Family-Friendly Church*, 9.

8. Nel, *Youth Ministry*. A search of this text using "relationships" will take the reader to many sources concerning this critical theological departure point in youth ministry.

9. Osmer, "Formation in the Missional Church," 50–51.

10. Osmer, *Practical Theology*, 11ff.

Ministering toward Identity Discovery

God loves his people so dearly that we can trust him for helping us become who we already are in Christ (cf. Phil 3). Preaching, teaching, and all other ministries play tremendously important roles in discovering our true God-given identity.[11] The reason why these ministries may not be bearing the fruit of a rich understanding of, and appreciation for, this given identity is often twofold:

- The legalistic approach in ministry: continually reminding members of what they have not become yet, instead of reminding them of who they already are—because of what God did and is doing! The gospel helps one realize that what God did is far more important than what we have not become yet.
- A lack of intentionality in all ministries—with a clear and consistent focus on who we are. As Osmer once said: "Rediscovery is the activity of discerning once again the meaning and power of tradition that has been repressed or forgotten. Recovery goes further. It involves the positive evaluation and appropriation of that tradition, using what has been rediscovered to structure present patterns of thought and action."[12]

Once again, I applaud each of the authors who participated in this project. I consider myself blessed to be associated with this volume of essays on such a critical challenge—"*Investing in Emerging Generations*."

Malan Nel
June 2019

Bibliography

Callahan, Kennon L. *Twelve Keys Leaders' Guide: An Approach for Grassroots, Key Leaders, and Pastors Together*. San Francisco: Jossey-Bass, 2010.

Dick, Dan R. *Vital Signs: A Pathway to Congregational Wholeness*. Nashville: Discipleship Resources, 2007.

Freudenburg, Ben, and Rick Lawrence. *The Family-Friendly Church*. Loveland, CO: Vital Ministry, 1998.

Moltmann, Jurgen. *The Church in the Power of the Spirit: A Contribution to Messianic Ecclesiology*. San Francisco: Harper & Row, 1977.

11. Cf. Nel, *Identity Driven Churches*, 70ff.; Nel, *Youth Ministry*, 217–44.
12. Osmer, *Teachable Spirit*, 141.

———. *The Church in the Power of the Spirit: A Contribution to Messianic Ecclesiology.* Translated by M. Kohl. Minneapolis: Fortress, 1993.

Nel, Malan. *Identity Driven Churches: Who Are We and Where Are We Going?* Wellington, South Africa: BibleCor, 2015.

———. *Youth Ministry: An Inclusive Missional Approach.* HTS Religion and Society 1. Cape Town: AOSIS, 2018. https://doi.org/10.4102/aosis.2018.BK83.00.

Osmer, Richard R. "Formation in the Missional Church: Building Deep Connections between Ministries of Upbuilding and Sending." In *Cultivating Sent Communities: Missional Spiritual Formation*, edited by Dwight J. Zscheile, 29–55. Grand Rapids: Eerdmans, 2012.

———. *Practical Theology: An Introduction.* Grand Rapids: Eerdmans, 2008.

———. *A Teachable Spirit: Recovering the Teaching Office in the Church.* Louisville: Westminster John Knox, 1990.

Powell, Kara, et al. *Growing Young: 6 Essential Strategies to Help Young People Discover and Love Your Church.* Grand Rapids: Baker, 2016.

Quinn, Robert E. *Deep Change: Discovering the Leader Within.* San Francisco: Jossey-Bass, 1996.

Acknowledgments

I AM grateful for the ten authors who wrote chapters for this book. The completion of this project was possible thanks in large part to their willingness to contribute their effort and expertise. Working with authors from Australia, South Africa, England, and the United States has been an enriching and horizon-expanding experience. I am honored to have these fine scholars as colleagues and am glad to have had this excuse to collaborate with each of them.

I also wish to express my appreciation for Professor Malan Nel. Though he has recently entered the ninth decade of life, he continues to model a vital, earnest concern for today's children and youth. He is respected around the world as an accomplished practical theologian and as a leading voice among youth ministry scholars. It has been more than a decade since I completed my University of Pretoria PhD studies under his supervision. However, the investment he made in my development as a Christian scholar continues to influence me deeply, while the qualities he exemplifies remain an inspiration to me. It is a great honor to be able to include a foreword from Professor Nel in this volume.

This is a book about churches that invest in the lives of children and youth. It thus seems fitting to acknowledge the churches that played such a crucial role in my own formation as a Christian young person. I am grateful for First Baptist Church of Goodrich, North Dakota, and Bismarck Baptist Church in Bismarck, North Dakota. During my childhood and teenage years, these churches provided me the opportunity to learn about Jesus, follow him in baptism, grow in faith, and discern my life's calling. My memories of participating in the life of these congregations are precious to me. I am grateful for the adults who modeled a life of mature faith, took note of me, encouraged and affirmed what they saw God forming in me, and invited me to take my first steps in ministry. Over the years, I have come to recognize more and more how deeply my journey has been affected by the important investments that these people made in my life during those critical early years.

I also must express my gratitude for Central Baptist Church, a congregation that I have served as pastor for more than six years now. This 120-year-old congregation has continued to have a significant impact locally, regionally, and globally throughout several generations. I know how blessed I am to be serving within such a healthy and vibrant congregation. I love working with the other members of our staff and am especially grateful for our Emerging Generations Team, a passionate and creative group of leaders who are on the front lines of nurturing the next generation in the faith. I am learning a lot as we experiment, learn, and grow together. Attempting to keep one foot in pastoral ministry and one foot in the world of academia is not always easy; I am so thankful that Central Baptist has been willing to permit me to carve out this sort of vocational space.

Some of the ideas outlined in this book's introductory and concluding chapters were first tested in a series of seminars I presented at Alberta Baptist Association churches across our province. I am grateful for the churches that hosted these seminars and for the participants who came out to discuss their shared commitment to invest in the members of rising generations. Thanks to our regional minister, Dr. Terry Fossen, for providing this opportunity and to the ABA's Leadership Development Team for partnering with me in this endeavor.

Finally, I am especially thankful to my family. I am fortunate to have grown up within a family that carries a multigenerational legacy of faith. I have been shaped profoundly by growing up in such an environment. I also am thankful for the interest and encouragement my family has shown toward my activities as a researcher, writer, and pastor. I am especially grateful for my wife, Teresa, and for my teenage daughter, Savannah. I am blessed daily by their love and support.

Cory Seibel

Introduction

Introducing the Generative Church

Cory Seibel

Investing in Younger Generations

In the fall of 2016, after several months of searching, a museum in Ohio finally located a time capsule that had been created by a local Episcopal church 150 years earlier. The church originally had enclosed this time capsule in the cornerstone of its building in 1866 but removed it a hundred years later while the structure was undergoing renovations. Some church members who were around at that time recalled that the capsule had been handed over to the local historical society. When they went looking, however, no one could find it.[1]

Before the time capsule was sealed in 1866, the collection of items placed within it included some historical records and a gold coin. The most intriguing item, and perhaps the centerpiece of the time capsule's contents, was a check addressed to "generations yet unborn." While a bank would never recognize this check as valid, it still held great value. It reflected this church's commitment to invest in the future in ways that would have a lasting impact for generations to come.

Those who first opened the capsule a century and a half later were surprised to discover that several items were missing.[2] Most noteworthy was the absence of the check written to future generations. Somewhere along the way, someone had decided to remove this item. At the time when this story

1. Bahney, "Church Anniversary."
2. Bahney, "Church Discovers Pieces."

was reported in the local newspaper, the question of what happened to the check remained a mystery. It was believed to be lost to history.

This story provides a fitting metaphor to describe a struggle that is being experienced within many churches today. While few churches have ever literally written a check to "generations yet unborn," virtually every congregation—at some point in its history—has identified making an investment in succeeding generations as an important priority.

Howard Vanderwell argues that this commitment is integral to every congregation's true calling. Noting that the church's ongoing witness and vitality is made possible by "the faithful work of Christ and the powerful work of the Spirit," he adds that "there is also a third consideration":

> Because the church will and must continue, each generation must shape the next generation so that each will know of God's mighty acts. The interplay of the generations in reminding each other of the truth of the gospel and the acts of God is an indispensable element of the continuation of the church. . . . When Ethan the Exrahite proclaims in Psalm 89, "I will sing of your steadfast love, O Lord, forever; with my mouth I will proclaim your faithfulness to all generations" (Ps. 89:1), he seems to have in view a people of God who continue through the generations because each age tells the next. So the continuation of the Christian church in society will depend on the faithfulness of the Christ who builds and protects the church, the Holy Spirit who empowers it to reach out, and the generations that form and teach each other.[3]

Properly understood, adults' efforts to help children and youth become established in the faith should not be motivated by a self-interested impulse to survive. As one Anglican vicar expresses, the reason for this commitment "isn't because we want to guarantee ourselves a future."[4] Instead, it is because of our confidence that God wishes to accomplish good purposes in the lives of these children and youth and through them as a generation. As this vicar asserts, "We are committed to young people because Jesus Christ came, taught, healed, suffered, died, and rose again for every single one of these young people."

Despite their best intentions, some churches manage to lose track of this mandate over time. Just as few have likely penned checks to future generations, few churches come to a definitive moment when they decide to suspend their efforts to invest in the generations that come after them. In

3. Vanderwell, "Biblical Values," 27–28.

4. Quoted in Crawford, "Church and Youth."

many cases, this commitment simply becomes misplaced as the adults of the church focus their energies on a host of competing priorities. Without church members necessarily even noticing this has occurred, the determination to influence rising generations can become outrightly lost.

Evidence seems to suggest that this commitment has indeed gone missing in many congregations today. One source providing such evidence is Thom Rainer's book *Autopsy of a Deceased Church*. Rainer makes the troubling claim that roughly "100,000 churches in America are showing signs of decline toward death."[5] He devotes his book to summarizing the insights he gained from conducting fourteen "church autopsies" in his work as a church consultant. Over time, each of these churches had suffered what he describes as "slow erosion." As Rainer explains, "Growth may come rapidly, but decline is usually slow, imperceptibly slow. This slow erosion is the worst type of decline for churches, because the members have no sense of urgency to change. They see the church on a regular basis; they don't see the gradual decline that is taking place before their eyes."[6]

In the churches he studied, Rainer discovered several common indicators of decline. The list of patterns that he identified includes the following:

1. They developed an unhealthy preoccupation with the past.[7]
2. They were not concerned to reflect the demographic makeup of their communities.[8]
3. Their budget became focused on their own interests.[9]
4. They lost sight of the priority of making disciples.[10]
5. They became driven by their own preferences.[11]
6. They lacked a clear purpose.[12]

These facets of the *slow erosion* experienced within many churches are sure to hinder any congregation's capacity to invest in emerging generations. Rainer notes this outrightly at a couple of key points in *Autopsy of a Deceased Church*.[13] Slowly but surely, the members of the churches he

5. Rainer, *Autopsy of a Deceased Church*, 7.
6. Rainer, *Autopsy of a Deceased Church*, 12–13.
7. Rainer, *Autopsy of a Deceased Church*, 17–23.
8. Rainer, *Autopsy of a Deceased Church*, 25–30.
9. Rainer, *Autopsy of a Deceased Church*, 31–37.
10. Rainer, *Autopsy of a Deceased Church*, 39–45.
11. Rainer, *Autopsy of a Deceased Church*, 47–53.
12. Rainer, *Autopsy of a Deceased Church*, 71–76.
13. For example, in his chapter entitled "The Church Refused to Look Like the

studied had managed to misplace their commitment to impact the generations coming after them. As a result, these congregations, like so many others with similar stories, have themselves been lost to history.

At the same time, it is encouraging to recognize that there are many vibrant congregations today that intentionally prioritize rising generations. In *Growing Young*, Kara Powell, Jake Mulder, and Brad Griffin summarize the findings from a Fuller Youth Institute study conducted among churches with a proven track record of investing in youth and young adults.[14] They note that the qualities needed for a church to "grow young" are not necessarily what we might assume them to be.[15]

Instead, they found six "core commitments" to be widely evident among churches that have proven most effective at engaging rising generations:

1. They empower young people to take an active and meaningful role within the life of the church rather than exercising centralized control.
2. They demonstrate empathy toward young people instead of judging and criticizing.
3. They welcome the young into "a Jesus-centered way of life" rather than expecting them to accept "formulaic gospel claims."
4. They seek to foster "warm peer and intergenerational friendship" instead of focusing on "cool worship or programs."
5. They do not merely give "lip service to how much young people matter"; instead they "look for creative ways to tangibly support, resource, and involve them in all facets" of the church's life.
6. They enable young people to "neighbor well" both locally and globally, rather than "condemning the world" beyond the walls of the church.[16]

A commitment to invest in rising generations is an important facet of the work to which the church has been called. Yet we can see that, within

---

Community," Rainer describes how some churches lose touch with the younger families within their communities (26). In the chapter "The Preference-Driven Church," he explores how churches' determination to serve their own "preferences" limits their effectiveness in engaging younger adults (48).

14. Powell et al., *Growing Young*, 25–27.

15. They specifically note the following ten characteristics which their research has led them to conclude are *not* essential for churches to "grow young": a precise size; a trendy location or region; an exact age; a popular denomination or lack of denomination; an off-the-charts cool quotient; a big modern building; a big budget; a "contemporary" worship service; a watered-down teaching style; a hyper-entertaining ministry program (Powell et al., *Growing Young*, 25–27).

16. Powell et al., *Growing Young*, 43.

any given local church, ongoing fidelity to this calling over time is not guaranteed. Some churches remain actively committed to this goal. Others lose sight of it and cease to act in ways that are faithful to it. The insights provided by Rainer and the Fuller Youth Institute team highlight for us how essential it is for churches to be intentional in their efforts to make a difference in the lives of the members of younger generations.

Introducing Generativity

This book is devoted to exploring what it means for churches to exercise intentionality in investing in rising generations. Its title is influenced by the work of the twentieth-century developmental psychologist Erik Erikson.[17] Erikson coined the term *generativity* to describe an "interest in establishing and guiding the next generation."[18] I am intrigued by the potential this term holds as a way of talking about the church. We could say that a *generative church* is one that demonstrates an active commitment to establish and guide the next generation in the faith. This book's title is inspired by a desire to explore what might be learned when we connect *generativity* and *church* in this way. It will be important, therefore, for me to unpack this connection further. Before returning to this focus later in this chapter, however, I first will set the stage for an exploration of congregational generativity by summarizing several key points from Erikson and others who have written insightfully about this concept in the context of human development.

To grasp how Erikson viewed the significance of generativity, we first must understand how he envisioned human development. Erikson conceived of the life course as involving a person's progression through a series

17. While Erikson's work has been widely influential, it is important to acknowledge that it also has been subject to critique. For example, in *Aging as a Spiritual Journey*, Eugene Bianchi offers these observations about the "male bias" in Erikson's work: "Erikson tends to apply his categories of intimacy and generativity with a male focus. For him, female adulthood is defined less by participation in the world of work than by the cultivation of 'inner space.' These observations, especially in a time of changing roles for men and women, warn us to be leery of psychological ideologies. How easy it is to accept the status quo as the essential and necessary pattern for a particular gender" (Bianchi, *Aging as a Spiritual Journey*, 29). While it is good to recognize that concerns have been raised about Erikson's work, we also must note that even many of Erikson's critics still engage appreciatively with his theories and find value in his overall contribution. Indeed, after providing a lengthy summary of the criticisms lodged against Erikson's work, Gilleard and Higgs proceed to argue in their article "Connecting Life Span Development with the Sociology of the Life Course" that Erikson's work offers important insight not only for developmental psychologists, but also for sociologists of the life course (301–15).

18. Erikson, *Identity: Youth and Crisis*, 138.

of developmental stages. During each of these stages, one is confronted with a specific developmental *task* native to that season of life. Through the person's efforts to face and resolve the challenges inherent in this task, he or she develops certain strengths. As Evelyn Eaton Whitehead and James Whitehead explain, "These essential strengths become habitual attitudes and consistent behavior in one's character."[19] Appropriating terminology from the Aristotelian tradition, Erikson described these strengths, developed through one's engagement with the challenges of life, as *virtues*.

According to Erikson, generativity becomes the central developmental task a person faces as he or she progresses into middle adulthood. The development of this capacity to invest in younger generations factored prominently in Erikson's understanding of the life course. In assessing Erikson's work, Don Browning suggests that generativity "is the normative center of Erikson's thought."[20] Browning claims that, while Erikson may actually have said less about this stage of development than any other, he saw it as constituting the very "center of life."

For Erikson, *care* is another way of describing the core virtue developed during this stage of life. Adults develop the capacity to care by being responsive to—and responsible for—the needs of the young.[21] The virtue of generativity, thus, entails a "broadening of concern" that absorbs the adult's inclination to prove and express oneself into a capacity to give of oneself for the sake of others.[22] In fact, suggests Browning, *love* as understood historically within the Christian tradition might actually be an appropriate synonym for what Erikson had in mind when he spoke of *care*.[23]

As these initial observations reflect, generativity is inherently intergenerational. This is perhaps obvious but is important enough that it needs to be stated. As Daniel Levinson explains, one's development of generativity is rooted in a budding attentiveness to "the flow of generations" and "concern for the upcoming generation."[24] Takatoshi Imada similarly notes that generativity necessitates "generational exchange," the "passing of that which is valued from one generation to the next."[25]

19. Whitehead and Whitehead, *Christian Life Patterns*, 32.

20. Browning, *Generative Man*, 181.

21. Whitehead and Whitehead, *Christian Life Patterns*, 120, 124.

22. Whitehead and Whitehead, *Christian Life Patterns*, 131, 120.

23. Browning, *Generative Man*, 194.

24. Levinson, *Seasons of a Man's Life*, 254.

25. Imada, "Generativity as Social Responsibility," 83–95.

While generativity entails interaction between the members of two or more generations, this can be expressed in a variety of contexts and roles.[26] For Erikson, parenthood served as the ultimate archetype of generativity. Parenthood "manifests dramatically many elements of the larger psychological challenge" posed during the middle adult season of life.[27] Yet the ability to be generative is not limited solely to those who are parents. Erikson noted that "there are people who, from misfortune or because of special and genuine gifts in other directions, do not apply this drive to offspring but to other forms of altruistic concern and of creativity, which may absorb their kind of parental responsibility."[28] Thus, while "generativity questions" arise within the family, they also surface in the workplace and in one's civic activities.[29]

Generativity can be exercised through "teaching, mentoring, leadership, and a host of other activities that aim to leave a positive legacy of the self for the future."[30] The commonality in all of these contexts is that adults adopt "a personally appropriate style" of expressing care and exercising influence to help pave the way for a better future.[31] As James Loder articulates, a generative persons aims to "set the standard for the future and reach the younger generation," yet approaches this task "with his or her own feelings and sensitivities derived from his or her past history."[32] Regardless of whether they are teachers, leaders, or mentors, generative adults are guided by a sense of purpose and spirit of initiative that leads them to invest their skills and energies for the benefit of emerging generations.[33]

According to Erikson, the foundation for one's capacity to be generative is laid during earlier stages of life.[34] He saw the root of generativity as being the love one receives throughout one's earliest formative years, which later is transformed into the care one is able to give to others in adulthood.[35] In addition, as one progresses into young adulthood, his or her "resources of intimacy" begin to emerge; this growing capacity to foster relationships

26. Capps, *Decades of Life*, 133, 139.
27. Whitehead and Whitehead, *Christian Life Patterns*, 121.
28. Erikson, *Identity and the Life Cycle*, 97.
29. Whitehead and Whitehead, *Christian Life Patterns*, 33.
30. De St. Aubin et al., "Generative Society," 4.
31. Whitehead and Whitehead, *Christian Life Patterns*, 123, 121.
32. Loder, *Logic of the Spirit*, 290.
33. Browning, *Generative Man*, 185.
34. Browning, *Generative Man*, 157.
35. Quoted in Browning, *Generative Man*, 194.

of intimacy in turn sets the stage for the emergence of one's "generativity resources" that develop fully during middle adulthood.[36]

Why does this formation during earlier stages have such bearing upon the development of generativity later in life? Dan McAdams and Regina Logan explain that "once a person has a clear sense of who he or she is (identity) and has established a relationship of intimacy, then he or she is psychologically ready to focus energies on promoting the well-being of the next generation."[37] Browning's response to this question also provides helpful insight: "And because he [*sic*] has within himself a workable identity and a sense of what is trustworthy in himself and in life, generative man can present himself to succeeding generations as a tangible identity from whom they can learn and against whom they can test their own emerging self-definitions. He can also present himself as one who can be trusted, just as he can help guide others to their own discovery of that which is worthy of their commitment and loyalty."[38]

Another important facet of Erikson's view of human development is his understanding that, in each life stage, development is a process by which opposing extremes are, to some degree, resolved and integrated.[39] For Erikson, the opposition with which a person must grapple during middle adulthood is one between the impulses of generativity and *stagnation*, between one's generative and self-centered inclinations.[40] Whitehead and Whitehead emphasize that this is a decisive and critical time in one's life:

> Some resolution must be reached. The person may decide not to face this new challenge, not to deal with the new questions raised. . . . But there is no reprieve. To choose not to face a new developmental challenge is to choose not stasis but stagnation. The "strengths" of earlier stages of development remain so only as they are tested and transformed at later stages. Without this subsequent transformation, earlier strengths atrophy into defended or immature responses.[41]

For many adults, the tension between generativity and stagnation will be manifested in the form of a *crisis*. As Whitehead and Whitehead explain, "For some, this will be a period of conflict, stress, and disorientation. For many, however, the developmental struggle of this period will not manifest

36. Whitehead and Whitehead, *Christian Life Patterns*, 87.

37. McAdams and Logan, "What Is Generativity?," 17.

38. Browning, *Generative Man*, 193.

39. Levinson, *Seasons of a Man's Life*, 30.

40. Whitehead and Whitehead, *Christian Life Patterns*, 32.

41. Whitehead and Whitehead, *Christian Life Patterns*, 31.

itself as a 'crisis' in this sense. But it will remain, in Erikson's more technical sense, a crisis: 'a critical step—critical being a characteristic of turning points, of moments of decision between progress and regression, integration and retardation.'"[42] This echoes Browning's description of the human journey toward mature generativity as one "punctuated by a series of confrontations with the darker, more destructive dimensions of life." Generativity, he posits, "is born out of a series of confrontations with mistrust, doubt, limitation, powerlessness, and confusion."[43]

Erikson cautioned that it would be an error to reduce our understanding of human development to only its positive dimensions and thus fail to appreciate the importance of the negative components. As Whitehead and Whitehead observe, "The negative impulses that are released in each of the stages of adult development—impulses toward isolation, self-concern, resentment, and doubt—'are and remain the dynamic counterpart.'"[44] The goal of each developmental stage, then, is not to eradicate those dimensions that are seen as undesirable. Instead, "Lasting strengths of the adult personality result from the balance of both positive and negative impulses in a ratio that is appropriate to the individual and consistent with his or her life commitments."[45]

Erikson's term for this is *synthesis*. As Browning expresses, "A virtue is always a matter of synthesis. It refers to the ego's capacity to gain a favorable synthesis out of the positive and negative dimensions of life's developmental crises and nuclear conflicts."[46] He adds that a virtue can be described as an "active capacity for synthesis which enables one to take due account of the negative aspects of each of these nuclear conflicts while still tilting the crisis in favor of the positive."[47]

Erikson's concept of synthesis provides an important clarification to help us grasp the relationship between generativity and stagnation. As Levinson observes, "Both generativity and its opposite pole, stagnation, are vital to a man's development. To become generative, a man must know how it feels to stagnate—to have the sense of not growing, of being static, stuck, drying up, bogged down in a life full of obligation and devoid of self-fulfillment. He must know the experience of dying, of living in the shadow

42. Whitehead and Whitehead, *Christian Life Patterns*, 34; this quote includes a citation from Erickson's *Childhood and Society*, 270–271.

43. Browning, *Generative Man*, 180.

44. Whitehead and Whitehead, *Christian Life Patterns*, 45; this quote includes a quote from Erickson's *Childhood and Society*, 274.

45. Whitehead and Whitehead, *Christian Life Patterns*, 46.

46. Browning, *Generative Man*, 160.

47. Browning, *Generative Man*, 160–61.

of death."[48] It is essential that this impulse toward stagnation not be permitted to prevail; rather, it must be allowed to propel one toward living generatively. Otherwise, as Donald Capps cautions, "when stagnation prevails, there is a self-constriction: no life, no vitality flows out of oneself into that which has been generated."[49]

A key facet of generativity's focus on the next generations is "handing on the tradition."[50] Generative adults play an important role as "keepers of the meaning,"[51] those who strive to pass on their understanding of "the good" to the members of rising generations.[52] Browning explains the importance of this by noting that all persons, "most especially young people," are in need of a belief system to support and provide substance to their identity.[53] Generative adults thus fulfill an essential function through their efforts to connect rising generations to their most cherished cultural questions and traditions.[54] As they do so, they endeavor to impart to the next generation a coherent, cohesive heritage.[55]

While the goal of handing on tradition is an important aspect of what it means to be generative, it also is frequently a source of tension. As McAdams and Logan express, "It is not easy to pass on the good from one generation to the next."[56] They note that this is true in part because of the various forces at work within society that work against the transmission of tradition. However, "generativity tensions" also sometimes arise as a result of the differences in perspective and values that exist between young and old.[57] Kai Erikson notes that "the lessons one generation is prepared to pass on to the next are, by definition, attuned to realities that are very likely to change at least a little by the time the new generation has replaced the old."[58] As a result, younger generations may react against their elders by insisting

48. Levinson, *Seasons of a Man's Life*, 30. Levinson's use of masculine pronouns reflects his book's focus on the developmental journey of adult males. While his insights reflect that focus, his observations about generativity have relevance for all adults.

49. Capps, *Decades of Life*, 126.

50. Whitehead and Whitehead, *Christian Life Patterns*, 148.

51. De St. Aubin et al., "Generative Society," 6; the authors include a quote from George Vaillant.

52. McAdams and Logan, "What Is Generativity?," 26.

53. Browning, *Generative Man*, 167.

54. De St. Aubin et al., "Generative Society," 8.

55. Whitehead and Whitehead, *Christian Life Patterns*, 170.

56. McAdams and Logan, "What Is Generativity?," 26.

57. Imada, "Generativity as Social Responsibility," 89.

58. Kai Erikson, "Reflections on Generativity and Society," 52.

that times have changed and by expressing their desire to focus on addressing problems that the older generations "have not even thought of."[59]

Generativity thus entails "a balancing act" between continuity and change.[60] The generative person must be willing to "enter into an extended, intense, and often agonizing dialogue with succeeding generations."[61] This may involve helping the members of the rising generation decide which traditional values to retain and which new values they might need to adopt. The young must be empowered "to participate in the generation and regeneration of cultural forms that aim to promote the advancement and well-being of future generations."[62] Generativity thus requires that the ties adults maintain to the past remain "flexible."[63]

A mark of maturity for the generative adult, therefore, is the ability to "let go." The generative adult will be more concerned with *care* than with *control*.[64] A technical term for this posture is *detachment*; as Whitehead and Whitehead explain, "Detachment is that peculiar virtue that allows one to let go of control."[65] For generative adults, there are at least three key dimensions to this *letting go*. First, they learn to let go of the members of the next generation progressively over time. The goal of caring for the next generation is not to create relationships of ongoing dependence, but rather to nurture a child's movement away from dependence upon them as he or she matures into adulthood.[66] Generative adults are concerned to support the members of the next generation as they form their own identities.[67] Over time, however, they must wrestle with "how to 'hold on' appropriately as long as needed and how to 'let go' appropriately as soon as needed."[68] Letting go thus means championing the members of the next generation without taking undue responsibility for their destiny.[69]

Second, generative adults also possess a capacity to let go of the tradition they have sought to pass along to the next generation. As Whitehead and Whitehead express, "As 'traditioners,' rather than reproducing the next

59. Loder, *Logic of the Spirit*, 284.
60. McAdams and Logan, "What Is Generativity?," 20.
61. Browning, *Generative Man*, 188.
62. De St. Aubin et al., "Generative Society," 8.
63. Browning, *Generative Man*, 186.
64. Imada, "Generativity as Social Responsibility," 94.
65. Whitehead and Whitehead, *Christian Life Patterns*, 150.
66. Whitehead and Whitehead, *Christian Life Patterns*, 120.
67. Imada, "Generativity as Social Responsibility," 93.
68. Whitehead and Whitehead, *Christian Life Patterns*, 122.
69. Whitehead and Whitehead, *Christian Life Patterns*, 123.

generation in our image and thus repeating ourselves, we gradually turn over to the next generation our society. . . . The challenge of mature generativity is to trust in the generational process, for certainly the next generation will alter what we hand on to them."[70] While each generation does its best to impart its values and traditions to the next generation, in truth, as Imada notes, there is little benefit in "controlling or demanding adherence to the preceding generation's values and institutions," because each new generation "will adopt or reject the values of the preceding generation" in the course of developing its own identity.[71] Generative adults, then, develop the capacity to trust "the potential of the next generation" and "to share with the next generation the control of the present and the design of the future."[72]

Finally, letting go is ultimately about releasing control of the future. Whitehead and Whitehead capture this poignantly: "In its responsible resignation, the senior generation can release the next generation from its own domination without leaving scars of exploitation and control. The next generation is left free to face the future in its own way, but supported by the strengths of a vital heritage whose validity is affirmed in the vigor of its elders."[73] Maturity in generative adults entails the awareness that, most truly, what is let go is "the illusion that I can control my world." Generative adults thus can let go of what has been generated—their cherished values and traditions and the members of the younger generation—without becoming cynical or bitter.[74]

It is crucial to note that, while the members of rising generations clearly profit in significant ways from the generative investments of adults, Erikson emphasized that the benefits of the intergenerational interplay between adults and youth do not merely flow in one direction. To express this, he employed the term *cogwheeling*. This colorful term describes the interconnectedness and interplay between the generations.[75] Reflecting upon this concept, Kathleen Calahan explains that individuals at different stages in life "connect with and draw forth capacities of those at another stage. For example, the child's need for care draws out the mother's generative need for caregiving. . . . A child's abilities and strengths 'dovetail' as they interlock with the abilities and strengths of people 'arranged around' her."[76] In other

70. Whitehead and Whitehead, *Christian Life Patterns*, 148–49.
71. Imada, "Generativity as Social Responsibility," 93.
72. Whitehead and Whitehead, *Christian Life Patterns*, 132.
73. Whitehead and Whitehead, *Christian Life Patterns*, 122.
74. Whitehead and Whitehead, *Christian Life Patterns*, 132.
75. Miller-McLemore, "Childhood," 56.
76. Calahan, "Calling over a Lifetime," 19.

words, there is a mutuality of dependence and benefit in the relationship between young and old. Both have an active role to play and an essential contribution to offer one another.[77]

As noted above, some adults fail to transition into generative maturity. Whitehead and Whitehead observe that this may occur for a variety of reasons: "I may be reluctant to move beyond the security of my intimate world. I may see my children or the works of my hands as possessions or simply as confirming signs of my own worth. I may resist the demands and inconveniences of social responsibility. I may be unable to nurture without control."[78]

The results of this failure are unfortunate, even tragic. As Whitehead and Whitehead express, "If fear or self-centeredness blocks my impulse to participate in the social world, the result can be growing self-absorption. The resources of personality appropriate to this stage of adult maturity become atrophied and a sense of boredom and personal stagnation set in."[79] Browning describes the outcome in equally regrettable terms: "Individuals who fail to achieve this delicate synthesis which generativity demands often become 'stagnated' and 'begin to indulge themselves as if they were their own—or one another's—one and only child.'"[80]

There is a discernable parallel between what we have explored here with reference to maturing adults and what was stated earlier in this chapter about congregations: both possess the potential for investing in younger generations, but both sometimes also choose to resist this aim and fall into stagnation. The concept of generativity helps us to understand this struggle within the human life course. I would like to suggest that employing generativity as a category for thinking about the life of the church also has the potential to provide us with valuable insight into the experiences of congregations today.[81] But in order to explore this premise, we will need to broaden

77. Capps, *Decades of Life*, 127.

78. Whitehead and Whitehead, *Christian Life Patterns*, 122. Donald Capps suggests another reason why an individual may experience stagnation—"namely, the situation in which an older adult's need to be needed by one or more members of the younger generation is not reciprocated by those who are younger. . . . Erikson's emphasis on the older adult's need to be needed by members of the younger generation suggests that this lack of reciprocity is most conducive to stagnation not when it originates from members of one's own generation but from members of the younger generation. Thus, the generativity vs. stagnation conflict is the most self-evidently *intergenerational* of all conflicts" (Capps, *Decades of Life*, 127).

79. Whitehead and Whitehead, *Christian Life Patterns*, 122.

80. Browning, *Generative Man*, 163.

81. As noted previously, there are those who object to aspects of Erikson's work or who discount it categorically. Our intentions here are not to defend Erikson's program

our discussion of generativity and shift its focus from the individual life course to the shared life of congregations.

Extending the Discussion

This is not the first time an attempt has been made to broaden how the concept of generativity is applied. While Erikson's work on generativity focused largely on its importance within the development of human persons, with time others have sought to explore the implications of generativity for contexts beyond the individual life course. The chief example of this is the book *The Generative Society: Caring for Future Generations*, edited by Ed de St. Aubin, Dan P. McAdams, and Tae-Chang Kim. These authors acknowledge that social institutions play an important role in the discussion of generativity because adults "express generativity in social contexts and through social institutions." This is certainly true of the church. One chapter in their book reports that generativity in adults is "positively associated with church attendance and with involvement in church activities."[82]

The central aim of *The Generative Society*, however, is to extend the horizon of the discussion of generativity by exploring "how social institutions themselves, and even societies writ large, may or may not function in generative ways."[83] This shifts the discussion of generativity away from the middle-aged adult by placing the focus upon institutions and their communal character. This effort to appropriate the language of generativity as a way of investigating the life of social institutions resonates deeply with the issues raised here regarding local churches' efforts to invest in rising generations. Indeed, *The Generative Society* provided the spark of inspiration for this introductory chapter of *The Generative Church*. In this book, I essentially am setting out to explore what it means for a specific social institution—namely churches—to function, or not function, in generative ways.

---

in its entirety. While providing an overview of key theoretical concepts developed by Erikson has been essential for developing our argument here, the validity of this argument is not contingent upon making a case for Erikson's work overall. Rather, we are seeking to engage one key concept developed by Erikson and to explore its potential utility for the church.

82. McAdams and Logan, "What Is Generativity?," 22. Whitehead and Whitehead similarly argue that it is important for a church "to provide both the expectation and the structure for . . . a transition to generative leadership in its adults." When this is not permitted, "the community will be deprived of a healthy variety of ministers" and "the handing on of the faith" is imperiled" (Whitehead and Whitehead, *Christian Life Patterns*, 140).

83. De St. Aubin et al., "Generative Society," 5.

The Generative Society argues convincingly that, for an institution to realize its generative potential, intentionality is essential. John Kotre speaks to this in his chapter on "Generativity and Culture." He notes that "no culture is permanently generative"; instead, cultures "have their moments—moments to which they rise, moments from which they fall."[84] Even when institutions value generativity in principle, it is not guaranteed that they will operate in generative ways. This certainly is consistent with what I noted earlier about local churches. As the Fuller Youth Institute's research demonstrates, many churches could be described as flourishing generative institutions. Others struggle in this regard. As Rainer's research highlights, some churches have lost their generative impulse nearly altogether. While *The Generative Society* can help us begin to develop a framework for thinking about the immense generative potential that local churches possess, it also enables us to appreciate that the actualization of this potential requires intentionality. This accentuates one of the hopes underlying *The Generative Church*.

The authors of *The Generative Society* suggest that, in our contemporary context, "We have little by way of language, little by way of a comfortable discourse for expressing generative inclinations."[85] As we contemplate the implications of this statement for the life of the church, we can recognize that a wealth of resources is available to aid churches in describing and discussing their hopes for the members of rising generations. There is no shortage of books, training seminars, and other resources dedicated to helping churches talk about their efforts to impact the children, youth, and young adults within the orbit of their influence. Nonetheless, many churches continue to struggle to find common language to talk meaningfully about the intentional investments they are striving to make in the lives of young people.

Resources like the Fuller Youth Institute's *Growing Young* are excellent aids for churches desiring to undertake these conversations.[86] My hope is that this book also has a distinctive contribution to make. By harnessing the language of generativity as a way of talking about the church, and by inviting engagement with the diverse perspectives reflected here, I hope to help concerned parties within local congregations, denominations, and theological schools engage in fruitful conversation about their collective *generative inclinations*.

84. Kotre, "Generativity and Culture," 35–49.

85. De St. Aubin et al., "Generative Society," 7.

86. The list of other helpful resources that could be referenced here is certainly too lengthy to mention. Two books that I have found particularly valuable are Dori Grinenko's *Greenhouses of Hope* and Nick Shepherd's *Faith Generation*.

Introducing the Generative Church

What might it mean for a local church to be generative? The chapters that follow will help us explore this question from a variety of cultural, methodological, and theological perspectives. Thus, it would be counterproductive for me to attempt to provide a comprehensive or systematic answer at this point. I nonetheless will outline a few initial observations to set the stage for what lies ahead. My aim in offering these thoughts is not to place constraints on this discussion and thereby prematurely *shut down* conversation, but rather to *open up* the discussion by providing some indication of its focus, parameters, and substance.

Contemplating the local church in conversation with the description of generativity provided earlier in this chapter can help us identify a handful of important themes. This is not meant to suggest that Erikson's thought should be allowed to function authoritatively or frame the agenda for the church. Rather, the purpose of this exercise is to reflect theologically on ideas introduced earlier in the chapter and attempt to tease out whatever helpful parallels might be identified between Erikson's concept of generativity and the communal life of the church. This is merely a creative thought experiment—an extended analogy—to help us begin exploring generativity within the congregational context.

Much as Erikson identified the development of generativity in adult persons as a virtue, there is a sense in which we can also understand the presence of generativity within the church as a matter of virtue.[87] In *A Community of Character*, Stanley Hauerwas makes a compelling case for thinking about the church as a community that is enabled by God to grow in virtue as its life is shaped by the biblical narrative.[88] Thus, while the active expression of congregational generativity certainly requires intentionality, congregations that evidence a vital commitment to generativity recognize that they do so not chiefly as a duty or a strategy, but as an outflow of God's transformative grace; they "are surprised and grateful to be graced with the strengths that allow them to love well and to care for what they and others have generated."[89]

87. In making this statement, I admittedly am playing with words somewhat. There certainly is not complete correspondence between how Erikson employed the term "virtue" and the meaning with which this term has been invested historically within the Christian ethical tradition. I do not mean to suggest that these two meanings should be conflated. Rather, I am merely seeking to connect them analogously.

88. Stanley Hauerwas, *Community of Character*.

89. Whitehead and Whitehead, *Christian Life Patterns*, 43.

As with adult persons, this commitment to care for the young constitutes the very heart of the virtue of generativity within the church. As Capps expresses, God cares, so we should too;[90] thus, he concludes, we should be moved to invest emotionally in the next generation.[91] Consistent with Hauerwas's approach, the generative church's efforts to care for the next generation are guided by a distinctively Christian vision of what it means to do so. Whitehead and Whitehead argue that this vision calls the church to be built up as a "loving and just community, while handing on the faith to the next generation."[92] It challenges adults within the church to relate to the next generation with a "peculiar and difficult combination of care and detachment, formed by faith in God's presence in the world." It provides church members a sense of purpose that moves them to engage in "action for others" steeped in the Christian vision.

I noted above that generativity is expressed by adults in a variety of ways and in a variety of contexts. Congregational generativity also is inherently contextual. Generativity does not merely entail "importing" successful strategies or programs developed elsewhere into the local church. Instead, generative churches take their contexts seriously as they strive to invest in the lives of specific young people in specific times and places. They seek to engage with the particular social, cultural, and historical circumstances that impact the daily lives of the members of rising generations for whom they care. As a result, while congregational generativity is sure to entail dynamics of teaching, mentoring, and other key activities, these will be expressed in distinct ways in different settings.

Much as generative adults develop a *personally appropriate style* that enables them to invest their skills and abilities for the benefit of the next generation, each generative church also learns to express generativity according to its own appropriate style. Generative churches are not plagued by a sense of inferiority or insecurity that drives them to compete with or mimic other ministries. Instead they endeavor to invest in the younger people who have been entrusted into their care in ways that are faithful to their congregational size, character, and God-given *charisms*. They may take steps to develop skills and competencies that enable them to express their generative inclinations more effectively.[93] However, the focus of these skills and competencies will be to help them more fully and more faithfully

90. Capps, *Deadly Sins and Saving Virtues*, 100.

91. Capps, *Deadly Sins and Saving Virtues*, 58.

92. Whitehead and Whitehead, *Christian Life Patterns*, 135.

93. Browning, *Generative Man*, 191; Whitehead and Whitehead, *Christian Life Patterns*, 45.

express the virtue of generativity within the concrete realities of their own congregational life, rather than to become something they are not.

The ability of adults to be generative is due in part to their prior development of identity and intimacy. Something similar can be said of churches. A church's capacity for generativity flows from its awareness of its identity as a community that is loved by Christ, invited to live in fellowship with him, and called to share this love with others. The sufficiency of this love—and the security of identity that it provides—liberates and invigorates generative churches to live in ways that prioritize the purposes of God's kingdom. Those who experience a vital connectedness to the love of Jesus through the Holy Spirit will be eager to share this love with the members of emerging generations. One might even posit that any church that has lost sight of its calling to be generative also likely has lost sight of its true identity in, and intimacy with, Christ.

Erikson observed that adults frequently experience the challenge of generativity as a crisis. This often is true of churches, as well. Concerted efforts to engage the members of younger generations sometimes cause crises to arise among adult churchgoers. They must wrestle with the implications of these efforts for their own valued traditions, comfort levels, and preferences. In truth, the struggle to be generative within the church stands in opposition to the impulse toward stagnation, as it does for adult persons. Capps draws a connection between stagnation and the "deadly sin" of apathy.[94] He cautions that stagnation leads to an inability to invest emotionally in younger generations or to sustain an interest in them. He writes of it as a "spiritual withdrawal" from the member of rising generation characterized by indifference toward them. When stagnation is allowed to gain a foothold, asserts Capps, the consequences are harmful not only for adults, but also for the younger people for whom we have been called to care.[95]

Over the course of its life cycle, every congregation will contend at times with the forces of stagnation at work in its midst.[96] A congregation's awareness of this prospect can serve as a reminder of its need for ongoing renewal. In reliance upon God's Holy Spirit, generative churches thus foster a capacity to experience renewal, to remain vital, and to stay focused upon

94. Capps, *Deadly Sins and Saving Virtues*, 59.

95. Capps, *Deadly Sins and Saving Virtues*, 63.

96. While there are many excellent resources dedicated to explaining the tendency toward stagnation within churches, I find Alan Roxburgh and Fred Romanuk's exposition of this topic in chapter 3 of *The Missional Leader* especially compelling and enlightening. Roxburgh and Romanuk describe the points in a congregation's life cycle where it is likely to be prone to fall into stagnation and provide a framework for intervention and renewal.

their shared purpose. By God's grace, these churches successfully resist falling into an irreversible state of stagnation.

Much like generative adults, generative churches strive to impart to their children and youth a vital tradition. In an article I coauthored with Malan Nel, I reflect on this point:

> The importance of the church's intergenerational calling presents it with the challenge of perpetuating its faith tradition from one generation to the next. Leith (1990:34, 36) views this as involving a process of "traditioning," which entails the incorporation of "each new person and generation" into the community of faith. The church, as a bearer of tradition, endeavours to provide a setting in which individuals might gain a vital experience of faith and an authentic sense of identity and in which successive generations might be incorporated into the Christian tradition.[97]

As in other arenas of human experience, churches often find this *traditioning* process to be a source of difficulty. Much has been written throughout recent decades about the challenges that cultural change has posed for the transmitting of tradition generation-to-generation within the church. Rather than fighting to preserve a particular expression of the Christian tradition, generative congregations recognize that the process of traditioning is "dynamic, with change as an inherent characteristic and asset."[98] The generative congregation thus is willing to engage in an ongoing process of "fluid traditioning," which requires that "members understand themselves not only as 'receivers' of tradition, but also as makers of future tradition."[99]

Generative churches also recognize their need to welcome the members of younger generations into active participation in this process of *fluid traditioning*. In the article I coauthored with Nel, I describe why this is important:

> The congregation should be willing to empower each rising generation with the freedom to make their distinctive mark upon the shape of that tradition. Kraft (2005:247) puts it as follows: "It is crucial that each new generation and people experience the process of producing in its own cultural forms an appropriate church vehicle for the transmission of God's meaning." In

97. Seibel and Nel, "Generation X." This quotation contains a reference to Leith's *From Generation to Generation*.

98. Seibel and Nel, "Generation X."

99. Seibel and Nel, "Generation X"; quotation includes references to concepts drawn from Diana Butler Bass's *Practicing Congregation*.

> essence, the continual process of fluid traditioning must be seen as having an intergenerational trajectory. . . . If a congregation's members truly consider their corporate witness of primary importance and intend for it to endure beyond their own life span, they must be willing to set aside their personal preferences about church to enable "a new ethos to be born."[100]

Like adults, generative congregations thus know that they must be willing to let go. They are enabled to do so because they are grounded in trust in the faithfulness of God. This allows them to surrender their illusions of control and to be filled with a confident hope for the future.

Finally, much as Erikson's concept of *cogwheeling* expresses, within generative churches, the intergenerational interactions between young and old are understood to be mutuality beneficial. In *Youth Ministry: An Inclusive Missional Approach*, Malan Nel cautions that conceiving of youth merely as "the church of the future" is a fallacy.[101] Because many young people already are part of the body of Christ[102] and are endowed with gifts for ministry, it is unhelpful to draw a distinction between "generative churches" and "youth" as though these are somehow separate categories. Generative churches recognize that young people already have a valid, vital contribution to make within the life of the congregation. They too can be generative!

This being said, Chap Clark notes that, while all people within the church "are siblings—children of the same Father, whether they are eighty or fifteen years old," those members who are more mature and who possess greater influence "must take the lead" in caring for, including, empowering, and nurturing the faith development of those who are vulnerable.[103] Clark argues that this principle "obviously applies" to youth and children. Generative congregations understand this. They recognize that, while younger persons are already capable of contributing meaningfully to the life of the church, mature members also bear a special responsibility to invest in the development of the children and youth God has entrusted into their care.

100. Seibel and Nel, "Generation X"; quotation includes references to Kraft, *Christianity in Culture*, and Thompson, *Treasure in Clay Jars*.

101. Nel, *Youth Ministry*, 195.

102. This statement reflects the assumptions of the Baptist ecclesiology from which I operate, one that emphasizes confession of faith and baptism by immersion as essential steps toward full inclusion in the church's membership. Adherents to other theological positions—including some of the authors who contributed to this volume—would see, and thus express, this point quite differently. The diversity of views on this point is covered well in Harwood and Lawson, *Infants and Children in the Church*.

103. Clark, "Adoption," 3.

An Invitation to Conversation

The remainder of this book represents an effort to explore various facets of generativity as a characteristic within local churches. I shared this introductory chapter with each of the authors included in this volume and invited them to contribute something to this discussion from their own work. The chapters that follow contain their responses. While they employ the language of generativity to varying degrees, their chapters are included here because they have something of value to offer our understanding of what it means for congregations to invest in rising generations. At the beginning of each chapter, I provide a brief introduction in which I identify how I see its contents contributing to this discussion.

The remainder of this book is divided into three sections:

- Part 1—Theoretical Conversations: This section includes five chapters that invite us to explore important theoretical issues with which any church striving to invest in rising generations must grapple. The authors of these chapters draw upon a diverse range of theological and sociological resources. While some of these authors reflect upon the practical implications of their ideas, they all offer theoretical insights that are broadly applicable to churches in a variety of contexts.
- Part 2—Contextual Conversations: In this section, two authors contribute chapters in which they wrestle with realities they face within their own contexts—one a South African and the other an American. Like the previous section of book, these chapters include some rich theoretical reflections. However, they also model thoughtful wrestling with the challenges that accompany efforts to invest in the members of rising generations within specific cultural settings. These chapters are sure to provide you with fresh insights that will help you in contemplating your own context.
- Part 3—Pastoral Conversations: The final section of this book is composed of two deeply insightful chapters with clear pastoral implications. These chapters will provide ministry leaders with much to think about in their own personal journeys and in their practice of ministry.

Rather than attempting to provide a systematic overview, the chapters that follow represent diverse perspectives. The authors whose work is included in this volume come from five different countries and a variety of Christian traditions. As you read through their chapters, you may identify tensions in the viewpoints the authors articulate. Rather than trying to harmonize these perspectives, I have chosen to entertain the diversity of the various voices reflected here. My desire in doing so is that you will receive this book as an invitation to conversation. There is a place for your voice in this conversation, too. With this in mind, I include a set of discussion questions following each chapter. I hope that you will take the opportunity to discuss this material with others.

I trust that the diversity of perspectives captured within the pages of this book will stimulate your imagination and help you to see new possibilities for what the virtue of generativity might look like in your congregation. May this volume inspire you with fresh insight into how your church might make lasting investments in rising generations of children and youth.

Bibliography

Bahney, Jennifer. "Church Anniversary Shines Light on Missing Time Capsule." *Circleville Herald*, August 11, 2016. https://www.circlevilleherald.com/news/church-anniversary-shines-light-on-missing-time-capsule/article_7d59fce2-bb3d-570e-9f44-e63858295f5b.html.

———. "Church Discovers Pieces of Missing Time Capsule." *Circleville Herald*, October 25, 2016. https://www.circlevilleherald.com/news/church-discovers-pieces-of-missing-time-capsule/article_c0083e35-b20e-5ba1-b7fb-c09cda3b9c1c.html.

Bass, Diana Butler. *The Practicing Congregation: Imagining a New Old Church*. Herndon, VA: Alban Institute, 2004.

Bianchi, Eugene C. *Aging as a Spiritual Journey*. New York: Crossroad, 1982.

Browning, Don S. "An Ethical Analysis of Erikson's Concept of Generativity." In de St. Aubin et al., *Generative Society*, 241–55.

———. *Generative Man: Psychoanalytic Perspectives*. New York: Westminster, 1975.

Calahan, Kathleen A. "Calling over a Lifetime: In Relationship, through the Body, over Time, and for Community." In Calahan and Miller-McLemore, *Calling All Years Good*, 12–32.

Calahan, Kathleen A., and Bonnie J. Miller-McLemore, eds. *Calling All Years Good: Christian Vocation throughout Life's Seasons*. Grand Rapids: Eerdmans, 2017.

Capps, Donald. *Deadly Sins and Saving Virtues*. Minneapolis: Augsburg Fortress, 1987.

———. *The Decades of Life: A Guide to Human Development*. Louisville: Westminster John Knox, 2008.

Clark, Chap, ed. "Adoption—Reenvisioning Youth Ministry and the Family of God." Introduction to *Adoptive Youth Ministry*, 1–8.

———. *Adoptive Youth Ministry: Integrating Emerging Generations in the Family of Faith*. Grand Rapids: Baker, 2016.

Crawford, Geoff. "Church and Youth: 'If Someone Said Come to Church I Would Have Laughed.'" *Church Times*, February 9, 2018. https://www.churchtimes.co.uk/articles/2018/9-february/features/features/church-and-youth-if-someone-said-come-to-church-i-would-have-laughed.

De St. Aubin, Ed, et al., eds. *The Generative Society: Caring for Future Generations*. Washington, DC: American Psychological Association, 2004.

———. "The Generative Society: An Introduction." In de St. Aubin et al., *Generative Society*, 3–13.

Erikson, Erik H. *Identity and the Life Cycle*. New York: International Universities Press, 1959; republished by Norton, 1980.

———. *Identity: Youth and Crisis*. New York: Norton, 1968.

Erikson, Kai. "Reflections on Generativity and Society: A Sociologist's Perspective." In de St. Aubin et al., *Generative Society*, 51–61.

Fowler, James W. *Becoming Adult, Becoming Christian: Adult Development and Christian Faith*. San Francisco: Jossey-Bass, 2000.

Gilleard, Chris, and Paul Higgs. "Connecting Life Span Development with the Sociology of the Life Course: A New Direction." *Sociology* 50 (2016) 301–15.

Grinenko, Dori, ed. *Greenhouses of Hope: Congregations Growing Younger Leaders Who Will Change the World*. Herndon, VA: Alban Institute, 2010.

Harwood, Adam, and Kevin E. Lawson, eds. *Infants and Children in the Church: Five Views on Theology and Ministry*. Nashville: Broadman & Holman Academic, 2017.

Hauerwas, Stanley. *A Community of Character: Toward a Constructive Christian Social Ethic*. Notre Dame: University of Notre Dame Press, 1981.

Imada, Takatoshi. "Generativity as Social Responsibility: The Role of Generations in Social Continuity and Change." In de St. Aubin et al., *Generative Society*, 83–95.

Kotre, John. "Generativity and Culture: What Meaning Can Do." In de St. Aubin et al., *Generative Society*, 35–49.

Levinson, Daniel J. *The Seasons of a Man's Life*. New York: Ballantine, 1978.

Loder, James E. *The Logic of the Spirit: Human Development in Theological Perspective*. San Francisco: Jossey-Bass, 1998.

McAdams, Dan P., and Regina L. Logan. "What Is Generativity?" In de St. Aubin et al., *Generative Society*, 15–31.

Miller-McLemore, Bonnie J. "Childhood: The (Often Hidden yet Lively) Vocational Life of Children." In Calahan and Miller-McLemore, *Calling All Years Good*, 38–62.

Nel, Malan. *Youth Ministry: An Inclusive Missional Approach*. Cape Town: AOSIS, 2018.

Powell, Kara, et al. *Growing Young: 6 Essential Strategies to Help Young People Discover and Love Your Church*. Grand Rapids: Baker, 2016.

Rainer, Thom S. *Autopsy of a Deceased Church: 12 Ways to Keep Yours Alive*. Nashville: Broadman & Holman, 2014.

Roxburgh, Alan J., and Fred Romanuk. *The Missional Leader: Equipping Your Church to Reach a Changing World*. San Francisco: Jossey-Bass, 2006.

Seibel, Cory, and Malan Nel. "Generation X, Intergenerational Justice and the Renewal of the Traditioning Process." *HTS Teologiese Studies / Theological Studies* [online] 66 (2010).

Shepherd, Nick. *Faith Generation: Retaining Young People and Growing the Church*. London: SPCK, 2016.

Vanderwell, Howard. "Biblical Values to Shape the Congregation." In *The Church of All Ages: Generations Worshiping Together*, 17–33. Herndon, VA: Alban Institute, 2008.

Whitehead, Evelyn Eaton, and James D. Whitehead. *Christian Life Patterns: The Psychological Challenges and Religious Invitations of Adult Life*. New York: Crossroad, 1992.

Part One

Theoretical Conversations

1

Some Theological Perspectives on Generativity

Jan Grobbelaar

§

EDITOR'S INTRODUCTION: The description of generative congregations provided in the introduction to this volume suggests that "the generative church's efforts to care for the next generation are guided by a distinctively Christian vision of what it means to do so." In other words, the conversation about the generative church is an inherently *theological* enterprise. Our vision of guiding the next generation in the faith, if it is to be faithful to God's true intentions, must be rooted in the testimony of Scripture. Grobbelaar's chapter is a great aid to us in this regard. He provides a thorough, penetrating account of the call to generativity within the pages of Scripture. Generativity, Grobbelaar helps us to appreciate, begins with who God is and constitutes an integral dimension of who God has created us to be as human beings. The biblical vision he sketches out is expansive, yet deeply accessible. It challenges us to contemplate the long-term impact of our present attitudes and actions—an impact that shapes the current generations of children and youth who have been entrusted into our care and that stretches into the future. This chapter invites us to listen carefully to the voice of Scripture, to allow our imagination to be shaped by its counsel, and to welcome the instruction and inspiration it provides to live more fully generative lives.

§

An Important Question

The title of this book, *The Generative Church*, raises an important question: Is the term "generativity" a theological concept or not? It is not so easy to give a clear answer to this question. Perhaps, the only answer to give at the beginning of this chapter is the ambiguous answer of both "No" and "Yes." Therefore, this chapter is a search to get more clarity on answering this question.

The "No" Answer

No, generativity is not a theological concept. It is not an expression used in the Scriptures. The term originates as a psychosocial concept, coined by Erik Erikson in his work on human development. In his book *Childhood and Society*, published in 1950, Erikson formulated a new theory on the human life course, which he called "eight stages of man."[1] According to Erikson, the long midlife of adults, the seventh stage, is the phase of generativity. He defines this as "primarily the interest in establishing and guiding the next generation."[2] Generativity can be linked to concepts like genesis, generate and generator, generous, and even regenerate. All these terms share the idea of "life-giving." It refers to the ability to produce, create, originate, procreate, be fruitful, or give birth. The generativity construct possibly implies three kinds of actions or behavior: "creating, maintaining, and offering."[3]

According to Erikson, generativity is the central developmental task for people in middle adulthood, usually starting around their early thirties when they are more settled in the adult world,[4] when they start to develop a "parental kind of responsibility" toward the younger generations.[5] It is in this stage of their lives that people become more and more interested in questions about what they will leave behind when they depart from this life or what their legacy for the next generation will be. It is in midlife that we

1. Erikson, *Childhood*, 219–34.
2. Erikson, *Childhood*, 231.
3. McAdams et al., "Anatomy of Generativity," 25.
4. Bach, "Culture of Generativity," abstract.
5. Erikson, *Childhood*, 231.

discover a "desire to invest one's substance in forms of life and work that will outlive the self."[6]

Generativity, thus, is a concern about the well-being of the next generation, about caring, nurturing, loving, blessing, cultivating, preserving, assisting, guiding, teaching, mentoring, raising, protecting, parenting—in short, about adults' responsibilities toward the succeeding generations. It is also about adults "generating: creating and producing things, people, and outcomes that are aimed at benefiting, in some sense, the next generation, and even the next."[7] It is, therefore, not just a concern, but a commitment to beneficiary acts toward the coming generations and the world they will live in.

Engaging in generative acts as a developmental task in midlife improves the psychological health and well-being of the adult actors themselves, and of the children who receive the benefits of these practices.[8] Generativity evokes mutuality. It enhances life for both the generative adult and the receiver of generativity. In this sense, the unique characteristic of generativity is its other-orientedness. It is a development in the adult's life away from focusing on the self to a focus on the well-being of other people, especially the younger generations.

But the concept of generativity is about much more than only the midlife developmental task that arises in every adult's life. "Generativity is a concept that links the individual and society."[9] It also includes generativity on the levels of society and culture—communal generativity—because "adults express generativity in social contexts and through social institutions. Generativity is shaped by political, economic, religious, and cultural forces."[10] Therefore, McAdams, Hart, and Maruna concurred: "There are generative people, generative situations, and generative societies."[11]

It is this aspect of generativity that confronts every society and social institution with some crucial questions: Are we interested in and concerned about the next generation? Do we contribute to the well-being of future generations or not? How do we improve or hinder their well-being? These are questions that also concern the church. Does the church function, live, and act in ways that enhance the spiritual growth and welfare of the next generations? Even more, does the church improve their lives holistically? Is

6. Kotre, *Outliving the Self*, 10.

7. McAdams et al., "Anatomy of Generativity," 7.

8. McAdams, "Redemptive Self," 81–100.

9. Friedman, "Erik Erikson on Generativity," 258.

10. De St. Aubin, "Generative Society," 5.

11. McAdams et al., "Anatomy of Generativity," 7.

the church genuinely generative? Even more probing, will there be Christian faith communities for the generations to come, and will there be a sustainable world for them to live in? Will the church outlast our current generation? This question is vital because the church is always only but a generation away from being extinguished.[12] Furthermore, in the light of the growing ecological crisis of our world, do we provide enough eco-care to God's creation to outlast our current generation?

Thus, to be generative is very important for being the church. Acknowledging this fact brings us to the point of considering the possibility that the concept generativity is, perhaps, also a theological concept.

The "Yes" Answer

Yes, the above question can also be answered with a "Yes." Generativity is much more than just a psychosocial concept. Don Browning wrote:

> Even since writing *Generative Man* (1973, 1975), I have believed that Erikson's concept of generativity was more than a psychological construct that defines the nature of adult maturity. . . . I have been convinced instead that it was a mixed concept that artfully interwove psychological, ethical, and even metaphysical levels of discourse. . . . I also have held the conviction that his idea of generativity was philosophically defensible from an ethical point of view, even though Erikson never attempted to test it from that perspective.[13]

In light of this statement by Browning, it is possible to see generativity also as a concept in which theological levels of discourse are interwoven. In general, "the most powerful discourses for generativity may come from the great religious traditions."[14] Surely, Christianity can be a constructive partner in any discourse on generativity. Generativity, as described in the above section, calls forward various Christian themes. It is loaded with a great quantity of theological implications.

Enshrined in generativity is an ethic of selfless care for other people, which was expressed at its best in the life, work, and teachings of Christ. Erikson even stated: "We recognize the perfection of charity in the words of Jesus . . . against the background of the last passion."[15] The heart of Er-

12. Wiersbe, foreword to *Children's Ministry Resource Bible*, v.

13. Browning, "Ethical Analysis," 241.

14. De St. Aubin et al., "Generative Society," 7.

15. Erikson, *Insight and Responsibility*, 151.

ikson's ethics and his view of generativity is the principle of the Golden Rule.[16] Describing his ethical view, Erikson wrote: "My baseline is the Golden Rule, which advocates that one should do (or not do) to another what one wishes to be (or not to be) done by [another]."[17] Although Erikson is of the opinion that the basic formulation of the Golden Rule is a universal concept expressed in many religions and many great sayings by highly esteemed people,[18] he states that the core of the Golden Rule is very much incorporated in Jesus's admonition to "love thy neighbor as thyself."[19] Against this background, we can declare with Dillon and Wink that "from a Western theological perspective, the ultimate generative act may be seen in Jesus Christ dying on the cross so that through his death and redemption humankind could have eternal life."[20] Jesus's death on the cross was the ultimate life-giving generative act for this world. Through his teachings and ministry, through his life and death, through his resurrection, Jesus made—generated—real life and a new world for all human beings.

Being generative sounds so much like the gospel. Although Erikson did not use generativity as a theological concept, we may consider using the construct Christian or theological generativity. Generativity was a new concept in Erikson's time, but the idea behind this concept was not new. The notion of generativity is quite old. It is very much present in the Bible. To such an extent that it is impossible to discuss in this chapter all the scriptural content that evokes the idea of generativity, this discussion will only attend briefly to some perspectives from the Bible. It will start right at the beginning because generativity is already present on the first pages of the Bible.

The Biblical Creation Story in Genesis 1:1—2:3

The intention of this discussion is not to do an in-depth exegetical study of the biblical Creation Story. It will rather attend only to those perspectives relevant for the topic under discussion.

16. Erikson, *Insight and Responsibility*, 217–43.
17. Erikson, *Insight and Responsibility*, 220.
18. Erikson, *Insight and Responsibility*, 221.
19. Erikson, *Insight and Responsibility*, 221, see 232–33.
20. Dillon and Wink, "American Religion," 153.

In the Beginning, God . . .

The book of Genesis starts with this gripping statement: "In the beginning, God created . . ." (Gen 1:1 ESV). In the Hebrew tradition, the phrase "in the beginning" became the name by which this book was known. The name "Genesis" comes from the Greek. Its meaning is "origins." Although the Creation Story provides a description of the origins of everything that exists, the emphasis in this sentence is not on the beginning, also not on what is created, but rather on God, the Creator. The biblical Creation Story in Genesis 1:1—2:3 deliberatly starts with God as the subject of this story. Actually, the word "God" dominates the whole story and is used thirty-five times.[21] By using the generic Hebrew word *ĕlōhîm*, and not the personal name *Yahweh*, to refer to God, "God's universality as creator and his [*sic*] transcendent power over all things"[22] is emphasized. Israel's God is not one god among many other creators as in the other Near Eastern creation stories. The God of Israel is the only living Creator. The term *create*, used forty-six times in the Old Testament,[23] is constantly used with God as the agent.[24] It underlines the fact that only Israel's God created everything. Indeed, God is the central figure in this whole Creation Story. Genesis 1:1—2:3 stresses the fact that the whole creation is God's work and everything that exists is dependant upon God.

The biblical Creation Story is not a scientific theory or a formulation of a doctrine, nor a history report about the origin of our universe.[25] It is so much more. It rather expresses a faith statement written in a poetic narrative form[26] or a praising song[27] like the creation psalms,[28] most probably for liturgical usage.[29] Provan confirms this view, saying that the Creation Story was written in a liturgical style and has a liturgical "feel."[30] It is a credo stating clearly Israel's faith that the Creator is the one and only God of the whole creation.[31] In the context of the ancient Near East where the nations

21. Kidner, *Genesis*, "Prologue"; Wenham, *Genesis 1–15*, "In the Beginning—Form/Structure/Setting."

22. Kissling, *Genesis*, "1:1 In the Beginning God."

23. Kissling, *Genesis*, "Created."

24. Kidner, *Genesis*, "Prologue."

25. O'Connor, *Genesis*, "Translation Challenges of Genesis 1:1."

26. Brueggemann, *Genesis*, 22.

27. O'Connor, *Genesis*, "Poetic Narrative."

28. O'Connor, *Genesis*, "Creation Psalms."

29. Brueggemann, *Genesis*, 22; Day, *From Creation*, 5.

30. Provan, *Discovering*, 75, 78.

31. Speiser, *Genesis*, "Comment."

worshipped immanent gods, Genesis 1:1—2:3 is a proclamation that the only Creator who should be worshipped by all people is a personal, but transcendent, God.[32] It challenged and rejected all the rival tales of the creation of the world by immanent gods told in their context. It also proclaims much more about God and God's creation:

> God and God's creation are bound together in a distinctive and delicate way. This is the presupposition for everything that follows in the Bible. It is the deepest premise from which good news is possible. God and his creation are bound together by the powerful, gracious movement of God towards that creation. The binding which is established by God is inscrutable. It will not be explained or analyzed. It can only be affirmed and confessed. This text announces the deepest mystery: God wills and will have a faithful relation with earth. The text invites the listening community to celebrate that reality. The binding is irreversible. God has decided it. The connection cannot be nullified.[33]

. . . It Was Good

The binding between God and God's creation came more and more to the fore through the sequence of deliberate steps taken by God in a highly structured way to create an organized and wonderful world, in God's view a good world. In creating the universe God did not play dice.[34] In the beginning, according to Genesis 1:2, "The earth was without form and void." This also can be translated as "unformed and unfilled."[35] Yes, there was no life-giving space to live in.

But God desired that the earth would be habitable, filled with living inhabitants. Therefore, God created on the first three days a habitat, an environment in which creatures could exist (Gen 1:3–13). God took good care to provide everything that the creatures would need for their existence and well-being in God's created habitat. All God's creative actions on the first three days were beneficiary acts to enhance life for the creatures to be created.

Then, on days four to six, God created all the creatures to fill the living spaces created for them (1:14–31). God filled the expanse of the heavens

32. Provan, *Discovering*, 76.

33. Brueggemann, *Genesis*, 22–24.

34. Armstrong, *In the Beginning*, 17.

35. Kissling, *Genesis*, "Formless and Empty."

with lights. God filled the waters with swarms of living creatures and the heavens with winged birds. God filled the earth with livestock and creeping things and beasts. Lastly, with everything in place to make human life possible, God created humankind, male and female. In making everything, God purposefully followed a specific creative pattern as demonstrated in the repetition of certain important words: God "said," "saw," "separated," and "called."[36]

God was so concerned with human life on earth that God, in advance, carefully planned and created everything human beings needed to live by before they were created. God's actions were "completely benevolent" and life supporting to all humanity.[37] God acted as a caring, nurturing, loving, cultivating, preserving, protecting, supporting Parent. This is who the Creator God is. From the beginning, the Creation Story clearly witnesses about the generative acts performed by the generative God.

Throughout this narrative, these generative actions are repeatedly judged by their Creator as "good" (Gen 1:10, 12, 18, 21, 25). At the end, God declared about the whole of creation that "it was very good" (Gen 1:31). Everything—the heavens, the earth, and the seas; the vegetation, plants, and trees; the two great lights and the stars, the sea creatures, and the birds; all livestock, creeping things, and beasts on the earth; the human beings made in God's image—was very good. "The verdict of 'good' (*ṭôb*) means not only that the finished product is worthy and well executed but also that it is beautiful";[38] it is "lovely, pleasing."[39] God was satisfied, delighted with the aesthetic quality of all the components of the created artwork.

God's satisfaction with creation is emphasized by the fact that on the seventh day God rested from all the work God had done. Barth's opinion is that "the fact that God rested means quite simply, and significantly enough, that He [*sic*] did not continue His work of creation, i.e., that He was content with the creation of the world and man."[40]

God's rest placed a huge responsibility on all human beings. In this regard O'Connor states, "All of creation is good, and all is worthy of respect and appreciation by humans who are part of it. The text invites ecological awareness, a recognition that we too are part of the living organism that is the cosmos."[41] Because of the fact that we are part of this "very good"

36. Armstrong, *In the Beginning*, 17.

37. Armstrong, *In the Beginning*, 17.

38. McConville, *Being Human*, 19.

39. Brueggemann, *Genesis*, 37.

40. Barth, *Church Dogmatics*, 214–15.

41. O'Connor, *Genesis*, "Goodness."

living organism, we must keep the habitat and the inhabitants—everything created by God—"very good" in God's eyes. Keeping everything good is emphasized by the functions God entrusted to human beings in Genesis 1:28. Until today it is the calling of the older generation to preserve all of creation so that it can be a good habitat for the following generations. This asks from us generative actions that will secure a very good, life-giving habitat for the future inhabitants of God's creation. This is a great challenge and a big responsibility in this age with so many looming ecological crises. We can no longer remain ignorant and inactive toward the threats that can turn God's *very good* created habitat into "very bad" for the generations who will inherit God's creation from us. The "good" future of God's created habitat as a "very good" living space for future generations is in our hands. God's rest does not mean that God is inactive in preserving a very good, life-enhancing habitat for all human beings, but by choice God wants to sustain this very good creation through our hands and our involvement in this wonderful creation.

. . . In Our Image

Our responsibility for the future in stressed by the fact that we as human beings were created in the image and likeness of God. God's generative acts reached their climax in the creation of human beings "in our image, after our likeness" (Gen 1:26). It is the first and only place in the whole Creation Story that these expressions are used. According to van Huyssteen, "being created in the image of God highlights the extraordinary importance of human beings: humans are walking representations of God, and as such are of exquisite value and importance."[42] But what exactly is the meaning of the concept *image*? Kilner states, "Simply put, image is about connection in a way that may also involve reflection."[43] A human being is not an exact copy of God, but in some way reflects something of God.

How should we understand the combination of the expressions *image* and *likeness*? Are they two totally different elements, together constituting a human being? In this regard Collins states,

> Many earlier Christian theologians have taken the image and likeness as separate components of created human nature—often with the idea that one was lost by the fall of Genesis 3, while the other remains. Since about the time of the Reformation,

42. Huyssteen, *Alone in the World?*, 121.

43. Kilner, *Dignity*, 54.

> scholars have recognized that this does not suit the text itself. First, there is no "and" joining "in our image" with "after our likeness." Second, in Genesis 1:27 we find simply "in God's image."[44]

It seems that these two phrases rather "reinforce one another."[45] Provan's view is "that 'according to our likeness' is in fact an explanatory gloss on 'in our image,' and that both are ways of saying the same thing."[46] Van Zyl is even of the opinion that these two words are synonyms.[47] Mngqibisa emphasizes that "the use of these two terms side by side vigorously declares that by creation humanity bears an image actually corresponding to the divine original."[48] Referring to these two terms Kilner aptly says, "God intends people ultimately to become the 'likeness' of God, where the special connection with God and the reflection involved entail similarity rather than identity."[49] Therefore, it is impossible to reflect on the nature of human beings without taking into account who God is. Ultimately, "all biblical anthropology turns out to be theological anthropology, which means that a human being is defined by his or her relationship with God and God's other creatures."[50] McConville even states, "The life of the human being, in biblical terms, takes form and meaning in God's world and in relation to him [*sic*]. The study of humanity cannot but be theological."[51] Thus, human beings' understanding of the image of God will be influenced by their understanding of and their relationship with God.

Taking Genesis 1 on its own, it is quite difficult to understand who God is, and what the exact meaning of the concept *image of God* is or implies. Jensen declares, "The biblical text is conspicuously silent in defining the *imago Dei*."[52] The meaning of the image of God is not explained in the Creation Story, nor in the rest of the Old Testament.[53] The use of this expression in the Old Testament is limited to only two more texts, both in the earlier chapters of Genesis (5:3; 9:6), and they do not help much to formulate a better understanding of this construction. The rest of the Old

44. Collins, *Genesis 1–4*, loc. 703–5.
45. Kidner, *Genesis*, "Sixth Day."
46. Provan, *Discovering*, 81.
47. Van Zyl, "Genesis," 5.
48. Mngqibisa, "Relationship," 47.
49. Kilner, *Dignity*, 59.
50. Towner, "Clones of God," 50.
51. McConville, *Being Human*, 10.
52. Jensen, *Graced Vulnerability*, 14.
53. Herzfeld, "New Member," 238.

Testament is also not very helpful because the focus is rather on God's actions than on abstract reflections about the nature of God.[54] The Creation Story itself also does not discuss or explain human nature.

Therefore, the creation of human beings in the image of God was interpreted quite differently through the ages by exegetes and systematic theologians.[55] These differences were also influenced and enhanced by the fact that *image* means different things for different cultures, and it is very easy to import one's own cultural ideas into this term.[56] All these interpretations were classified by different theologians in different ways. Broadly, the following categories, with much variation in each one, can be identified:[57]

The Classical or Substantive Interpretations

According to the substantive view, the image of God is found in one or another capacity or faculty within human nature which differentiates us from the animal world. The implication is that human beings are, in some part of their substance, like God. Collins calls it the *resemblance view*, because the image of God is reflected in some divine-like quality which humans possess.[58] The text does not give any indication of the location of this divine-like quality within humans. Through the ages a variety of qualities have been identified by scholars. Some of them saw the image as a physical characteristic and others have found it in a mental or spiritual capacity.[59] Migliore expresses the following view in this regard:

> Perhaps the dominant Western interpretation of the image of God has been that it resides in the *rational nature of human beings*. In the view of many classical theologians, including Thomas Aquinas, the exercise of human reason is a participation in and the reflection of the divine *logos* or reason by which the world was created.[60]

54. Durand, *Skepping*, 164.

55. Towner, "Clones of God," 343–44.

56. Kilner, *Dignity*, 48.

57. Herzfeld, *In Our Image*, 10–32; Mngqibisa, "Relationship," 47–53; Shults, *Reforming*, loc. 2346–592; Huyssteen, *Alone in the World?*, 26–144.

58. Collins, *Genesis 1–4*, loc. 710–13.

59. Herzfeld, *In Our Image*, 16.

60. Migliore, *Faith Seeking*, 140.

Herzfeld expresses a similar view by stating that, until the Reformation, most writers connected the image of God in some way to human beings' intellectual capacity or rationality.[61]

Existential or Relational Interpretation

This view connects in one way or another the image of God to human beings' capacity to build relationships with God and other people. According to this view, "man is fully man when in relationship with God and the human community."[62] A relational view, in Hall's words, "conceives of the *imago* as an inclination or proclivity occurring within the relationship."[63]

The Reformation broke away from the substantive view of the image of God. Both Luther and Calvin's point of departure for their understanding of the image of God was always a relational comprehension of our world.[64] The great theologian of the twentieth century Karl Barth followed in their footsteps. According to Barth, the plural speech used by the Creator—"let us make man in our image" and "in the image of God he created him; male and female he created them"—are community texts showing that the image of God is not an individual concept, but rather a social or relational concept.[65] Migliore aptly states that

> the symbol "image of God" describes *human life in relationship* with God and with the other creatures. . . . The image of God is not like an image permanently stamped on a coin; it is more like an image reflected in a mirror. That is, human beings are created for life in relationships that mirror or correspond to God's own life in relationship.[66]

Eschatological Interpretation

The eschatological interpretation understands the image of God primarily from God's promised future. According to this view, the ideal relationship between human beings and God cannot be constructed from the past. It can only be constructed from the future, from the end. In this regard Moltmann

61. Herzfeld, *In Our Image*, 16.
62. Collins, *Genesis 1–4*, loc. 719–20.
63. Hall, *Imaging God*, 98.
64. Hall, *Imaging God*, 98–106.
65. Barth, *Church Dogmatics*, 176–210; Grenz, *Theology for the Community*, 175.
66. Migliore, *Faith Seeking*, 141.

argues that "the true likeness to God is to be found, not at the beginning of God's history with mankind, but at its end."[67] The implication of this view is that the image of God is only a disposition to what it will become when God's kingdom finally arrives. "This teleological focus implies that the image is not yet actualized but exists as a predisposition to the operation of providence that draws us toward the final state of being in God's image."[68] According to Moltmann the image of God is thus not a stable, unchanging condition, but a continuous process with an eschatological conclusion.[69]

Functional or Dynamic Interpretation

The functional understanding of the image of God emphasizes the actions and the calling of human beings. "Generally speaking, theologians in the twentieth century felt that the Bible focuses on function rather than ontology: that is, on what people do rather than what they are."[70] Regarding what exactly this function is, theologians from different theological subdisciplines have different opinions. According to Herzfeld, Old Testament scholars mostly interpret the image of God in terms of the discourse of the text as *dominion*:[71] "Then God said, 'Let us make man in our image, after our likeness. And let them have dominion over the fish of the sea and over the birds of the heavens and over the livestock and over all the earth and over every creeping thing that creeps on the earth'" (Gen 1:26). This is followed up in Genesis 1:28 with God's commission for human beings to have dominion over all the creatures. As God's representatives and agents, humans represent God on earth as rulers on God's behalf.

The *image* concept was well known to Israel, especially as practiced in the royal ideology of the nations of the ancient Near East. Goldingay explains it as follows:

> Being made in God's image might have made Israelites think of the way Middle Eastern kings sometimes placed statues in different parts of their realm to represent the king to his subjects. It reminded them of who is king here. It asserts his authority and reminds them to obey him. Humanity's being made as God's image would therefore make a neat link with the declaration that humanity is to master the earth. As God's visible image,

67. Moltmann, *God in Creation*, 225.

68. Shults, *Reforming*, loc. 2520–21.

69. Moltmann, *God in Creation*, 227.

70. Collins, *Genesis 1–4*, 711–12.

71. Herzfeld, "New Member," 239.

> humanity represents God in the world in its responsibility to hold sway over the earth's creatures on God's behalf.[72]

As the image of God, human beings make God's presence in this world visible. "God, the king of kings, has statues representing the divine self in every corner of the world, but unlike the immobile marbles of the kings, God's statues walk and talk."[73]

In their walking and talking, human beings must subdue the earth and rule over all creatures. This lays a huge responsibly on the shoulders of all human beings, "for the work of humankind is to care for the earth even as the Creator has already begun to care, to protect and enhance the earth as God's creation."[74] In this regard, Towner makes the important remark that, just as Joseph served the pharaoh in Egypt, human beings are "God's viziers in the world."[75] He explains it as follows:

> To be God's vizier is to serve at God's pleasure and to preserve that which belongs to God. It is to serve as mediator and conduit of goodness and health between the source of all goodness and the good creation. In short, the name of the mode and style in which the old narrative tradition of the Bible understand human dominion to be exercised is *stewardship*.

As God's stewards, humanity's rule over creation must serve the well-being and prosperity of creation. Brueggemann rightly declares, "The image images the creative use of power which invites, evokes, and permits. There is nothing here of coercive or tyrannical power."[76] Humans did not receive a license to exploit creation unrestrained for their own benefit without taking into consideration the well-being of nature and all other creatures. It was expected from ancient oriental kings

> to be devoted to the welfare of their subjects, especially the poorest and weakest members of society (Ps 72:12–14). By upholding divine principles of law and justice, rulers promoted peace and prosperity for all their subjects. Similarly, mankind is here commissioned to rule nature as a benevolent king, acting

72. Goldingay, *Genesis*, "Genesis 1:26"; Enns, *Evolution of Adam*, 49, 139; Wolff, *Anthropology*, 160.

73. Towner, *Genesis*, 26.

74. Brueggemann, *Reverberations*, 106.

75. Towner, *Genesis*, 29.

76. Brueggemann, *Genesis*, 32.

as God's representative over them and therefore treating them in the same way as God who created them.[77]

Only One Interpretation?

Do we have to choose between the four interpretations of the image of God as discussed above? Not necessary. Collins is of the opinion "that they need not be mutually exclusive."[78] Vorster is even of the opinion that the author of the Creation narrative in Genesis 1 intentionally wrote the narrative in such a way that the idea of the human being as the image of God has an "open" meaning, which indicates that it can be interpreted in different ways and, therefore, requires more theological investigation.[79] Although the concept offers different interpretative possibilities, it seems that in the context of Genesis 1 most Old Testament exegetes prefer to emphasize the functional view; but this view can be enriched when the best intentions of the other interpretations are incorporated into the functional interpretation.[80] This is especially true when the interpretation of the image of God is not restricted only to Genesis 1:26–28; but understood in light of the witness of the whole of Scripture. Vorster declares that "the New Testament imbues the *imago Dei* with a Christological and eschatological sense that is essential for a correct understanding of the concept."[81]

Our understanding of the image of God can be broadened when we connect it with the New Testament idea of the image of Christ. Shults convincingly explains that, for the authors of the New Testament epistles, "the concepts of the image and likeness of God refer directly to Jesus Christ."[82] These two concepts do not oppose each other but rather express the same theological idea. "From a New Testament perspective, Jesus *is* the image of God, and the ultimate reality and possibility of being human require sharing in his life."[83] It is the Christian calling to follow in the footsteps of Jesus Christ. Human beings must subdue the earth and have dominion over all creatures as God in Christ would do it. In this regard Shults states, "If we are called to be like Jesus, then our 'rule' of the earth will take the form of

77. Wenham, *Genesis 1–15*, verse 28.
78. Collins, *Genesis 1–4*, loc. 723.
79. Vorster, *Created in the Image*, 4.
80. Huyssteen, *Alone in the World?*, 161.
81. Vorster, *Created in the Image*, 4.
82. Shults, *Reforming*, loc. 2557–58.
83. Huyssteen, *Alone in the World?*, 125.

servanthood, not oppressive domination over the creation of which we are an integral part."[84]

Is this not exactly what generativity means? Although not deliberately, Erikson captured much of the essence of living out the image of God in his concept of generativity, especially in his emphasis on the importance of the Golden Rule, understood as neighbor love. As explained above, generativity is about the values and actions of caring, nurturing, loving, blessing, cultivating, preserving, assisting, guiding, teaching, mentoring, raising, protecting, and parenting directed toward the succeeding generations. Was this not expressed most fully in the life and death of Jesus Christ? As image-bearers of God, human beings have the calling to live out generativity in a Christ-like manner, creating a life-enhancing habitat for the coming generations, and contributing to their development in living themselves more and more according to the godly-image they have received.

God Blessed Them

God did not merely make the creation and then leave it to its own destiny but guaranteed and ensured its sustainability. The sustainable acts of God emerged in the statement that God blessed humankind: "And God blessed them" (Gen 1:28a). Through this divine blessing God continued acting kindly and generously toward humankind and the rest of creation. This blessing is expressed in these words: "Be fruitful and multiply and fill the earth" (Gen 1:28b). This clause makes it clear that this blessing is chiefly about fertility. God's blessing is thus not only the continuation of God's creative works, but it is also the empowerment of human beings to emulate God's creative actions by multiplying, producing new bearers of God's image.[85] "Through procreation, conception, and birth the blessing produces the chain of generations"[86] who were the role players in the rest of the Genesis narrative.

It is, therefore, no surprise that "blessing" continued to play a crucial role throughout the remainder of the Genesis narrative. It is one of the themes that integrate the different stories in Genesis into one unit. The text states that God blessed the animals (1:22), humankind (1:28), the Sabbath (2:3), Adam (5:2), Noah (9:1), and frequently the patriarchs (12:3; 17:16, 20). Without divine blessing, God's creation, included human beings, would not have been sustainable. It is clear that, throughout the Genesis narrative,

84. Shults, *Reforming*, loc. 2543–44.

85. Wenham, *Genesis 1–15*, verse 22.

86. Westermann, *Genesis*, 11.

the divine blessing was "the power which enabled all beings to live in the most profound and comprehensive sense. Men, women, animals, plants, and fish were filled with the sacred force that enabled them all to fulfill their natures and to live in their element."[87]

Genesis tells us the story of the fulfillment of God's ordained blessing upon the whole of creation. The earth is filled with animals and humankind. After the flood it is filled for a second time. The narratives of the patriarchs overflow with children, despite their struggles with infertility. They were prosperous and successful. Despite their wrongdoings and sin, God protected and blessed them, guiding them into the future, generation by generation. Westermann makes the important observation that in the succession of these generations fulfilling their natures, "lies the beginning of history. History grows out of the blessing conferred on the human family." God's blessing makes the ongoing history of humanity—as expressed through the generative actions of generation after generation—possible, but it only becomes reality through humanity's life-giving generativity, creating living-space for the future generations. That is humanity's calling, to be generative, to be a blessing to each other, especially toward the younger generations. The older generations always have the responsibility to bless, from generation to generation to generation until the arrival of God's new created heaven and earth in all its splendor. Without God's blessing, and people living as God's image-bearers blessing the whole of creation, creation would return to the chaos of its beginning.

Being Generative People

We only arrived where we are today because of the wonderful blessings God bestowed upon God's creation and the continuous generational care that flowed from it and directed our paths. Today, we have the paths of the future generations in our hands, to enhance or endanger their well-being. This applies to our interactions with nature, culture, and the future generations created in the God's image. They need our generative acts according to the pattern of God's generative acts toward all creation.

In living out generativity we always must remember that we "have no right to play God with other creatures, or to commit genocide or 'specicide.'"[88] Brueggemann stresses that being created in the image of God

87. Armstrong, *In the Beginning*, 25.

88. Towner, *Genesis*, 29.

> provides a theological basis for the intense valuing of human life. Every human person—including the unattractive, the unacceptable, the disabled, the unproductive—is entitled by his or her very existence to the dignity and worth befitting the creature who alone among the creatures bears the irreducible markings of dignity and dominion from the Creator's own grant.[89]

This includes the smallest and the youngest of humankind, because children are also created in God's image. To be the image of God is not something that you become when you grow up into adulthood, but all children already—from the day of their birth—bear the image of God in all its fullness.[90] This fact is especially illustrated in Genesis 5:1–3 (ESV):

> This is the book of the generations of Adam. When God created man, he made him in the likeness of God. Male and female he created them, and he blessed them and named them Man when they were created. When Adam had lived 130 years, he fathered a son in his own likeness, after his image, and named him Seth.

The first two verses echo the words of the Creation Story in Genesis 1:26–27, emphasizing the fact that human beings were created "in the likeness of God." Fretheim makes the important observation that the genealogical structure of Genesis 5 "makes God the 'father' of Adam."[91] The *father* created his image in his *son*. When Adam as a father creates a son, this son is described as being in his own likeness, after his image. In these verses there is no indication of any contradiction between the image of God and the image of Adam. So, the image of God became via Adam part of Adam's descendants. In this regard Fretheim states, "Human beings are now the ones who create further images of God. In other words: this first generation of children *is* created in the image of God (even after the fall into sin)."[92] Each baby birthed into this world is from the moment of conception blessed with the image of God. From their first breath and crying sounds they represent everything that is associated with being the image of God. Therefore, each baby—every child and teenager—carries "an intrinsic theological value,"[93] and they should be received and handled accordingly. They have human dignity, even "godly" dignity; they are the image of God and Christ. Jesus

89. Brueggemann, *Reverberations*, 107.
90. Fretheim, "God Was with the Boy," 4.
91. Fretheim, "God Was with the Boy," 4.
92. Fretheim. "God Was with the Boy," 4.
93. Prest, *God's Word*, 3.

himself said: "Whoever receives one such child in my name receives me" (Matt 18:5).

Receiving children into this world bears with it the responsibility of being generative, of being a blessing, of being the image of God toward them—respecting and protecting them, nurturing and guiding them, caring for their well-being, creating living spaces for them. Kloppers says that, in respect of children, human beings must rule, cultivate, and preserve, not only regarding their physical well-being, but also regarding their life contexts and anything that can endanger and harm them.[94] Generativity toward children attends not only to their spiritual needs, but holistically to the totality of their needs: physical, ecological, educational, emotional, familial, medical, social, and all other needs arising in their lives. Through generativity, adult human beings must serve the younger generations, making this world a life-giving home for them and developing them toward their full potential to help ensure their future. According to van Huyssteen, a discussion of the image of God should always include an emphasis on human rights.[95] This same principle is applicable in discussing the image of God in relation to children. It should also always include an emphasis on children's rights. Attending to and enhancing children's rights is part and parcel of being a generative church. In a gripping article exploring Genesis 37:34–35, Jeremiah 31:15, and Matthew 2:18, Brueggemann indicates that we, just as Rachel, have to remember and weep. Being a generative church, "we weep—and remember—perhaps enough to make a difference."[96]

To make a difference, we must become more and more a generative church. As an expression of generative and generational care, *blessing* needs to become embedded in the culture of every church. Perhaps Fujimura's work on culture care and his approach to generative thinking can help the church in this regard.[97] Being a generative church, we must enhance generational thinking. A generative life expresses itself in generosity. It works with a mindset of abundance and not of scarcity or survival. Grateful for the many blessings received from God, generativity is expressed in giving abundantly of ourselves and our resources to the coming generations. In doing this we have to be on the lookout for the genesis moments of our personal lives and the life of the church. It is these moments that possess the potential for the church to create unexpected flourishing for the younger generations. As a people of "makers," we are able to experience the joy of generating new

94. Kloppers, "Kindersorg," 295.

95. Huyssteen, *Alive in this World?*, 158, 161.

96. Brueggemann, "Remembering," 383.

97. Fujimura, *Culture Care*, loc. 134.

generations who can also become people of blessing for this world—people who, by living according to the image of God, will continue to carry blessing into the future for the generations still to come.

Hopefully this will be the legacy of our current generation, fulfilling—in Erikson's view—the central developmental task for people in middle adulthood; or, in the view of Genesis, living as bearers of the image of God in this world and thus becoming more and more a generative church for the sake of coming generations.

Bibliography

Armstrong, Karen. *In the Beginning: A New Interpretation of Genesis*. London: Vintage, 1996. E-pub.

Bach, Mara J. "The Culture of Generativity: Exploring the Manifestation of Generativity in the Manifestation of Generativity in the Mexican/Mexican-American Population." PhD diss., Marquette University, 2014. https://epublications.marquette.edu/dissertations_mu/408/.

Barth, Karl. *Church Dogmatics: The Doctrine of Creation*. Part 1. Translated by Geoffrey W. Bromiley and Thomas F. Torrance. London: T. & T. Clark, 2004. Logos Bible Software.

Browning, Don. "An Ethical Analysis of Erikson's Concept of Generativity." In *The Generative Society: Caring for Future Generations*, edited by Ed de St. Aubin et al., 241–55. Washington, DC: American Psychological Association, 2004.

Brueggemann, Walter. *Genesis*. Interpretation: A Bible Commentary for Teaching and Preaching. Louisville: Westminster John Knox, 2010. Kindle edition.

———. "Remembering Rachel's Children: An Urban Agenda for People Who Notice." *Word & World* 14 (1994) 377–83.

———. *Reverberations of Faith: A Theological Handbook of Old Testaments Themes*. Louisville: Westminster John Knox, 2002.

Collins, C. John. *Genesis 1–4: A Linguistic, Literary, and Theological Commentary*. Phillipsburg, NJ: P&R, 2006. Kindle edition.

Day, John. *From Creation to Babel: Studies in Genesis 1–11*. Library of Hebrew Bible / Old Testament Studies 592. London: Bloomsbury, 2013. Google Books.

De St. Aubin, Ed, et al. "The Generative Society: An Introduction." In *Generative Society*, 3–13.

———, eds. *The Generative Society: Caring for Future Generations*. Washington, DC: American Psychological Association, 2004.

Dillon, Michelle, and Paul Wink. "American Religion, Generativity, and the Therapeutic Culture." In de St. Aubin et al., *Generative Society*, 153–74.

Durand, Johannes Jacobus Fourie. *Skepping, Mens, Voorsienigheid* [Creation, man, providence]. Pretoria: N G Kerk boekhandel Tvl., 1982.

Enns, Peter. *The Evolution of Adam: What the Bible Does and Doesn't Say about Human Origins*. Grand Rapids: Brazos, 2011. Kindle edition.

Erikson, Erik H. *Childhood and Society*. New York: Norton, 1950.

———. *Insight and Responsibility: Lectures on the Ethical Implications of Psychoanalytic Insight*. New York: Norton, 1964.

Fretheim, Terrence E. "'God Was with the Boy' (Genesis 21:20): Children in the Book of Genesis." In *The Child in the* Bible, edited by Marcia J. Bunge et al., 3–23. Grand Rapids: Eerdmans, 2008.

Friedman, Lawrence J. "Erik Erikson on Generativity: A Biographer's Perspective." In de St. Aubin et al., *Generative Society*, 257–64.

Fujimura, Makoto. *Culture Care: Reconnecting with Beauty for Our Common Life*. Downers Grove: InterVarsity, 2017. Kindle edition.

Goldingay, John. *Genesis for Everyone*. Part 1. Louisville: Westminster John Knox, 2010. Olive Tree edition.

Grenz, Stanley J. *Theology for the Community of God*. Grand Rapids: Eerdmans, 2000.

Hall, Douglas J. *Imaging God: Dominion as Stewardship*. Grand Rapids: Eerdmans, 1986.

Herzfeld, Noreen L. *In Our Image: Artificial Intelligence and the Human Spirit*. Minneapolis: Fortress, 2002.

———. "A New Member of the Family? The Continuum of Being, Artificial Intelligence, and the Image of God." *Theology and Science* 5 (2007) 235–47.

Huyssteen, J. Wentzel van. *Alone in the World? Human Uniqueness in Science and Theology*. Grand Rapids: Eerdmans, 2006.

Jensen, David H. *Graced Vulnerability: A Theology of Childhood*. Cleveland: Pilgrim, 2005.

Kidner, Derek. *Genesis: An Introduction and Commentary*. Tyndale Old Testament Commentaries 1. Nottingham: InterVarsity, 2008. Olive Tree edition.

Kilner, John F. *Dignity and Destiny*. Grand Rapids: Eerdmans, 2015. Kindle edition.

Kissling, Paul. *Genesis*. College Press NIV Commentary 1. Joplin, MO: College Press, 2004. Logos Bible Software.

Kloppers, M. H. O. "Kindersorg" [Child care]. In *Die diens van Barmhartigheid en die Nederduitse Gereformeerde Kerk* [The compassion services and the Dutch Reformed Church], edited by J. J. De Klerk, 295–306. Kaapstad: N G Kerk-Uitgewers, 1990.

Kotre, John. *Outliving the Self: How We Live On in Future Generations*. New York: Norton, 1996.

McAdams, Dan P. "The Redemptive Self: Generativity and the Stories Americans Live By." *Research in Human Development* 3 (2006) 81–100.

McAdams, Dan P., et al. "The Anatomy of Generativity." In *Generativity and Adult Development: How and Why We Care for the Next Generation*, edited by Dan P. McAdams and Ed de St. Aubin, 7–43. Washington, DC: American Psychological Association, 1998.

McConville, J. Gordon. *Being Human in God's World: An Old Testament Theology of Humanity*. Grand Rapids: Baker Academic, 2016.

Migliore, Daniel L. *Faith Seeking Understanding: An Introduction to Christian Theology*. 2nd ed. Grand Rapids: Eerdmans, 2004.

Mngqibisa, Oscar Themba. "The Relationship of Humankind and Nature according to Psalm 8." DTh diss., University of Stellenbosch, 2006.

Moltmann, Jürgen. *God in Creation: A New Theology of Creation and the Spirit of God*. Translated by Margaret Kohl. San Francisco: Harper & Row, 1985.

O'Connor, Kathleen M. *Genesis 1–25A*. Smyth & Helwys Bible Commentary. Macon, GA: Smyth & Helwys, 2018. Logos Bible Software.

Prest, Eddie. *God's Word on Children*. Pinelands: TFL, 1999.

Provan, Iain. *Discovering Genesis: Content, Interpretation, Reception*. London: SPCK, 2015. E-pub.

Shults, F. LeRon. *Reforming Theological Anthropology: After the Philosophical Turn to Relationality*. Grand Rapids: Eerdmans, 2003. Kindle edition.

Speiser, Ephraim Avigdor. *Genesis: Introduction, Translation, and Notes*. Anchor Yale Bible 1. New Haven: Yale University Press, 2008. Logos Bible Software.

Towner, W. Sibley. "Clones of God. Genesis 1:26–28 and the Image of God in the Hebrew Bible." *Interpretation* (2005) 341–56.

———. *Genesis*. Westminster Bible Companion. Louisville: Westminster John Knox, 2001.

Van Zyl, A. H. "Genesis." In *Verklarende Bybel (1983 vertaling)* [Explanatory Bible (1983 translation)], edited by A. H. van Zyl, 1–63. Cape Town: Lux Verbi, 1989.

Vorster, Nico. *Created in the Image of God: Understanding God's Relationship with Humanity*. Eugene, OR: Pickwick, 2011. Kindle edition.

Wenham, Gordon J. *Genesis 1–15*. World Biblical Commentary 1. Dallas: Word, 1987. Logos Bible Software.

———. "Genesis." In *New Bible Commentary 21st Century Edition*, edited by D. A. Carson et al. Leicester: InterVarsity, 1994. Logos Bible Software.

Westermann, Claus. *Genesis*. Translated by David E. Green. Text and Interpretation. London: T. & T. Clark International, 1988.

Wiersbe, Warren W. Foreword to *Children's Ministry Resource Bible*, edited by Child Evangelism Fellowship. Nashville: Nelson, 1993.

Wolff, Hans W. *Anthropology of the Old Testament*. Philadelphia: Fortress, 1981.

Questions for Reflection and Discussion

1. In this chapter, Grobbelaar provides several biblical themes and images to help us think about generativity as a theological concept. Which of these biblical connections are most thought-provoking to you? Why?
2. How does Grobbelaar's view of children bearing the image of God impact your attitudes toward children? How might this perspective influence the way that your church relates to children?
3. Grobbelaar encourages us to engage in "generational thinking." As he states, "Generational thinking considers how our lives were influenced positively by the generations before us and how we can contribute to those generations who will remain after our departure." Which adults had the greatest influence upon you during your formative years? In whose lives are you being called to have a positive influence at present?

2

Discipleship and Intergenerationality

Interrelated Concepts at the Core of Christianity

Joe Azzopardi and Kayle de Waal

§

EDITOR'S INTRODUCTION: In my introductory chapter, I suggest that generative churches desire to "provide a setting in which individuals might gain a vital experience of faith and an authentic sense of identity" rooted in Christ. Azzopardi and de Waal help us explore this idea further by drawing our attention to a crucial New Testament category: the call to discipleship. They also focus upon an essential characteristic of generative churches—interaction between the generations—by pointing us to the intergenerational congregation as the ideal context for growing as a disciple of Christ. They describe flourishing intergenerational churches as those that foster an environment of interdependence between generations, that empower people of all ages to participate meaningfully in ministry, and that encourage the generations to make accommodations for one another's sake. These themes resonate deeply with the picture of congregational generativity sketched out in the introductory chapter. This chapter concludes with an exploration of the importance of mentoring, a relational dynamic frequently associated with generativity. Azzopardi and de Waal insist that mentoring also is a crucial component of a vibrant culture of discipleship within the church.

This chapter helps us recognize that a truly generative church is a disciple-making church and invites us to consider what this means in practice.

§

DISCIPLESHIP and intergenerationality go hand in hand to deepen the core of Christianity and advance the kingdom of God. In fact, the Bible provides both the spiritual and conceptual framework within which to understand intergenerational congregations as the ideal context for discipleship. Before addressing the notion of an intergenerational church, it is important in our view to understand the place of the individual disciple. Being a disciple is the heart of Christianity. "And He said to them, 'Follow Me, and I will make you fishers of men'" (Matt 4:19 NASB). The call to be a disciple is first and foremost a call to follow Jesus. It means "to adhere to," "to walk behind," "to stay close to"—all of this is directed toward Jesus.[1] It entails a personal commitment to Jesus and whole-hearted allegiance to him.[2] While there is a range of definitions of discipleship, we propose that discipleship could be defined as becoming who God desires us to be while helping others to become who God wants them to be.[3] A relationship with Jesus provides the foundation for the disciple to serve, connect, grow, lead, and worship in the context of an intergenerational church. This provides an essential framework to help us understand what it means to be a generative church.

1. Putman et al., *DiscipleShift*, 47–50, attempt to define discipleship by using Matthew 4:19, and suggest that "follow me" represents the acceptance of Christ at a head level, "and I will make you" represents a transformation at the heart level, and "fishers of men" represents a change in one's actions or hands.

2. Morris, "Disciples of Jesus," 116.

3. Burrill, *Radical Disciples for Revolutionary Churches*, 29–30, says that discipleship is to be in a living relationship with Jesus who is discipling you. In this relationship, one is to be constantly learning more about the Person, while at the same time living in subjection to that Person. "The person being discipled is never completely discipled, but always in the process of being discipled." Earley and Dempsey, *Disciple Making Is . . .*, 22–26, attempts to define the word "disciple" by identifying ten traits: (1) one who considers the cost, (2) loves others, (3) abides in Christ and bears fruit, (4) continues in the Word and experiences freedom, (5) follows Christ's desires, (6) makes disciples, as well as one who is (7) committed, (8) sacrificial, (9) willing to give up possessions, and (10) full of the Holy Spirit. Green, *Gospel of Luke*, 565, suggests the discipleship language in Luke 14:25–27 is a call of Jesus for "the reconstruction of one's identity, not along ancestral lines or on the basis of one's social status, but within the new community."

Discipleship: The Prerogative for Intergenerationality

We would like to explore two biblical themes that aid the development of an understanding of discipleship in the context of intergenerational churches, namely, the body of Christ and the gifts of the Spirit.

Body of Christ

One of the dominant models of thinking about the church is the metaphor of the body of Christ (Rom 12:4–5; 1 Cor 12:12, 27; Eph 4:12, 25; 5:23, 30; Col 1:24).[4] In the first-century context the metaphor was rooted in the idea of the Greco-Roman city-state as a body.[5] This metaphor provides the theological and structural underpinnings to understand the Pauline churches. The church is an organic whole, the living manifestation of Jesus Christ; he is not just in his church, but the church is in him (Acts 9:4). All disciples, regardless of age, possess the very life of God. It is this life that is present in an intergenerational church. Moreover, the notion of body simply—yet profoundly—illustrates the relationship between Christ and his church. Just as the body is an intricate and interdependent organism, so is the local church. Just as the body is a unified whole, so is the local church.[6]

The notion of the church as one body leads to another biblical metaphor—the family of God—to deepen our understanding of an intergenerational church. While a body is connected and unified, so too is a family (*oikos*).[7] The writers of the New Testament continually refer to this image because it highlights the central purpose of God—to be reconciled with us.

4. Berkhof, *Systematic Theology*, 557, goes so far as to call this designation the most "complete definition of the New Testament church."

5. Bird, *Evangelical Theology*, 716. For examples of ancient writers that personified the body and its parts see Ciampa and Rosner, *First Letter to the Corinthians*, 597–98.

6. MacArthur and Mayhue, *Biblical Doctrine*, 750.

7. This notion of *oikos* can be traced to the gospels. After healing the demon-possessed man, Jesus told him specifically, "Go home to your family (*oikos*) and tell them how much the Lord has done for you, and how he has had mercy on you" (Mark 5:19). Immediately following Zacchaeus's conversion, Jesus reflected on what had just happened by saying, "Today salvation has come to this house (*oikos*)" (Luke 19:9). When Jesus healed the politician's son, John said that "he and all his household (*oikos*) believed" (John 4:53). When Jesus called Levi (Matthew) to be his disciple, Mark recalled that, "while Jesus was having dinner [with] Levi's house (*oikos*), many tax collectors and sinners were eating with him and his disciples, for there were many who followed him" (Mark 2:15).

- "Consequently, you are no longer foreigners and aliens, but fellow citizens with God's people and also *members of his household*" (Eph 2:19).
- "Therefore, as we have opportunity, let us do good to all people, especially to those who belong to the *family of believers*" (Gal 6:10).
- "Do not rebuke an older man harshly, but exhort him as if he were your father. Treat younger men as brothers, older women as mothers, and younger women as sisters, with absolute purity" (1 Tim 5:1–2).
- "If I am delayed, you will know how people ought to conduct themselves in God's *household*, which is the church of the living God, the pillar and foundation of the truth" (1 Tim 3:15).

The New Testament writers draw on the image of *oikos* in describing the intimate nature of relations within the church, the development of its leaders and its growth, and how believers related to and understood God.[8] The use of the term family is indicative of not merely one, but several generations deeply connected to one another and functioning as a unit.

When churches today function in light of their identity as the body of Christ and the family of God, there is a fundamental shift in how those churches look and act. There is a shift from programs to relationships, from independence to interdependence and from fragmentation to wholeness.

Gifts of the Spirit

The body of Christ metaphor also provides the substance for Paul's teaching on spiritual gifts.[9] Paul is convinced that every member of the church must have the opportunity for Jesus to shape and transform their lives into conformity to his plan and will (Rom 8:29; 12:1–2; Eph 4:23–24). Our faith tradition understands that it is at the time of baptism, as in the case of Jesus (Matt 3:13–17), that the Holy Spirit fills all believers and grants them his gifts for ministry. According to Grudem, "a spiritual gift is any ability that is empowered by the Holy Spirit and used in any ministry of the church."[10] The

8. For a study that demonstrates the close relationship between members of the Pauline churches, see Aasgaard, *My Beloved Brothers and Sisters!* Another study that demonstrates a range of maternal metaphors used by Paul that deepen our understanding of the notion of the family of God is Gaventa, *Our Mother Paul*. Gaventa expounds upon Gal 4:19; 2 Thess 2:11, 12, 17.

9. See Fortune and Fortune, *Discover Your God-Given Gifts*, 29–31, for how the body of Christ motif functions in relation to the spiritual gifts.

10. Grudem, *Bible Doctrine*, 396. Stuart, "Charism in the Light of Scripture," 325–34, states that Paul's use of gift (*charisma*) can be understood in four ways: (1) charismata are eschatological, signs of the presence of the Holy Spirit given in the Last

granting of spiritual gifts is the prerogative of the Spirit and he grants them according to his purpose and with no distinction with regard to gender, age, or nationality (1 Cor 12:4–11; 11:11–12; Gal 3:13, 28; 5:1). The early Christian communities were not structured around positions, personalities, or power, but instead were organized around the gifts of individual members of varying ages. Since the spiritual giftedness of members was the key to the operation of the early church, function was more important than office.[11]

Paul also gave four lists of ministries, each at least somewhat different from the other (Rom 12:6–8; 1 Cor 12:4–11; Eph 4:8–13). In fact, Peter exhorts, "As each has received a gift, use it to serve one another, as good stewards of God's varied grace" (1 Pet 4:10 ESV). The word "varied" (*polikos*) means "having many facets, having rich diversity." God has provided the local church with all it needs to serve him faithfully.[12]

Interestingly, Paul provides no organizational system or flow chart for how these gifts are to be used. He does, however, say that everything should be done "decently and in order" (1 Cor 14:40 ESV). Paul informs the church at Corinth, "Now about spiritual gifts, brothers, I do not want you to be uninformed" (1 Cor 12:1–13). His conviction is that spiritual gifts will strengthen the local church fellowship, extend the church's witness and ministry, and paint a relevant picture of Christ; one which is not merely theoretical but practical in impacting people's lives. The wider New Testament teaches that spiritual gifts cannot be earned through our efforts (Eph 4:7), that it is in fact a sin to waste the gifts God gives (1 Cor 4:1–2; Matt 25:14–30), and that believers are to develop the gifts God gives them (1 Pet 4:10). As we think about the application of this concept, a question that ought to be asked is, "Are those of every generation being given the opportunity to use and develop their spiritual gifting?"

The body of Christ metaphor and the doctrine of the gifts of the Spirit convey the deeply relational nature of the local church.[13] They highlight

---

Days, when the New Age breaks into the Old; (2) charismata are ecclesial, set in the corporate interdependent life of the body of Christ. Again and again Paul emphasizes that the charismata given to individuals are for the sake of others, to build up the body in love; (3) charisma is vocational; and (4) charisma is egalitarian. The egalitarian nature of the gifts in the early church suggests that both men and women were active in leadership roles in the church. See Osiek et al., *Woman's Place*, and Ellingsen, *Reclaiming Our Roots*, 42, who note that women played a prominent role in the leadership of the early church.

11. Verhey and Harvard, *Ephesians*, 165.

12. Grudem, *Bible Doctrine*, 399.

13. In 2 Cor 13:14 Paul prays that the "fellowship (*koinonia*) of the Holy Spirit" may be with the Corinthian believers. And in Phil 2:1 Paul speaks of the "fellowship (*koinonia*) in the Spirit." These two verses highlight the vertical and horizontal relationship of

the fact that every member, no matter what generation they may be in, is called and equipped for ministry; that every member and the ministry entrusted to them is of equal value; and that the local church is to grow in connectedness, ministry, and love.

Intergenerationality: The Context for Discipleship

Having seen the evidence of the Holy Spirit enabling not only the individual believer in the New Testament but empowering every generation within a Christian community, we now turn our attention to exploring how intergenerational communities can play a significant role in providing the context for discipleship through the diversity of believers who are united in Christ and his mission. But what characterizes an intergenerational church? Is it just a matter of putting a bunch of people of different age groups into the same building each week while trying to keep the peace? Truthfully, intergenerational congregations do take a lot of hard work, as it is much easier to work with a uniform group of people.[14] We will devote the remainder of this chapter to exploring some of the work that is most essential. We will argue that there are five factors that must be present for intergenerationality to flourish.[15]

The first three factors—positive interactions, connectedness, and interdependence—are progressive steps toward building a healthy relationship. The last two factors—accommodation and empowerment—concern inclusivity, which is an essential characteristic of a Christian community.[16]

---

koinonia. The vertical dimension is a believer's fellowship with God, while the horizontal aspect of *koinonia* is with other believers through the Holy Spirit.

14. Conway, "In It for the Long Haul."

15. It is worth noting the work of Bengston and Mangen, "Generations, Families, and Interaction." Bengston and Mangen's work on intergenerational solidarity within the family used six factors in understanding how to strengthen the bonds of cohesion within multigenerational families. While the factors discussed in this chapter are in regard to a generalized (as opposed to a family) context, Bengston's factor of "associational solidarity" has similarities with "Positive Interactions," while his factor of "functional solidarity" is somewhat akin to "Interdependence." For an exploration of how Bengston's theory of intergenerational solidarity relate to the life of the church, see Seibel, "Intergenerationally Sticky Church."

16. Crispin, "Theology of Accommodation."

Factor 1: Positive Interactions

The first factor found in intergenerational communities is basic to any cohesive community, and that is the existence of positive interactions between community members.[17] This is not to say that there are no negative interactions (such perfection does not exist on Earth); however, as with any healthy relationship, the positive interactions should outweigh the negative. This factor is foundational in that, without interaction, there is no relationship to speak of; therefore, for the rest of the factors yet to be mentioned to take place, they must be preceded by positive interaction.

Aside from the occurrence of cordial and respectful exchanges, there are other aspects of positive interactions that need to be stressed. For congregations to become intergenerational, individuals of every generation must find a way to push past the temptation of conversing only with those who are like themselves or else fall into remaining a segregated community, a category to which most multigenerational churches belong. Multigenerational means that there are several generations coexisting together at the same time and place. However, this in itself is not intergenerational, even if everyone is in the same place and at the same time, if they do not have relationships with each other.[18]

Intentionality is essential for positive interactions to occur. While spontaneous pleasantries are encouraged and expected in Christian gatherings, intentionality is required if lasting relationships are to be built.[19] This is particularly relevant in a diverse community where individuals with different backgrounds are less likely to spend time together.[20] Over time, an intentional choice to interact with an individual who is different may lead to a healthy relationship simply through a commitment to engaging in conversation.[21] Positive interactions done regularly with intentionality are likely to elicit meaning and purpose, which lead to several other factors found in flourishing intergenerational communities.

Factor 2: Connectedness

Having positive interactions between members of different generations in a congregation will provide the groundwork for the second factor of

17. Allen and Ross, *Intergenerational Christian Formation.*
18. Allen and Barnett, "Addressing the Two Intergenerational Questions."
19. Powell and Clark, *Sticky Faith.*
20. Snailum, "Integrating Intergenerational Ministry."
21. Massi et al., "Impact of Dialogic Intergenerational Activities."

intergenerational churches, which is connectedness. Connectedness goes beyond mere interaction in that individuals actually become bound together in unity despite diversity in age.[22] Indeed, without the characteristic of connectedness it is rather difficult to call a group of people a community.[23] Intergenerational churches do the majority of their activities together and see themselves as a family, participating in worship, service, and learning together.[24] This is not to say that everything is done together, as there are some aspects of life that ought to be done according to life stage.[25] The importance of connectedness is evidenced by the fact that most literature on the topic of intergenerationality revolves around uniting the diverse age groups of a community and helping every generation feel as though they are accepted and belong.[26] Clearly, connectedness is a basic factor of intergenerational congregations since it is part of what defines intergenerationality itself.

Factor 3: Interdependence

After positive interactions become the established norm, the age-diverse congregation becomes interconnected with each other. This interconnection leads the congregation to a point of interdependency and mutuality, since connectedness increases the awareness and therefore the impact of the gifts and abilities of each generation.[27] You can tell a church has reached some level of interdependency when an aged-based event takes a generation away from the congregation for a time, and the church finds itself functioning more poorly for it; for example, a youth rally disables various ministry teams and leaves everyone feeling a longing for them to return. This makes sense when one realizes that each generation has something beneficial to offer the rest—the elders pass on wisdom and skills to those younger, while the younger provide purpose and vitality.[28] This aspect of intergenerationality is one of its main attractions as a characteristic, and it further demonstrates the power of the body of Christ in action.[29]

22. Cohen-Mansfield and Jensen, "Intergenerational Programs in Schools."

23. *Cambridge Dictionary*, s.v. "community."

24. Ross, "Four Congregations That Practice Intergenerationality."

25. Snailum, "Implementing Intergenerational Youth Ministry."

26. Andreoletti and Howard, "Bridging the Generation Gap"; Cortellesi and Kernan, "Together Old and Young"; Nesbit Sbanotto and Blomberg, *Effective Generational Ministry*; Grignoli et al., "Development of a European Learning Model."

27. Menconi, *Intergenerational Church.*

28. Murayama et al., "Effect of Intergenerational Programs."

29. Eikenberry, "Developing an Intentional and Transparent Intergenerational

Factor 4: Empowerment

The last two factors of intergenerationality are probably the most challenging for congregations to embrace, since both involve sacrifice on the part of church members and leaders. They are empowerment and accommodation. To empower means to give power or authority to another, and churches that are intergenerational have leaders who are willing to give authority to people from a variety of age levels.[30] If intergenerationality is truly a core value of a community and every generation is considered valued then every generation should have the opportunity to participate in all ministries and, when possible, to lead.[31] For younger people to develop responsibility, they must first be given responsibility. Further to this, great leaders create great leaders; the younger generation needs to be mentored for continuity of the ministry (and therefore legacy) to be achieved.[32] Unfortunately, empowerment is a characteristic that many in leadership struggle with, not only in intergenerational affairs, but in general. However, if we truly accept the concept in 1 Peter 2:9 of the priesthood of all believers, then we as leaders must recognize that all members of the body of Christ, whether they are sixteen or sixty, are indeed Christ's ministers and therefore need to be considered in leadership. Each generation has strengths and weaknesses. However, an advantage of working as a united body is that the weaknesses of one member are compensated for by another, which therefore can lessen the likelihood of failure. Consequently, while sharing power with others can be difficult it has immense benefits.[33]

Factor 5: Accommodation

As with empowerment, the characteristic of accommodation is challenging for many congregations as it is all about giving something up for the benefit of others. For intergenerationality to flourish, however, accommodation must be exercised since the perspectives and needs of every generation

---

Ministry."

30. Snailum, "Implementing Intergenerational Youth Ministry."

31. There are limits of course, as a base experience and cognitive level are necessary, especially with some positions. For example, having a ten-year-old in charge of the church budget would likely be a poor decision considering both typical maturity and mathematic ability of that age group.

32. Andreoletti and Howard, "Briding the Generation Gap"; Powell and Clark, *Sticky Faith.*

33. Stollings, "Unlocking the Power of Intergenerational Leadership."

should be considered equitably.[34] Unlike empowerment, however, accommodation is a challenge for everyone, not just the leadership. For example, if one or two generations control the music played and prevent styles other than their own preference from taking the stage, it sends the message (subtly or otherwise) that those with different musical tastes are not valued. We have personally seen this happen to both younger and older members in different congregations, and the result commonly is bitterness, anger, and, far too often, their departure.

There are three aspects to accommodation: empathy, sacrifice, and surrender. To accommodate one must be able to empathize with others, meaning to put oneself in the shoes of another and try to see things from their angle.[35] To accommodate one also often must sacrifice, which entails offering something of significant value for someone else's desires or need to be fulfilled. Surrender is a word that often is perceived as unpleasant, as it requires humility. A closely related—and equally unappealing—term is submission, which entails an individual choosing to give up their own authority and allow someone else to preside. When one looks at Jesus, however, we see the ultimate example of a servant leader, one who pulled out all of the stops to accommodate our sinfulness so that we might be heirs to his kingdom.[36] As Christians, we can affirm that accommodation is not inherently unpleasant; it is the way of Jesus.

In summary, intergenerationality flourishes in the presence of five factors: positive interactions, connectedness, interdependence, empowerment, and accommodation. Congregations who strive to be intergenerational need to incorporate these characteristics into their cultural fabric. However, there is one other aspect of intergenerationality that must be mentioned; while it is not a foundational dimension of intergenerationality, it does provide evidence of healthy intergenerationality: mentoring.

Mentoring: The Evidence of Intergenerationality

When looking at research studies, most benefits resulting from intergenerationality cited in research either directly or indirectly relate to mentoring.[37]

34. Crispin, "Theology of Accommodation."

35. Shaw, *Generational IQ*.

36. Bonhoeffer, *Cost of Discipleship*.

37. Cortellesi and Kernan, "Together Old and Young"; Hsu et al., "Effectiveness of Intergenerational Program"; Agmon et al., "Relationship between Mentoring"; Massi et al., "Impact of Dialogic Intergenerational Activities"; Raven, "Impact of Mentoring Reconsidered"; Andreoletti and Howard, "Bridging the Generation Gap"; Grignoli et al.

While many church members seem intimidated with the idea of being a mentor to someone else, it is worth noting that members of intergenerational congregations often participate in informal mentoring without realizing it, as it simply involves intentionally pouring into someone with less experience than oneself to aid them in their life journey; this can be as simple as going out of your way to talk to a certain younger person every week at church.[38] While these are two separate concepts, intergenerationality is intrinsically connected to mentoring. The positive interactions and connectedness that form between two individuals from different generations is how mentoring begins.[39] Long-term mentoring results in interdependency, as both young and old contribute important things to their relationship.[40] Mentoring requires accommodation and should result in empowerment for both parties involved.[41] Therefore, upon reflection, a flourishing mentoring culture (whether formal or informal) could be considered the crowning piece of evidence that a church has developed a healthy culture of intergenerationality.

Thinking back on our discussion of discipleship, we can see another way this concept of mentoring becomes even more significant. Considering that discipleship could be defined as becoming who God desires us to be while helping others to become who God wants them to be, then is not the mentoring relationship the basic unit of discipleship? Can there be true discipleship without one mentoring someone else in some capacity? Since discipleship should not be understood merely as focused on self-help or personal growth with God's assistance, but rather as a direct response to the Great Commission to actively make disciples as we go about our lives, could intergenerational churches provide the ideal context for discipleship? As a setting in which there is rich potential for mentoring relationships to emerge, might intergenerational churches be the missing puzzle piece that has prevented us from truly being the people God has called us to be?[42]

"Development of a European Learning Model"; Ayton and Joss, "Empowering Vulnerable Parents."

38. Campbell, *Mentor like Jesus*; Shaw, *Generational IQ*.

39. French et al., *Bsomebody2someone*.

40. Roberto, "Our Future Is Intergenerational."

41. Parrott, *Transforming Together*.

42. Bonhoeffer, *Cost of Discipleship*.

Concluding Thoughts

In this chapter, we have argued that the call to discipleship, when understood in light of the biblical concepts of the body of Christ, the family of God, and the gifting of the Spirit, validates the importance of intergenerationality. Having explored how the core factors of intergenerationality help to create an ideal context for discipleship, we hope others will join us in recognizing the importance of nurturing and pursuing intergenerationality within the church under the direction of the Spirit. The Spirit desires to deepen the intergenerational dynamics of the church as its members exercise the gifts with which he has endowed them. As the Spirit plays this essential role in deepening our relationships, this enables our theological ideals about the body of Christ and the family of God to move from abstract notions to experiential reality.

Bibliography

Agmon, Maayan, Cheryl, et al. "The Relationship between Mentoring on Healthy Behaviors and Well-Being among Israeli Youth in Boarding Schools: A Mixed-Methods Study." *BMC Pediatrics* 15 (2015). http://dx.doi.org/10.1186/s12887-015-0327-6.

Allen, Holly Catterton, ed. *InterGenerate: Transforming Churches through Intergenerational Ministry*. Abilene, TX: Abilene Christian University Press, 2018.

Allen, Holly Catterton, and Chris Barnett. "Addressing the Two Intergenerational Questions." In Allen, *InterGenerate*, 17–24.

Allen, Holly Catterton, and Christine Lawton Ross. *Intergenerational Christian Formation: Bringing the Whole Church Together in Ministry, Community and Worship*. Downers Grove: IVP Academic, 2012.

Andreoletti, Carrie, and Jessica L. Howard. "Bridging the Generation Gap: Intergenerational Service-Learning Benefits Young and Old." *Gerontology & Geriatrics Education* 39 (2016) 46–60. http://dx.doi.org/10.1080/02701960.2016.1152266.

Ayton, Darshini, and Nerida Joss. "Empowering Vulnerable Parents through a Family Mentoring Program." *Australian Journal of Primary Health* 22 (2015) 320–26. http://dx.doi.org/10.1071/py14174.

Bengston, Vern L., and David J. Mangen. "Generations, Families, and Interaction: An Overview of the Research Program." In *Measurement of Intergenerational Relations*, edited by David J. Mangen et al., 10–14. Newbury Park, CA: Sage, 1988.

Berkhof, Louis. *Systematic Theology*. Grand Rapids: Eerdmans, 1958.

Bird, Michael F. *Evangelical Theology: A Biblical and Systematic Introduction*. Grand Rapids: Zondervan, 2013.

Bonhoeffer, Dietrich. *The Cost of Discipleship*. 6th revised and unabridged ed., containing material not previously translated. London: SCM Press, 1959.

Burrill, Russell. *Radical Disciples for Revolutionary Churches*. Fallbrook, CA: Hart Research Center, 1996.

Campbell, Regi. *Mentor like Jesus*. Nashville: Broadman & Holman, 2009.
Ciampa, Roy E., and Brian S. Rosner. *The First Letter to the Corinthians*. Pillar New Testament Commentary. Grand Rapids: Eerdmans, 2010.
Cohen-Mansfield, Jiska, and Barbara Jensen. "Intergenerational Programs in Schools." *Journal of Applied Gerontology* 36 (2017) 254–76. http://dx.doi.org/10.1177/0733464815570663.
Conway, Joseph P. "In It for the Long Haul." In Allen, *InterGenerate*, 121–27.
Cortellesi, Giulia, and Margaret Kernan. "Together Old and Young: How Informal Contact between Young Children and Older People Can Lead to Intergenerational Solidarity." *Studia Paedagogica* 21 (2016) 101–16. http://dx.doi.org/10.5817/sp2016-2-7.
Crispin, Gareth. "A Theology of Accommodation as a Resource for Integrating Youth and Children into Intergenerational Church." *Christian Education Journal* 14 (2017) 7–22.
Earley, Dave, and Rod Dempsey. *Disciple Making Is . . . : How to Live the Great Commission with Passion and Confidence*. Nashville: Broadman & Holman, 2013.
Eikenberry, David. "Developing an Intentional and Transparent Intergenerational Ministry in a Small Congregation." DMin thesis, Trinity International University, 2013.
Fortune, Don, and Katie Fortune. *Discover Your God-Given Gifts*. Cootamundra, Australia: Peacemakers, 1987.
French, Wayne, et al. *Bsomebody2someone: Mentoring Training Series*. Silver Spring, MD: General Conference Youth Ministries Department, 2015.
Gaventa, Beverly Roberts. *Our Mother Saint Paul*. Louisville: Westminster John Knox, 2007.
Green, Joel B. *The Gospel of Luke*. New International Commentary on the New Testament. Grand Rapids: Eerdmans, 1997.
Grignoli, Daniela, et al. "The Development of a European Learning Model for Intergenerational Learning: Guts (Generations Using Training for Social Inclusion in 2020)." *Reģionālais Ziņojums. Pētījumu Materiāli* 11 (2015) 109–25, 92–93.
Grudem, Wayne. *Bible Doctrine: Essentials of the Christian Faith*. Leicester, UK: InterVarsity, 1999.
Hsu, S. C., et al. "Effectiveness of Intergenerational Program in Improving Community Senior Citizens' General Health and Happiness (Report)." *European Scientific Journal* 10 (2014) 46–63.
MacArthur, John, and Richard Mayhue, eds. *Biblical Doctrine: A Systematic Summary of Bible Truth*. Wheaton, IL: Crossway, 2017.
Massi, Giselle, et al. "Impact of Dialogic Intergenerational Activities on the Perception of Children, Adolescents and Elderly / Impacto De Atividades Dialogicas Intergeracionais Na Percepcao De Criancas, Adolescentes E Idosos (Texto En Ingles)." *Revista CEFAC: Atualizacao Cientifica em Fonoaudiologia e Educacao* 18 (2016) 399. http://dx.doi.org/10.1590/1982-0216201618223015.
Menconi, Peter. *The Intergenerational Church: Understanding Congregations from WWII to www.com*. Createspace Independent, 2010.
Murayama, Yoh, et al. "The Effect of Intergenerational Programs on the Mental Health of Elderly Adults." *Aging & Mental Health* 19 (2014) 306–14. http://dx.doi.org/10.1080/13607863.2014.933309.

Nesbit Sbanotto, Elisabeth A., and Craig L. Blomberg. *Effective Generational Ministry: Biblical and Practical Insights for Transforming Church Communities*. Grand Rapids: Baker Academic, 2016.

Parrott, Ele. *Transforming Together: Authentic Spiritual Mentoring*. Chicago: Moody, 2009.

Powell, Kara, and Chap Clark. *Sticky Faith: Everyday Ideas to Build Lasting Faith in Your Kids*. Grand Rapids: Zondervan, 2011.

Putman, Jim, et al. *DiscipleShift: Five Steps That Help Your Church to Make Disciples Who Make Disciples*. Grand Rapids: Zondervan, 2013.

Raven, Neil. "The Impact of Mentoring Reconsidered: An Exploration of the Benefits for Student Mentors." *Research in Post-Compulsory Education* 20 (2015) 280–95. http://dx.doi.org/10.1080/13596748.2015.1063265.

Reidar, Aasgaard. *My Beloved Brothers and Sisters! Christian Siblingship in Paul*. Journal for the Study of the New Testament Supplement 265. London: T. & T. Clark, 2004.

Roberto, John. "Our Future Is Intergenerational." *Christian Education Journal* 9 (2012) 105–20.

Ross, Christine. "Four Congregations That Practice Intergenerationality." *Christian Education Journal* 9 (2012) 135–47.

Seibel, Cory. "The Intergenerationally Sticky Church." In Allen, *InterGenerate*, 253–63.

Shaw, Haydn. *Generational IQ: Christianity Isn't Dying, Millennials Aren't the Problem, and the Future Is Bright*. Carol Stream, IL: Tyndale, 2015.

Snailum, Brenda. "Implementing Intergenerational Youth Ministry within Existing Evangelical Church Congregations: What Have We Learned?" *Christian Education Journal* 9 (2012) 165–81.

———. "Integrating Intergenerational Ministry and Age-Specific Youth Ministry in Evangelical Churches: Maximizing Influence for Adolescent Spiritual Development." EdD, Biola University, 2012.

Stollings, Jessica. "Unlocking the Power of Intergenerational Leadership." In Allen, *InterGenerate*, 111–19.

Verhey, Allen, and Joseph S. Harvard. *Ephesians: A Theological Commentary on the Bible*. Louisville: Westminster John Knox, 2011.

Wade-Benzoni, Kimberly A., and Leigh Plunkett Tost. "The Egoism and Altruism of Intergenerational Behavior." *Personality and Social Psychology Review* 13 (2009) 165–93. http://dx.doi.org/10.1177/1088868309339317.

Questions for Reflection and Discussion

1. Azzopardi and de Waal begin this chapter by advocating for the importance of three biblical concepts: the call to discipleship, the church as the body of Christ, and spiritual gifts. To what extent do these biblical concepts factor into the discourse about investing in rising generations within your context? How do you see these categories being expressed practically in your setting?
2. The authors of this chapter outline five key components of a vibrant intergenerational church: positive interaction, connectedness, interdependence, empowerment, and accommodation. How would you assess your own church context in light of these five indicators of intergenerational health? Where do you see evidence of these dynamics within your congregation?
3. Azzopardi and de Waal emphasize the importance of mentoring. Where is mentoring occurring within your church, whether formally or informally? What experiences of being mentored—or serving as a mentor—have been most impactful to you personally?

3

Intergenerational Ministry

Youth and Church in Context

Anita Cloete

§

EDITOR'S INTRODUCTION: In my opening chapter, I state that congregational generativity is "inherently contextual." As I express in that chapter, generative churches "seek to engage with the particular social, cultural, and historical circumstances that impact the daily lives of the members of rising generations." Anita Cloete takes up this theme in this chapter. Sociologists suggest that generational dynamics can be studied on two levels: the *macrosociological* approach analyzes relations between generations on a societal scale; the *microsociological* approach looks at intergenerational relationships within particular social groups within society.[1] In this chapter, Cloete shows us that both perspectives play a crucial role in helping churches think contextually about ministry among the members of rising generations. She begins at the macrosociological level by introducing the work of the South African generational theorist Nerina Jansen, whose insights enable us to consider how church members have been shaped through their experiences within the broader generational landscape of society. Cloete does not stop

1. Pillemer et al., "Intergenerational Relations," in *Encyclopedia of Sociology*, edited by E. F. Borgatta and R. J. V. Montgomery (New York: Macmillan, 2000), 1:1388.

there, however. Turning her attention to the microsociological context of the local church, she encourages us to explore the importance of the generations sharing life—learning and serving together. This chapter provides an insightful framework for understanding the generational contexts in which generative churches minister and for considering how to invite young people to discern God's purposes within the peculiarities of these contexts.

§

Introduction

ONE of the main arguments of this chapter is that both *church* and *youth* need to be understood in the local and broader global contexts in which they are situated. Moreover, a theological understanding of both youth and church should not be separated from a sociological understanding of both. Generational theory is proposed as a suitable lens to reflect on the relationship between youth and other generations at a given time in society, but more specifically in the church. Learning and serving together, as well as discernment as a communal theological process, are underscored as ways that could inform and shape intergenerational ministry. These processes could prevent youth ministry from being a one size fits all strategy by contextualizing ministry that is locally relevant, while at the same time resonating with global realities. Lastly, it is argued that intergenerational ministry is more than a strategy or program; instead, it is about being church and therefore an ecclesial matter.

Generational Theory

The idea that there exist different generations is not new and so neither is the need and plea for intergenerational ministry. Therefore, this chapter discusses generational theory as a preferred lens to identify and describe the different generations. Such a discussion aims at providing insight into the theoretical framework that underpins generational theory while also pointing to the limitations thereof. It is necessary to give an overview of generational theory because arguments for intergenerational ministry assume this theory but seldom reflect on its theoretical underpinnings. Although, for the most part, I am positive about the theoretical framework presented here, it is important to have a critical look at it because any theory has limitations and cannot explain reality completely.

My reflection on the theoretical framework for generational theory will draw primarily on the work of Nerina Jansen called *Generation Theory*. My motivation for choosing her work is the fact that her analysis responds to key questions of what generational theory entails and provides a relevant and suitable theoretical framework to analyze the relationship between institutions and people in a rapidly changing society. Moreover, her work presents a meaningful explanation for the tension between different generations in society and the church today. Lastly, she acknowledges how rapid societal changes influence generations and their coexistence in society and, therefore, focuses ultimately on the generation of young people and their central role in constructing social change.

Jansen has done a systematic sociological analysis of the core elements of generational theory for the purpose of interpreting human existence in society and variations in this existence.[2] Prerequisites for a generation include a certain time dimension, a particular historical context, and a certain lifestyle. The time factor refers to the biological fact of birth, linked to age. Although this biological dimension is important, a generation does not consist only of people who share a birth date and thus are the same age. Instead, a generation should be understood in terms of a *zone of dates* and a way of life. People within the same zone of dates design for themselves a similar way of life. Within the same generation, there are *contemporaries*, those who share similar birth dates, and *coevals*, the members of a cohort who exhibit the same way of life.[3]

Coevals live in a particular time and space that has a direct effect on how they design their lives. Coevals engage with their circumstances through interpretation of the ideas of the context in which they live, called *primary* or *absolute* ideas. These are the existing ideas in a context, which they did not help formulate. A generation reflects on these existing ideas and develops similar, though not radically different, perspectives in a process of meaning making. "A generation is the concrete social form of perspectives."[4] The collective perspective developed by a generation is embodied and expressed through a certain way of life.[5]

While there are other ways of explaining generations, I have chosen to utilize Jansen's outline. Jansen distinguishes between five generations, each consisting of those born within a fifteen-year time span between. In summary these are:

2. Jansen, *Generation Theory*, 10.
3. Jansen, *Generation Theory*, 11.
4. Jansen, *Generation Theory*, 13.
5. Jansen, *Generation Theory*, 15.

1. **Childhood (years 1 to 15):** Little social change takes place because the child is introduced to the existing world.
2. **Youth (years 15 to 30):** Although youth are more receptive and attentive, there are not significant changes taking place within this generation.
3. **The generation that initiates change (years 30 to 45):** This generation engages in conflict with the established ideas of the older generation, which has the potential to lead to change.
4. **The generation that dominates (years 45 to 60):** The members of this generation are normally leaders and, more importantly, bearers of authority and therefore occupy a dominating position toward other generations in society.
5. **Old age (years 60 to 75):** The generation that has been through all the previous stages and could witness to the time gone by.[6]

As noted above, there exist other ways of classifying different generations. For instance, today such classifications would not end at age seventy-five because people are living much longer than in the time this work was published. It is important to note that more than one generation coexist in any given time and space. Their coexistence is also responsible for continuation and discontinuation, or change, in the social structure. Although all these identified generations coexist, Jansen argues that only three are the most active: youth, the generation that initiates change, and the generation that has the dominant position of power in society.[7] The nature of the relationship between these three active generations is characterized by tension because of the questions of power that exist between them. The power relations between generations are described as asymmetric because their positions differ with regard to the power they hold. This unequal power positioning between younger and older generations is known as the generation gap. Jansen acknowledges that a closer look needs to be taken at the youth that are growing up in a rapidly changing society and the effect that the pace of change has on the relationship between different generations.[8] Older generations cannot adapt fast enough to the changes because they do not have a frame of reference to handle and interpret the new circumstances. The implications of rapid change for youth are even more far reaching because they are forced to create a new structure of life, a new world in

6. Jansen, *Generation Theory*, 35.
7. Jansen, *Generation Theory*, 36.
8. Jansen, *Generation Theory*, 87.

which they can develop a distinctive lifestyle. Therefore, youth today are affecting change much faster than previous generations.

In sum, the generational theory as discussed above implies that:

- People living in a certain time and space share a similar process of making meaning of their lives, resulting in certain shared characteristics.
- Both a context and the people who inhabit it are in a dynamic relationship with each other, shaping and changing one another.
- Power is central to the relationship between different generations.
- Interaction between coexisting generations brings about continuation and discontinuation (change) in society.
- Generational theory takes into account that generations consist of individuals but does not account for individual actions and ways of living.
- Due to the acceleration of change in society, all generations—not only three, as Jansen suggested—are actively shaping society today; as a result, a closer look is needed for new ways to analyze the power dynamics between generations.
- Intergenerational engagement provides historical memory, bridging the gap with the past, and has the potential to put the future into meaningful perspective.

The Plea for Intergenerational Ministry

It is important to stress that the need and call for intergenerational ministry is not new but one that has been coming for some time now. Publications by White, Harkness, and Gambone on different aspects of intergenerational ministry testify to the fact that the importance of intergenerational ministry has a significant history.[9] White draws on the work of George Mead (1934), who postulates that people are *becoming* through interaction with each other, and the developmental psychology of Erik Erikson (1963).[10] Furthermore, White starts his work with a social analysis of society, the context in which both people and church exist.[11] In other words, his work also emphasizes the relationship between different generations and their

9. See White, *Intergenerational Religious Education*; Harkness, *Intergenerational Christian Education*; and Gambone, *All Are Welcome.*

10. White, *Intergenerational Religious Education*, 91.

11. White, *Intergenerational Religious Education*, 1.

role in forming each other as well as the reality that such interactions take place within a specific time and context. In more recent works on intergenerational ministry, critique of age-specific ministry is central because it is regarded as the opposite, and even an enemy, of intergenerationality. Therefore, age-specific ministry is often described as generational fragmentation, artificially dividing the body of Christ.[12] Moreover, such age-specific ministry is deemed to lean too heavily on developmental psychology rather than on theological motivations.

Although such critique could be valuable, I would argue that developmental psychology and social theories as discussed in the first part of this chapter are central to understanding and developing an intergenerational ministry. Putting it differently, social theories and theological foundations could work together, especially because both the church and human beings are part of a social context that shapes them as much as our theological understanding of people and the world do. Therefore, I encourage an interdisciplinary approach where both theology and other disciplines assist us to develop an understanding of, and appreciation for, both our differences as generations and the context that shapes us. This does not imply that social theories should replace our theological grounding for ministry, but rather that these could complement each other in our endeavors to be true to the calling of being church in a rapidly changing society.

In 2016, at least three noteworthy books were published with reference to generations or with the explicit theme of intergenerational ministry. These publications are: *Adoptive Youth Ministry: Integrating Emerging Generations into the Family of Faith*, by Chap Clark; *Teaching the Next Generation*, edited by Terry Linhart; and *Effective Generational Ministry: Biblical and Practical Insight for Transforming Church Communities*, by Elizabeth Nesbitt Sbanotto and Craig Blomberg. All these publications shed light on this shared theme from different angles and perspectives; they share the notion that generations exist and should journey together to learn from each other about matters in everyday life, particularly in faith formation. Only Nesbit Sbanotto and Blomberg have done empirical work using grounded theory in a qualitative study with focus groups to explore at least three generations, namely the Baby Boomers (1946 to 1964), Gen Xers (1965 to 1981), and Millennials (1982 to 2001).[13] In their study they tried to establish how the fact that these identified age groups constituted specific generations has shaped their values, beliefs, and worldview. They however do not claim that every person in a particular generation is exactly the same, because

12. Glassford and Barger-Elliot, "Toward Intergenerational Ministry," 364.

13. Nesbit Sbanotto and Blomberg, *Effective Generational Ministry*, xiv.

numerous societal factors play a role in shaping people into who they are and who they are becoming. Nesbit Sbanotto and Blomberg provide an important hermeneutical key that connects, but at the same time distinguishes, generations from each other, namely lived and learned experience.[14] Lived experience means a generation has lived through a certain significant event and therefore has firsthand knowledge and experience thereof, while the next generation might only have come to learn about it afterward. Therefore, a defining event would be a lived experience of one generation but merely a learned experience for another. An example in South Africa would be apartheid, the political system that segregated people according to race group, oppressed black people, and benefited white people.

If we take Jansen's classification or arrangement of the three generations indicated above, all three generation would have lived experiences of apartheid; however, the older generations would have more intimate and personal experience of it than younger generations. On the other hand, the explosion in technological development that brought about digital living would be an experience that Generation X and the Millennials have more knowledge of than their parents and grandparents who constitute the generations before them. Their memories and experience of the same event would differ; therefore, engagement is needed in order to value all experiences, as one experience is not more valuable than the other. Acknowledgment of and engagement between generations seems to be crucial because, as Nesbit Sbanatto and Blomberg note, each generation tends to take for granted the good that went before and react against the bad from their own historical perspective.[15]

It could be concluded that the generations need each other not only for faith formation, which is sometimes the exclusive focus of ministry, but also for—and in—everyday living. The last section of this chapter will give at least two building blocks to create community though intergenerational ministry.

Learning and Serving Together

Often research on youth and youth ministry focuses only on youth as a group or generation in isolation from the larger society. Such a focus could create a very narrow understanding of both youth and ministry. As demonstrated by the discussion of generation theory above, there is never at any point of time only one generation in any given society, but multiple generations

14. Nesbit Sbanotto and Blomberg, *Effective Generational Ministry*, xix.

15. Nesbit Sbanotto and Blomberg, *Effective Generational Ministry*, xix.

coexisting. Does this mean all research on youth ministry should focus on distinct generations or intergenerational ministry? Not necessarily, but any youth ministry and research that does not take seriously the broader cultural context and its significance for religion neglects an integral part of any generation's experience or how to minister to it.

Neither people nor churches exist in a vacuum. According to Bonner, the two major cultural shifts in the past century are the loss of a shared corporate story (metanarrative) and the increased isolation of youth from adults resulting in an enormous gap between generations in society at large and in the church specifically.[16] Furthermore, changes in society have resulted in changes in the developmental phases of adolescents. These changes confirm the social embeddedness of youth, their interaction with the surrounding culture in a given context. I would like to single out Bonner's reflection on the objectification or systematic abandonment of youth and how this not only dehumanizes young people but also deepens the gap between youth and adults[17]—in the language of this chapter, between generations. I would like to argue that the emphasis on youth, and therefore the general focus upon one generation in youth ministry and research, is also a form of objectification of youth; it puts all the pressure on them to learn to participate and become what older generations assume they themselves already are. Youth and children are affirmed in Scripture as models of faith and therefore their contribution and participation should not be seen as being of less worth or dismissed as immature.[18] At the same time, youth should learn respect for other generations and be provided opportunities to learn about the history that has shaped them. Intergenerational dialogue, in which all parties are acknowledged and treated with respect, should be central in order for generations to be introduced to each other's worlds. At the same time, we should be aware that such closeness could create tension. I have argued elsewhere that ministry that focuses on all the generations could lead to creative tensions. These tensions could however be utilized in creative ways to build relationships instead of dividing people. Our differences should not turn us into enemies; instead they can enable us to create a deeper level of respect and engagement. I would like to single out the tension between closeness and distance that could exist. "The creative tension of closeness and distance does not pertain only to physical presence or absence, but also refers to the way we are together. When together, each generation needs to be appreciated for who they are and there should be openness to different ways of

16. Bonner, "Understanding the Changing Adolescent," 27.

17. Bonner, "Understanding the Changing Adolescent," 32.

18. See Matt 18:2–4; 1 Tim 4:12.

expressing spirituality together."[19] In intergenerational ministry, we should create an environment where all generations could find their own voice and create a way of expressing themselves, not at the cost of community but to express diversity, which is a key aspect of church as a community.[20]

Terry Linhart focuses on the importance of teaching, especially of the next generation, as indicated in title of the book he edited.[21] I would say that perhaps a weakness of the book is its lack of explicit focus on different generations as part of the learning process while overemphasizing that one (older) generation should teach the next (younger) generation. At the same time, the theoretical reflections introduced throughout the different chapters present valuable ways to foster intergenerational ministry. The book delves into educational philosophy and stresses the importance of the teacher in the process of teaching as well as a theological foundation for teaching. Yet it makes clear that teaching is not meant as only a cognitive exercise where certain facts are communicated. Instead, it highlights the important distinction that teaching does not necessarily result in learning, and therefore a holistic approach to learning is needed to create space where it can take place because of teaching. Learning as doing, experience, belonging, and becoming could be utilized not only among peer groups, but also across generational and age groups.[22] It is when generations learn together that they realize that all generations have something to teach and to learn from one another. Interpreting Scripture and tradition together facilitates community where different generations could not only participate but also contribute.

Participation may only signal being part of something, but belonging implies that an individual's contribution is accepted and legitimized in a group as one actively engages in the practices of the community.[23] I deem the distinction between participating and belonging of significance, because it does not merely constitute a wordplay but signifies a difference that is often overlooked in ministry. Often, we only hope for participation and do not go so far as to believe that people could really contribute and, for instance, reinterpret tradition from their perspective and worldview. Moreover, the movement between *knowing* and *acting* is important in intergenerational ministry, as staying with only knowing does not have enough significance. Root explains that ministry should invite different generations

19. Cloete, *Creative Tensions in Youth Ministry*, 4.

20. Cloete, *Creative Tensions in Youth Ministry*, 5.

21. Linhart, *Teaching the Next Generation*.

22. Ketcham, "Faith Formation with Others," 101–7.

23. Ketcham, "Faith Formation with Others," 106.

into opportunities to encounter the living Christ.[24] I would argue that knowledge could and should be part of such encounters; but participating, for instance in Christian practices, would facilitate such an encounter on a different level than only knowing.

Intergenerational ministry values diversity as a core element. Not even specialized age-specific ministry could escape the diversity that people, by their very nature, bring along. Intergenerational ministry implies bringing together different generational cultures, and therefore cultural sensitivity and awareness are among the primary skills required. If youth ministry is primarily about making space and trying to include youth, it operates from the premise that there are insiders and outsiders, which is not welcoming and uplifting. Intergenerational ministry should embrace and underscore the role of the sacraments that most church traditions practice, namely baptism and the Eucharist. These outward signs point toward the work of grace done by Christ and continued by the Holy Spirit. In light of this, I would suggest that ministry should put more emphasis on youth's identity in and through Christ—in other words, who and what they are already in Christ. Who we are in Christ and who we are becoming are two sides of the same coin and therefore youth ministry should proclaim and affirm both. Nel describes the congregation as a space where change is normal, where people become who they are already in Christ.[25] The church should therefore not be a space where only older generations have power and assume leadership roles, but a space where younger generations are nurtured because they can assist and lead in contextualizing ministry. From a theological perspective, intergenerational ministry is not merely a strategy to ensure the existence of the institutional church, but indeed a calling to be church in a rapidly changing context.

Discernment

Root cautions, "It is easy to say that youth ministry is about discerning God's continued actions in the world, but how do we do this in the midst of the complications of our contexts, our personalities and God's transcendent nature?"[26] I found it fitting to start this section on discernment with this difficult question, because I would not wish to suggest that the process of discernment is an easy road. It is, however, the only road for the church to be church in a changing world. Many would rather leave the faith community

24. Root, "Shape of Human Knowledge," 63.

25. Nel, *Youth Ministry*, 21.

26. Root, *Youth Ministry as Discerning Christopraxis*, 99.

than engage with this necessary, but difficult process. In a context where we prefer quick answers, this ongoing process could not be less attractive.

Osheim makes a noteworthy contribution to theological reflection on discernment from a Catholic perspective by providing a thought-provoking description of its foundation.[27] She gives an interesting account of different aspects of discernment, namely revelation and the reception of such revelations within the church, and how they intersect.[28] God reveals himself to us through his self-gift, Jesus Christ, who is understood as God's communication with the world and especially the church. Osheim understands this communication from a Trinitarian perspective, meaning God revealed himself through his Son Jesus Christ and continues the work through the Holy Spirit.[29] Through its reception of God's self-communication, the church came into existence and discovered her mission. I would like to emphasize the fact that the dialogue between God and the church necessitates community because, as Osheim puts it, "we seldom if ever come to know by ourselves. Instead, we are dependent on those who come before us: our communities, families and friends who help us learn."[30] This community of learning consisting of different generations implies that we learn anew in each generation how to express that revelation in our specific context and culture. Osheim's focus on the work of the Holy Spirit in the process of discernment is also noteworthy. The Holy Spirit assists us to grow in our understanding of the meaning of the divine revelation and our ability to express it in word and action.[31]

Wright's suggestion of ongoing critical and communal reflection is a crucial aspect of discernment that should inform intergenerational ministry.[32] Wright explains that reflective ministry should at least include critical reflection on the following areas:

- Our religious traditions, including the beliefs and practices thereof.
- Our individual lives before and in Christ.
- The world around us.[33]

27. Osheim, *Ministry of Discernment.*
28. Osheim, *Ministry of Discernment*, 2.
29. Osheim, *Ministry of Discernment*, 4.
30. Osheim, *Ministry of Discernment*, 7.
31. Osheim, *Ministry of Discernment*, 13.
32. Wright, *Reflective Youth Ministry*, 85.
33. Wright, *Reflective Youth Ministry*, 91.

Critical reflection as an integral part of intergenerational ministry signifies even more the participation of different generations by allowing younger generations to question the very practices and beliefs that remain so often unquestioned because of the assumption that questioning is a sign of unbelief. Wright anchors her emphasis on the idea of questioning by referring to how Jesus's ministry from childhood was characterized by questions;[34] he even responded to the actions of others with a question, like when he asked his mother, "Didn't you know I had to be in my Father's house?" (Luke 2:7). In addressing this topic, Root underlines the significance of doubt for faith seeking understanding.[35] Doubt is often expressed through disturbing questions about existential issues experienced in life. Doubt is, however, not a sign of unbelief but rather an important part of the life of faith and trust.

Wright also acknowledges that such questioning can be hard and therefore not automatically welcomed.[36] Questioning, however, could be a sign of showing interest and wanting to take ownership of what is presented to you in order to integrate it with your worldview and everyday life. Moreover, questioning can assist in the reinterpretation of traditional practices by evoking discussion, wrestling with existential issues, discomfort with easy answers, and even conflict between generations, which are crucial ingredients in the process of growing. Wright, however, cautions that questions do not necessarily need a fixed and complete answer from only one generation, but they do provide an opportunity to engage in theological reflection together and for each one in the community to exercise their shared responsibility to find responses to their questions.[37] Such a process also invites reflection on one's individual life before and with God. Questions about God and Christian living in most cases stem from our own life stories and experiences. Critical reflection on your own life as an individual and your vocation is of utmost importance for spiritual growth and even more so for young people who are intensely involved in a process of identity formation. Identity formation is not merely a biological or psychological process but also a spiritual one. Lastly, reflection should also be concerned with our responsibilities toward our immediate context as well as global issues. The outcome of the continuous process of discernment should inspire us to be an active church in the world. A discerning community can never turn away from the need and cry of the world but should be inspired and

34. Wright, *Reflective Youth Ministry*, 91–92.

35. Root, *Youth Ministry as Discerning Christopraxis*, 194.

36. Wright, *Reflective Youth Ministry*, 90.

37. Wright, *Reflective Youth Ministry*, 90.

willing to act in it. Faith has public significance and should therefore be embodied through the church by concrete action in the world.

I find the story about the calling of Samuel (1 Sam 3) a suitable illustration of how discernment shapes intergenerational ministry. Both Samuel and Eli were together in the same space (the tabernacle) and time (when the word and revelation of God was rare). Second, they represented different generations sharing the responsibility to discern God's will in their time. Samuel seemed to be alert because, even while he was sleeping, he heard the call, while Eli did not. Together they also shared the responsibility to discern the voice (word/revelation) of God. Several times Samuel reported to Eli because he assumed that it was Eli calling him, until Eli realized that it was God calling Samuel. It is significant that Samuel did not ignore the voice after Eli told him to go back to bed but responded every time until they together discovered the appropriate response to God's call. This interaction between Eli and Samuel demonstrates that discerning God's will is not an easy or a one-off process. Moreover, the message from God was a hard one for someone as young as Samuel, laying a tremendous responsibility on his shoulders. Thus, it demonstrates that God's revelation is not only reserved for a specific generation, but rather that God reveals himself to all generations. The revelation of God calls for obedience as Samuel demonstrated when Eli asked him about the word of the Lord to him. Eli's guidance to Samuel assisted him to recognize God's voice and call on the one hand, while Samuel's obedience led to a new dispensation. Until Samuel responded to the call of God, the word of Lord was scarce, but the process of discernment led to appropriate action and the Lord continuing to appear to Samuel.

Conclusion

This chapter has explored generational theory as a primary lens to describe what is meant by generations and how their interaction with each other and their context constructs social change. I have argued that generational theory should also form the basis of intergenerational ministry. A vivid overview of the plea for intergenerational ministry revealed that different perspectives have been generated on how intergenerational ministry should look. This chapter, however, underscores the need for an interdisciplinary approach to ministry where social theories are taken seriously to inform our theological reflection on ministry, not replace it. Learning and serving together, as well as discernment as a theological process of discovering God's will in a specific time and space, are singled out as primary processes that should inform and shape intergenerational ministry. Since our society is marked by fragmentation, intergenerational ministry will be counter-culture. As such, it will not happen automatically, but there should be an intentionality in shaping such a ministry. The church should not be the only space of intergenerational ministry, but it should have a strong missional approach of going into the world by serving in its immediate context. For generations to meet and share their life and faith stories, they will have to be prepared to take responsibility for each other not only in the church context but also in society. To fulfill that responsibility intergenerational ministry should not only be concerned with keeping youth in the church but also with sending them into the world.

Bibliography

Bonner, Steven. "Understanding the Changing Adolescent." In Clark, *Adoptive Youth Ministry*, 22–38.

Clark, Chap, ed. *Adoptive Youth Ministry: Integrating Emerging Generations into the Family of Faith*. Grand Rapids: Baker Academic, 2016.

Cloete, Anita. "Creative Tensions in Youth Ministry in a Congregational Context." *HTS Theological Studies* 71 (2015) 1–7.

Erikson, Erik H. *Childhood and Society*. New York: Harper & Row, 1963.

Gambone, James V. *All Are Welcome: A Primer for Intentional Intergenerational Ministry and Dialogue*. Crystal Bay, MN: Elder Eye, 1998.

Glassford, Darwin, and Lynn Barger-Elliot. "Toward Intergenerational Ministry in a Post-Christian Era." *Christian Education Journal* 8 (2011) 364–78.

Harkness, Allen G. "Intergenerational Christian Education: Reclaiming a Significant Educational Strategy in Christian Faith Communities." PhD diss., Murdoch University, 1996.

Jansen, Nerina. *Generation Theory*. Johannesburg: McGraw-Hill, 1974.

Ketcham, Sharon G. "Faith Formation with Others." In *Teaching the Next Generation: A Comprehensive Guide for Teaching Christian Formation*, edited by Terry Linhart, 100–111. Grand Rapids: Baker Academic, 2016.

Linhart, Terry, ed. *Teaching the Next Generation: A Comprehensive Guide for Teaching Christian Formation*. Grand Rapids: Baker Academic, 2016.

Mead, George H. *Mind, Self, and Society: From the Standpoint of a Social Behaviorist*. Chicago: University of Chicago Press, 1934.

Nel, Malan. *Youth Ministry: An Inclusive Congregational Approach*. Pretoria: Kitskopie, 2005.

Nesbit Sbanatto, Elizabeth A., and Craig L. Blomberg. *Effective Generational Ministry: Biblical and Practical Insights for Transforming Church Communities*. Grand Rapids: Baker Academic, 2016.

Osheim, Amanda C. *Ministry of Discernment: The Bishop and the Sense of the Faithful*. Collegeville: Liturgical, 2016.

Root, Andrew. "Youth Ministry as Discerning Christopraxis: A Hermeneutical Model." In *The Theological Turn in Youth Ministry*, edited by Andrew Root and Kenda Creasy Dean, 98–118. Downers Grove: InterVarsity, 2011.

———. "The Shape of Human Knowledge and Christian Ministry." In Linhart, *Teaching the Next Generation*, 56–64.

White, James W. *Intergenerational Religious Education: Models, Theory and Prescription for Interage Life and Learning in the Faith Community*. Birmingham, AL: Religious Education, 1988.

Wright, Almeda M. "Reflective Youth Ministry: Youth Ministry as Critical, Ongoing, Communal Reflection." In Clark, *Adoptive Youth Ministry*, 85–96.

Questions for Reflection and Discussion

1. In this chapter, Cloete provides us a framework for thinking about the generational dynamics we experience within our churches. What generational groups seem to factor most prominently in the life of your congregation at present? How would you describe the relationship between the generational cohorts present within your church?
2. Cloete encourages us to consider the importance of the generations within our churches learning and serving together. In what ways do you see this occurring within your church context? If this is not happening, why not?
3. Cloete provides an insightful account of the need for the generations within the church to engage in the Christian practice of discernment together. In what ways does this section of her chapter challenge or inspire you? What factors, if any, make it difficult for the generations within your congregational context to engage in the practice of discernment together?

4

The Relationship between Church and Home

A Theological Approach

Gareth Crispin

§

EDITOR'S INTRODUCTION: In the introductory chapter, I note that Erikson saw parenthood as the "ultimate archetype" of generativity. While Erikson insisted that generativity is not limited only to parents, mothers and fathers clearly play a crucial role in the lives of their own children. In this chapter, Crispin argues that a generative church must grapple with how it conceives of the relationship between its responsibility to nurture children and youth in the faith and that borne by the Christian parents within its ranks. Crispin introduces us to the various ways in which churches have sought to address this relationship. He then guides us through a full-fledged biblical vision of what this relationship can—and perhaps *should*—be. Ultimately, Crispin hopes to see young people become meaningfully linked to the broader life of the church and to find their place as active participants within it. However, he notes, this requires us to consider the importance of "letting go," a theme that he picks up from the introductory chapter. He focuses especially on the specific ways that parents must be prepared to "let go" as their children grow toward maturity. This chapter provides us opportunity to gain clarity about how we envision the crucial interplay between congregational generativity and the generative faith exercised within the home.

§

Like two deathless stars meant to burn forever, God and His church will always be married. Always be in love. Always be one. So much so that death will never part them, for even that will be no more.[1]

Introduction

THE old African proverb that it takes a village to raise a child captures nicely an important impasse within youth and children's ministry. Who has primary responsibility in ministry to youth and children? Is it the parents, or is it the village, the church? If both, how do the two relate?

In considering the concept of the generative church this is a vital question, as home and church are two key social institutions in the life of emerging generations. We have already seen how adults "express generativity in social contexts and through social institutions" and that "social institutions themselves may or may not function in generative ways." So exploring the relationship between these two key social institutions should shed light on an important way in which generativity functions.

While it is fair to say that dichotomies can obscure the detailed reality and nuance of any discussion, they also can help to pull open a debate; they can help us categorize phenomena for the sake of analysis. This is true in discussing the relationship between home and church. There is a range of views on this relationship, but there is also a sense in which we have two corners. In one we have the proponents of *Intergenerational Church* (IG) and in the other the champions of *Family Ministry* (FM). Sadly, there appears to be little engagement between these two.

This chapter will explore the arguments made by IG and FM writers and focus on the disagreement over the primacy of home or church in youth and children's ministry.[2] It then will explore how biblical theology and an ap-

1. Hill-Perry, *Gay Girl, Good God*, 184.

2. Because the focus of disagreement and discussion between IG and FM writers revolves around youth and children already in the church, this will also form the focus

preciation of the developmental processes of youth and children might provide a way to bring IG and FM positions together into coherent relationship and help us understand how this relationship can aid generativity.

Who Is Saying What? The Broad Contours of the Debate

Intergenerational Church: Definitions and Focus

In the last decade or so, IG has been put firmly on the agenda of youth and children's ministry, but what is it? And what do proponents of IG say about the relationship between home and the wider church?

Allen and Ross's text has become one of the key sources on recent IG thinking; in it they describe IG ministry as occurring

> when a congregation intentionally brings the generations together in mutual serving, sharing or learning within the core activities of the church in order to live out being the body of Christ to each other and the greater community.[3]

IG ministry thus is primarily concerned with the way that the church functions as church. There is a focus on mutuality, the old and young learning from one another,[4] a foundational facet of IG that is also picked up on by writers such as Csinos in his strategies for inclusion[5] and Snailum, who posits that "mutually influential relationships are the distinguishing characteristic of intergenerational community." Snailum also contrasts intergenerational settings to merely multigenerational ones, which "are those social environments in which several generations are in proximity with each other but not necessarily in relationship."[6] Harkness writes along similar lines in setting out his four constitutive factors of intergenerational ministry: mutuality between participants, collaboration, shared experiences, and bi-directional teaching.[7]

---

of this chapter. Questions around the missional possibilities of these approaches are important but will not be reviewed here.

3. Allen and Ross, *Intergenerational Christian Formation*, 17.
4. Allen, "Bringing the Generations Together," 331.
5. Csinos, *Children's Ministry That Fits*, 87–107.
6. Snailum, "Integrating Intergenerational Ministry Strategies," 8.
7. Harkness, "Intergenerational Christian Education," 222–23.

Reasons why IG writers believe this is the correct focus for ministry to youth and children will be explored later; for now let us explore the differences between IG and FM.

Family Ministry: Definitions and Focus

Like IG, FM is a relatively new entrant in contemporary thinking and writing on youth and children's ministry. As a category it covers a range of views helpfully summarized by Jones, who defines FM as

> the process of intentionally and persistently realigning a congregation's proclamation and practices so that parents are acknowledged, trained, and held accountable as the persons primarily responsible for the discipleship of their children.[8]

Within this, Jones perceives three models: Family-Based (FBM), Family-Equipping (FEM), and Family-Integrated Models (FIM).[9] FBMs are similar in look to traditional segmented-programmatic models; however, they take the normal segmented program and add the involvement of parents. FEMs take things one step further and ask how the church can restructure the entire program to equip parents in their primary role as disciplers of their children and the primary agents of outreach to other parents. FIMs (in theory) do away with age segregation altogether.

While FBMs and FEMs are focused on the primacy of parents in discipling youth and children, that does not mean there will be much if any intentional interaction between youth, children, and older generations during church services and activities. In theory, one could operate a FBM or FEM without youth and children ever really coming into contact with older members of the church; they might be taught and discipled separately, but their parents would be included, equipped, and partnered with. Thus, FBMs and FEMs are likely to look very different in practice from IG models.

While one might expect to see close similarities between FIMs and IG models, they are in fact very different, due to their divergent understandings of the value of learning theory and the relationship between the biological-legal family and the church family. Contra IG writers, as described above, proponents of FIMs essentially endorse the inclusion of youth and children within adult activities and services with little or no change in response to their presence.

8. Jones, *Perspectives on Family Ministry*, 40.

9. Jones, *Perspectives on Family Ministry*, 40.

So, in articulating a commitment to expository preaching, Renfro states that "sermons are geared for adults, yet we're amazed at what children get out of these messages"[10] and "they soak up far more than many people might think as *they watch* their parents worshipping, praying, listening, and humbling themselves week by week."[11] This is a far cry from the ideals of the participative, inclusive, and mutual approach encouraged by IG writers.

Disagreements over Learning Theory

These differences between IG and FM proponents are explicable in the first instance by a different approach to the use of the social sciences and learning theory. FM advocates can display a negative attitude to the social sciences[12] and promote what, on the surface, looks like a purer "scriptural approach."[13] IG authors, on the other hand, are much readier to explicitly embrace certain aspects of the social sciences.

Space precludes a detailed account of the discussion over the use of social science and in particular debates around learning and developmental theories. However, it is worth noting that many IG theorists argue against approaches that separate youth and children into age-specific groups by asserting that they are based, in part, on an unhelpful dominance of certain development theories (e.g., Piaget, Fowler). They see such theories as unhelpful because they focus only on a narrow definition of learning which is best suited to an academic approach as opposed to a broader understanding of formation that can occur within the life of a community of faith.[14]

Reacting to this, IG thinkers draw on leaning theorists such as Vygotsky to promote situative/sociocultural theories of learning. As Allen summarizes,

> This theory places a stronger emphasis on the social interaction of the learning environment than do cognitivist and behaviorist theories, and promotes the idea that the social setting itself is crucial to the learning process.[15]

10. Renfro, "Family-Integrated Ministry," 58.

11. Renfro, "Family-Integrated Ministry," 57, my emphasis.

12. Stinson and Jones, *Trained in the Fear of God*, 31.

13. See Stinson and Jones, 31–32; Rienow, *Limited Church*, 11–57.

14. See Glassford and Barger-Elliot, "Toward Intergenerational Ministry," 365–68; Harkness, "Intergenerational Christian Education," 26; Pazmino and Kang, "Generational Fragmentations and Christian Education," 382.

15. Allen, "Bringing the Generations," 324.

Vygotsky argues that to move through the zone of proximal development (the distance between someone's actual and potential development), individuals actually need to interact with those who are further down the line than they;[16] it is this interactive development which IG approaches seek to foster.

IG authors reach similar conclusions using other theorists such as Bailyn[17] and Westerhoff.[18] This approach is also comparable to Dean's idea of *legitimate peripheral participation*, which allows for "real, if tentative, opportunities to participate at the periphery of conversations until they gained sufficient fluency to join in fully."[19] In this way, IG writers reject the fragmentation of the segmented approaches and the nonparticipatory methods of the FIM authors to advocate a very specific model of church.

Church or Home?

The second reason for the difference between IG and FM thinkers is more germane to the matter at hand. IG and FM writers disagree over the relationship between the biological-legal family and the church family. As we will see, generally speaking, FM writers give most weight to parents, and especially fathers, whereas IG authors stress the church family more. This is no small matter as demonstrated by Harkness when he identifies the danger of family ministry models focusing so much on family units that intergenerational interaction within the church is stifled.[20] We can approach this discussion by way of examining Deuteronomy 6 almost as a test case.

Both Harkness and Beagles explicitly contend that, given the difference between modern understandings of the nuclear family and the Old Testament ideas of a wider kinship grouping or clan, the discipling commands of Moses in Deuteronomy 6 should be understood as relating to a grouping more akin to our modern church families than our modern biological-legal families.[21] While not denying the responsibility of parents found in Deuteronomy 6 and other Old Testament passages, Beagles asserts that the

16. Allen, "Bringing the Generations," 326.

17. Pazmino and Kang, "Generational Fragmentations," 381.

18. See Harkness, "Intergenerational Education," 438–39; Glassford and Barger-Elliot, "Toward Intergenerational Ministry," 373.

19. Dean, *Almost Christian*, 144.

20. Harkness, "Intergenerational Education," 435–36.

21. Beagles, "Growing Disciples in Community," 149; Harkness, "Intergenerational Christian Education," 44.

demands of discipling a child are too great for one small nuclear family; as he expresses, "it truly does take a village to disciple young people."[22]

Harkness concludes that the context of Deuteronomy 6 (Moses speaking to the covenant community of God's people) pushes us to understand the references to children as *collective* rather than *particular*; they are the children of the community rather than the children of particular people.[23] He argues further that even if we think Moses might be speaking to a smaller unit than the whole covenant community, the next unit down is the kinship group, which might be as many as fifty to one hundred people and would have included many adults. So, while there was obviously a responsibility on the part of biological parents, that "responsibility would have been spread in quite a natural way over all the members of the whole 'family' (= household) unit."[24]

FM proponents, however, see the balance the other way. Getting to the heart of the issue, Hamilton argues that discipleship of youth and children "doesn't take a village; it takes a father."[25] Writing contra Harkness and others, though without direct engagement with them, he focuses on Deuteronomy 6 and the fact that the Hebrew verbs in the commands in v. 7 are second person masculine singular in form. Thus, while Moses is addressing the covenant community about the covenant between them and God, the way in which the covenant community is to ensure its ongoing future obedience to God is specifically through fathers (reflected in the fact that the verb is masculine) teaching their own children (evident in the verb being singular).[26]

Hamilton goes on to look at the similarities between the commands to fathers in Deuteronomy 6 and the commands to kings in Deuteronomy 17. He argues that the king was to be like a father to the nation, to love and lead them as an example for fathers to follow within their own families. It follows then that FM writers taking this line would not hesitate to focus on the adults—and especially fathers—in worship services, as the role of church leaders is seen much the same as that of the king: to lead fathers to lead their families.[27]

But even among FM thinkers there is disagreement, with a fault line seemingly falling somewhere among the advocates of FEM. Sheilds (a FBM

22. Beagles, "Growing Disciples in Community," 157.
23. Harkness, "Intergenerational Christian Education," 44.
24. Harkness, "Intergenerational Christian Education," 43.
25. Hamilton, "That the Coming Generation Might Praise the Lord," 37.
26. Hamilton, "That the Coming Generation Might Praise the Lord," 35–38.
27. Hamilton, "That the Coming Generation Might Praise the Lord," 38–40.

supporter) writes that the FIM has a "'family of families' type of ecclesiology," but that the "New Testament church is not a family of families but the family of God."[28] While he does not share Harkness's views of the danger of undermining IG integration, Shields is concerned that the family of families view might result in a reduction of the wider church's efforts in evangelism (a classic critique of the "heavy" family integrationist position by a "lighter" integrationist).[29]

Even within the same volume as Hamilton, we see Plummer, in his chapter on the New Testament and early church, concluding that with respect to church leaders,

> the recognition of such gifting within the broader community suggests that children might benefit from gathering to receive teaching from God-given instructors other than their parents. In some cases, these gatherings might occur in age-organized contexts.[30]

This is hardly a move toward the intergenerationality of Harkness and others, but it does reveal a fissure running somewhere down the middle of FM approaches as to the precise relationship between the biological-legal family and the church family.

Attempts at a Middle Path

There are several movements that have attempted to bring together the home and church in constructive ways. We cannot review all of them here but will focus on the following: Joiner's *Think Orange*, Clark's *Adoptive Church* and *Adoptive Youth Ministry*, DeVries's *Family-Based-Youth Ministry*, Jones's *Family-Equipping Ministry*, and Stanton's ideas around transitioning.[31] In doing so we will pay particular attention to how they use biblical theology in their treatment of the church-home relationship and whether they do so more convincingly than the IF and FM writers above.

28. Shields, "Family-Integrated Ministry."
29. Shields, "Family-Integrated Ministry," 81.
30. Plummer, "Bring Them Up," 55.
31. Stanton, *Families*.

Thinking Orange

Think Orange helpfully captures the idea of church and home as different institutions coming together to create a partnership that is greater than the sum of its parts, or in Joiner's analogy, bringing red and yellow together to make a different color. On the thorny issue of exegeting Deuteronomy chapter 6, Joiner simply draws attention to the partnership between the home and the wider community of faith,[32] but as he unfolds his vision it becomes clear that it is squarely a FM rather than an IG vision.

For Joiner the family is primary in discipleship;[33] it is the family that does the nurturing.[34] He has a different definition for Family Ministry than Jones,[35] but in essence "thinking orange" means church leaders thinking about how best to synchronize efforts with the family by working with them and leveraging their natural potential to influence their children.

When Joiner flirts with the overarching story of the Bible he focuses on the genealogies "from Adam to Jesus, from Genesis to Matthew," musing that "maybe these lists are there to remind us that God is actively using families to link the past to the future so that they might broadcast His love to every generation."[36] This is helpful to an extent but lacks a fuller biblical-theological picture.

The result is that, while *Thinking Orange* gives us many good avenues for thought, it does not help us bring together the insights of FM and IG church, and neither does it adequately digest the implications of both biblical theology and the developmental processes of youth and children.

Adoptive Church / Youth Ministry

Chap Clark's *Adoptive Youth Ministry* has been one of the most significant developments in youth and children's ministry thinking in recent years. It brings more focus to the role of the local church in youth ministry and the way in which churches need to embrace youth in their midst as family, as siblings. Clark works against inviting "the young to Christ without offering them inclusion in the family God has for them."[37] For him, "the adoptive

32. Joiner, *Think Orange*, 78.
33. Joiner, *Think Orange*, 49.
34. Joiner, *Think Orange*, 79.
35. Joiner, *Think Orange*, 83.
36. Joiner, *Think Orange*, 49.
37. Clark, *Adoptive Church*, 182.

church is youth ministry with a destination: the household of God."[38] Perhaps what is most interesting about Clark's position is that it holds the local church and parents in high regard but does not neatly fall into either the IG or FM constituency.

Space precludes the detailed engagement with Clark that his work deserves. For the purposes of this chapter we will pick up on one area that is especially pertinent to our concerns. Clark is a youth ministry specialist and, while he is well attuned to adolescent development,[39] his approach takes less consideration of the movement from childhood to adolescence and adolescence into emerging adulthood and specifically how this might require a change in relationship between parents and the wider church.

For Clark,

> without an adoptive model of youth ministry, even those broader ministry strategies focused on parents as disciplers and the most solid youth programs cannot possibly provide intrinsic participation in the whole of the family of God that our young need to be convinced of their place and worth.[40]

Maybe, but equally, an integrationist approach to youth ministry (call it adoptive or whatever) is unlikely to work unless parents understand and are bought into the strategy. This is especially important when considering the large amount of influence the home context has over both what younger children do and their emerging attitude toward the wider church family. Clark spends a good deal of time on speaking about the other adults in the church (not parents or youth leaders), but not enough time is spent examining how the significant impact of parents can be weaved into an integrationist position.

In Clark's edited book on the adoptive approach, in considering how teens become part of the church, Cannister discusses things a church can do to integrate youth into the wider family. In doing so, among other things, he includes examples of how he encouraged his own children toward integration, but these are only mentioned incidentally. Parents are not placed at the heart of the model.[41] Diaz and Jackson[42] write in the same volume about the wider church and families, respectively, but neither directly addresses this question of the relationship between church and family. There

38. Clark, *Adoptive Church*, 4.

39. Clark, *Hurt 2.0*.

40. Clark, "Adoption View," 84.

41. Cannister, "Thinking Ecclesiologically," 142–43.

42. Diaz, "Call to Adoption"; Jackson, "Thinking Critically."

is a great deal to take from Clark's adoptive approach, but in the end it does not satisfactorily bring together home and church. It does a good job of thinking about one half of the issue (the welcome needed from the existing church family) but seemingly underplays the other (how parents fit into the picture).

Family-Based Youth Ministry

First published in 1994, DeVries's *Family-Based Youth Ministry* is one of the earliest and best contemporary treatments of the church/home relationship. He clearly and winsomely demonstrates the importance of both church and home before specifically delineating that "the primary task of family-based youth ministry is to 'pass the baton' of faith formation to the extended family of the church."[43]

He explicitly situates his approach in youth ministry rather than what he calls family ministry, meaning that instead of expecting parents to take responsibility, "the church takes the responsibility" with a focus on the youth ministry "accessing as much as possible the family and the extended family of the church."[44]

This raises the first of two significant questions when reading DeVries's work: it assumes that the baton belongs to the youth ministry to begin with. Functionally and experientially of course this may be the case, but without any engagement with the classic biblical texts (Deut 6 et al.) DeVries ends up bypassing the opportunity to biblically ground and justify his approach. It also perhaps, as with Clark, demonstrates the influence of DeVries's grounding as a youth pastor rather than a children's pastor.

Second, not only is there no engagement with the classic scriptural references, there is no engagement with biblical theology as a wider field, meaning *Family-Based Youth Ministry* lacks the biblical-theological guidance needed to help shape a conception of the church/home relationship. So while there is a great deal to commend in DeVries's approach, it would benefit from detailed engagement with biblical theology.

Jones's Family-Equipping Model

While firmly within the FM constituency, Jones, perhaps of all the FM writers, pays most attention to the wider church and also to biblical theology.

43. DeVries, *Family-Based*, 155.

44. DeVries, *Family-Based*, 175.

He is keen to stress the importance of the wider church in countering the prevalent segmentation of ministries along age lines.[45] Additionally, he perceptively uses biblical theology to show how parents might be tempted to see their children only in light of creation (loving them as made in God's image) and the fall (disciplining them as sinners), while leaving the questions about their redemption to the church.[46]

However, the main thrust of Jones's use of biblical theology is to help parents (and help churches to help parents) see their children "for who they really are" rather than shape the relationship between the home and church. This is all good and well, but as we will see, biblical theology suggests more than Jones allows.

Families: A Forgotten Factor?

Stanton's Grove booklet *Families: A Forgotten Factor* delves into the issue of the relationship between home and church and concludes that as children grow up, parents slowly pass the *activity* of discipling over to the church while maintaining the primary *responsibility* for it.[47] The focus on movement over time is very helpful, as is the consideration of responsibility and activity. However, as I will argue shortly, a focus on biblical theology suggests something more: a passing over not only of activity but also responsibility to the wider church.

Biblical Theology as a Way Forward?

It seems rare for IG and FM thinkers to engage and dialogue directly with one another. This is a shame given the positive and distinct reflections each brings to bear on questions of youth and children's ministry. In bringing the two together and focusing on this significant area of disagreement, I hope to provide a way to profit from the best aspects of both approaches by articulating a clear vision for how the church and home might fit together both theologically and practically.

I have argued above that, while both approaches seek a grounding in the Bible, they do so only by looking at narrow exegetical and contextual issues to the detriment of the wider picture given by biblical theology. Alongside their not paying sufficient attention to the arc of biblical theology, I will

45. Jones, *Family Ministry*, 127–29.

46. Jones, *Family Ministry*, 69–88.

47. Stanton, *Families*, 18–19.

contend that problems have emerged due to seeing *youth* and *children* as static categories and paying insufficient attention to the dynamic nature of the developmental process and how it impacts questions of the relationship between parents and the wider church.

I will argue that a biblical-theological approach to the relationship of church and the home that recognizes the dynamic nature of childhood and adolescence will help us map out a constructive and theologically robust path through the current disagreement. We must first define biblical theology and establish why it is to be considered normative in this discussion.

What Is Biblical Theology and Why Is It Normative in This Discussion?

Rosner defines biblical theology as "principally concerned with the overall theological message of the whole Bible. It seeks to understand the parts in relation to the whole."[48] It thus depends on a coherence which arises from both a canon of Scripture and the inspiration of that canon. Because of this, biblical theology as a discipline is nonsensical to those for whom the canon of Scripture or the inspiration of that canon are problematic; you could go as far as to say that, for those who hold such views, it does not exist.[49]

Most FM and IG proponents do not fall into this group, but rather seem to accept the canon and its inspiration and therefore the coherence of the whole message of the Bible, which means they affirm biblical theology's existence and see it as a valid theological approach. Biblical theology is therefore normative for IG and FM writers, which also enables the focus placed upon it within this chapter to contribute most meaningfully to this discussion.

The core activities of biblical theology are twofold. It seeks to draw out themes that "constitute the ligaments that hold the canon together: rest, temple, priesthood, kingdom, and so forth,"[50] but it also looks to draw these out in relation to "the great turning points in redemptive history."[51]

There are various ways of understanding these turning points, some more detailed than others. For this chapter, a fairly basic version will suffice; we will think of the grand story of the Bible as one based on the turning points of creation, rebellion, redemption, and consummation (or new creation).

48. Rosner, "Biblical Theology," 3.

49. Balla, "Challenges to Biblical Theology," 20–27.

50. Carson, *Christ and Culture Revisited*, 45.

51. Carson, *Christ and Culture Revisited*, 45.

In thinking about these turning points, Rosner emphasizes the centrality of analysis and synthesis in the biblical-theological endeavor. In seeking to understand the Bible as a whole there is necessarily an iterative process of analyzing the parts and synthesizing the whole. In this way, "biblical theology must never be thought of as independent of the other disciplines. It presupposes them."[52]

By "other disciplines," Rosner means systematic theology and biblical studies (exegesis, etc.). These disciplines seek to understand the Bible through different approaches than biblical theology but also help biblical theologians to understand the parts that make up the whole. The biblical theologian cannot do biblical theology without analyzing the Bible systematically and exegetically. At the same time, because there is a whole to speak of, "biblical study is incomplete until biblical theology has been done."[53] Carson makes a similar point forcefully in saying that the biblical-theological turning points "must control our thinking *simultaneously* and *all the time*." Because of this, he chooses to call them "the *non-negotiables* of biblical theology."[54]

The importance of biblical theology, however, is not merely intellectual or abstract. It is grounded and has profound implications for our practice. As Rosner confirms, biblical theology "is practiced by Christian communities and is intricately linked to their determination to shape their faith, life, worship and service in accordance with scripture under the guidance of the Spirit."[55] If "biblical study is incomplete until biblical theology has been done,"[56] then perhaps biblical theology is incomplete until it has been embraced as a practical theological project.

How might biblical theology then shape our "faith, life, worship and service"? Carson gives a helpful set of examples of possible impacts of biblical theology when he uses it to examine Niebuhr's options for conceiving the relationship between Christ and culture. The "Christ against Culture" paradigm, for example, is generated by stressing fall and redemption, assuming a backdrop of persecution and, by definition, downplaying creation and consummation.[57]

It is the argument of this chapter that most FM and IG proponents have done something similar when it comes to discussing the relationship

52. Rosner, "Biblical Theology," 4.

53. Rosner, "Biblical Theology," 4.

54. Carson, *Christ and Culture Revisited*, 59.

55. Rosner, "Biblical Theology," 5.

56. Rosner, "Biblical Theology," 4.

57. Carson, *Christ and Culture Revisited*, 59–60.

between church and home. There is not enough synthesis, not enough taking account of the whole—and not only the whole but the trajectory of that whole. And, as I suggested above, this occurs in conjunction with paying insufficient attention to the developmental processes of youth and children.

Because this discussion revolves around a tale of two families—biological and spiritual—we need now to turn to examining family and marriage—because biblically the two, while distinct, are intrinsically linked—through the lens of biblical theology. This entails undertaking the sort of thematic biblical theology mentioned earlier, while also ensuring it remains embedded within the arc of the creation, rebellion, redemption, and new creation turning points.

In Creation

Genesis 1 and 2 introduce us to the essence, nature, and purpose of marriage and family. Adam is given the role of stewarding the garden, but it is not good for him to do this alone (Gen 2:18). Adam is given a helper suitable for him, Eve. She is bone of his bone and flesh of his flesh (Gen 2:23); for this reason, he is to become "one flesh" with her. This idea of marriage being about one-fleshness will be crucial in a biblical-theological understanding of marriage and family. Adam and Eve in their one-fleshness are to multiply, create family, and steward the earth (1:26).

In the Fall

In Genesis 3 we read that the fall of humankind does not erase marriage and family, but neither do they remain unaffected (Gen 3). Humanity's relationship with God is marred (Gen 3: 8–10) and so therefore are all human relationships; marital relationships become strained (Gen 3:7, 16), and family life becomes deeply problematic (Gen 4).

In Redemption

Jesus'ss statements about the role of marriage and family are varied and, at first glance, appear to be in tension with one another. We will return to a consideration of these statements in due course. For now, from a biblical-theological perspective, we will focus on Ephesians 5:22–33, which is, as

Ortlund suggests, "the theological and hermeneutical intersection through which all biblical questions about marriage must eventually pass."[58]

Paul begins by talking about husband and wife, but at every point weaves in a comparison between that relationship and that of Christ and the church. As the passage develops, Paul makes clear that he is making a specific point about the relationship between the two: that earthly marriage points us toward the eternal marriage between Christ and his church.

Paul returns to the one-fleshness of Genesis 2 to show the extent to which a husband should love his wife (as he loves his own body, v. 28), but in doing so also demonstrates how this shows us something of Christ's love for his church, which is his body (v. 29). After quoting Genesis 2:24, Paul then makes the striking statement that, in doing so, he is talking about Christ and the church (v. 31). As Ortlund argues, "Paul's declaration in verse 30 that 'we are members of [Christ's] *body*' gives him the opportunity to show a typological connection with Genesis 2:24 ('one *flesh*') in verse 31."[59]

In the same way that uniting to husband or wife means leaving the previous family of the father, so too uniting to Christ means leaving our previous family of husband/wife or parent. Only Paul doesn't take it that far, at least not yet; his household codes (Eph 5 and Col 3) demonstrate that, until the final consummation of all things in Christ, the earthly family retains some of its allegiance. Union with Christ does indeed involve a leaving of the earthly family for the heavenly one, but this is a process that will only be completed finally when Jesus returns.

In Consummation

Notwithstanding the discussion to come about Jesus's various comments regarding marriage and family, he makes it clear that in the new creation there will be no marriage and therefore also no natural family (Mark 12:25). Revelation 21 shows us that this will be because of the marriage of the Lamb to his bride, the church (Rev 21:2). This union will be complete and other earthly unions that point to this final eternal union will be no more.

So biblically-theologically we see a biological family created through the coming together of male and female replaced eternally by a spiritual family created through the coming together of the Lamb and the church. We live in the in-between times, the *now* and the *not yet* in which the church exists and believers are in a very real sense already in union with Christ (Rom 12:5); but as this has not been fully consummated, we live in both

58. Ortlund, "Marriage," 656.

59. Ortlund, "Marriage," 656.

families at once. Given this, it is no surprise that we find Jesus's comments with respect to marriage and family life to be confusing and characterized by tension.

Jesus on Marriage and Family

Some of Jesus's teachings on family and marriage sound strong to our ears (Mark 3:31–35; Matt 10:34–38; Luke 14:25–27). As Hellerman points out, we have been only too happy to domesticate them, often limiting Jesus's words to the level of conviction rather than actual behavior.[60] Step by step, Hellerman addresses Jesus's references to brothers and sisters to show that the plain meaning of the texts of the gospels is that "exchanging one family for another is at the very heart of what it means to be a disciple of Jesus."[61]

Hellerman shows how for Jesus's hearers the individual was always seen as secondary to the family, including sibling relationships. Thus the moniker "brother," as used by early Christians, is doubly powerful; it is not merely a term of endearment or even an indication of theoretical commitment, but is a statement of complete change in family allegiance.[62] This is akin to a change of bloodline: the natural bloodline of earthly parents to the spiritual bloodline of being in God's family through the blood of Christ.[63]

This doesn't do away with the natural family but situates it within the church as the primary family. Hellerman concludes that

> an ideal and not uncommon situation, we might surmise, would see the conversion of a whole household, with the disciple's natural family embedded in, and serving the mission of, the dominant surrogate family of faith. In this case there would be no conflict of loyalties. But even here the natural family existed to serve the designs of the family of God, and not vice versa. The focus was on the church—not on the family. And where conflict between the natural family and God's family did arise, the faith family was to become the primary locus of relational solidarity.[64]

While Hellerman provides a convincing way of integrating Jesus's teachings, he does not take the discussion far enough. He alludes to the

60. Hellerman, *When the Church Was a Family*, 56.
61. Hellerman, *When the Church Was a Family*, 68.
62. Hellerman, *When the Church Was a Family*, 53–75.
63. Thanks to Russell Haitch for this observation.
64. Hellerman, *When the Church Was a Family*, 73.

question of the place of children when suggesting that whole households would be brought into the church family. However, he does not attempt to synthesize the teachings that place direct responsibilities on the shoulders of fathers alongside the more IG passages on spiritual formation within the biblical witness. Because of this, he also does not help us with the question in hand, that of bringing FM and IG positions together. He does not, for example, mention texts such as Ephesians 6:4 or the enduring relevance of Deuteronomy 6:4–9 (key texts for FM writers). No mention is made of what happens as a child grows into an adolescent and an adolescent into an adult.[65] Youth, children, FM, and IG are simply not the target of his discussion.

Bringing a More Comprehensive Biblical Theology to Bear

We recall that the direction of travel in biblical theology is from natural family to supernatural family, from biologically constituted to spiritually constituted relationships. We remember that we live in the now and the not yet of the biblical-theological arc, experiencing the tension of living in two families, while not forgetting that Ephesians 5 tells us that the natural exists to point to the supernatural.

Considering then that the natural family points to the church family, it is perhaps not unreasonable to conclude that this is how the relationship should develop over time. Doing so would mean that in the now and not yet of the present, natural families should be seeking to move children in an arc toward the future, toward the church family. It's important, however, to clarify what this does and does not mean.

It doesn't simply mean getting youth and children to pray a prayer to accept Jesus as their personal Savior. Hellerman's work pushes us to see how becoming part of the church is so much more than this and is deliberately and forcefully expressed in terms of a sibling bond. Natural families should not simply be seeking to promote some form of personal confession, but a life lived in light of the reality of the sibling nature of the church, a new allegiance to the church family. In contemporary society we are well used to seeing parenting generally as a launch pad, but in the church do we see the natural family's role specifically as launching youth and children into the church family?

65. Space precludes a detailed discussion of how conceptions of the journey from childhood to adulthood have changed over time. It will suffice to note that, while some significant differences exist, there remains a core similarity in the sense that children do mature to adulthood and do so over time in steps or a journey.

In saying this we don't simply mean the church universal. The now and the not yet of biblical theology reminds us that we are not yet in the new creation where the church will be one, with no need for gathered churches with local pastors. In the stage of the biblical-theological arc in which we currently find ourselves, God has provided pastors and teachers to look after local churches. Biblical theology, therefore, specifically encourages parents to launch their youth and children into local churches, into a defined local ecclesia in which they can continue to be nurtured in the faith.

Considering the Developmental Processes of Youth and Children

Before concluding we need also to pause to reflect on the developmental processes of children and youth (seemingly overlooked in the discussions around FM and IG). It is perhaps obvious to state that children begin as completely dependent on their biological or adoptive parents and bit by bit emerge into increasing social and emotional independence or maturity, but perhaps the full implications of this for youth and children's ministry have not been properly assessed, especially when setting this arc of development alongside the arc of biblical theology. How does the development into increasing autonomy or self-differentiation impact how we view the relationship between natural family and church family?

In his introduction to this volume, Seibel has already helpfully set out the importance of Erikson's concept of generativity for ministering to youth and children. He encourages us to see generativity in churches as a commitment to "establish and guide the next generation in the faith." While Erikson used parenthood as a model of generativity, it is not limited to parents; Seibel reminds us that it can be located in a variety of contexts and so brings our focus to the whole church as a generative institution. Central to this generative task is the process of letting go, caring rather than controlling.

It is here that the arc of biblical theology can provide a focus to both our view of the development of youth and children and our understanding of generativity. For the church to "let go" it, in the first instance, needs parents of youth and children in the church to let go. While in some ways parenthood is a model of generativity, parents also are a key component of the generative church. As children develop, they do so—especially in the early days—in relation to their parents and under their parents' care.

Keeping in mind the trajectory that biblical theology encourages us to consider, the letting go process from the perspective of the parent is not like standing back and folding their arms but more like walking alongside encouraging them in a certain direction. Teaching a child to ride a bike might serve as a helpful illustration.

As a child begins to show the wish and ability to cycle unaided, a parent can walk and run with them, holding the bike steady but loosening their grip so the child can begin increasingly to feel what it is like to balance the bike themselves. There comes a point when the parent gives a last little gentle push and lets go, even then jogging alongside to accompany the child. At this point the parent has launched the child with purpose and direction.

This idea of a process of letting go fits nicely as a mirror image of learning theories embraced by IG writers. As parents let go, they do not do so into a vacuum but into the family of the church and they do so not in one go, but over time, allowing and even encouraging their children into the peripheral participation noted above.

In Erikson's own words, one of the main underlying assumptions of his framework of psychosocial development is "that the human personality in principle develops according to steps predetermined in the growing person's readiness to be driven towards, to be aware of, and to interact with, a widening social radius."[66]

Biblical theology directs us to consider that in the life of youth and children this widening social radius includes the local church, and the reality of the influence of parents encourages us to see that they are crucial in this launching process, especially in the early years.

An Integrated, Dynamic Approach?

So what might it look like to bring biblical theology and a consideration of the development processes of youth and children to bear on IG and FM models? Put simply, it would be an approach which seeks to begin with placing more stress on FM the younger the children are, but which moves more and more toward IG as the youth and children grow. Not only this, but it would involve helping parents understand that this is the framework within which the church is working, equipping them to help integrate their children into the local church increasingly as they grow and develop. In this sense, raising children in the instruction of the Lord (Eph 6:4) includes teaching them that the wider church family members are their brothers and sisters, their real eternal family. In some senses this can be seen as a gradual passing over of pastoral responsibility from parents to church.

It is again important to note what is not meant by this. First, this does not mean that children somehow grow out of the parental relationship

66. Erikson, *Childhood and Society*, 261.

completely. Jesus was clear that ignoring the relationship between parents and children even in adulthood is not what he had in mind (Mark 7:11–12; John 19:26–27).

Second, and importantly for discussions around the generative church, the idea of passing over pastoral responsibility from parents to church leaders is not meant to ignore the increasing self-differentiation, agency, and autonomy of emerging generations or the mutuality and interdependence of church family life. Pastoral oversight and generative concepts such as "letting go" of emerging generations should not be seen as mutually exclusive.

It is interesting to note as we conclude that the position we have arrived at through bringing biblical theology and developmental processes into this conversation is very close to the position arrived at by Carol Lytch in her sociological analysis of teenage faith.[67] Through her significant qualitative research study Lytch concluded that

> in affirming that parents are the most influential factor in faith transmission, my study shows that they are so because of how they link teens to their churches, the primary place where they develop religious commitment through socialization and religious experience.[68]

Practically speaking, acknowledging this dynamic integrationist position will encourage churches, parents, and youth leaders to view each other as partners in the integration of youth and children over time, with an increasing focus as they get older on their integration into the church.

Churches will need to ensure that youth and children's groups don't become quasi-parachurch organizations that are in competition with the church as a whole. What this looks like will vary depending on the specific context of churches, but the general philosophy would be similar to that of the youth and children's minister who said that "everything we do apart is training us to be together."[69]

Parents will need to work toward a constructive approach to encouraging their children into the church family. Where possible, examples of this could include creating social situations where their children get to know adults in the wider church in an appropriate way and avoiding unconstructive negative comments about the church to guard against unintentionally developing critical spirits in their children.

67. Powell and Clark came to similar conclusions in their research study, *Sticky Faith*.

68. Lytch, *Choosing Church*, 200.

69. This quote is taken from the qualitative research interviews that make up the field research for the author's doctoral research.

Naturally, the wider church will also need to examine itself to see how it might need to change in order make this approach work. This will certainly involve changing church practices to accommodate youth and children,[70] but also will entail the adults in the wider church demonstrating the sibling bond implied in the "one-anothering" described throughout the New Testament. If we are seeking to integrate youth and children into the wider church, then we need to ensure perhaps first and foremost that it is the kind of family into which we would want them to be integrated.

Bibliography

Alexander, T. Desmond, and Brian Rosner, S. *New Dictionary of Biblical Theology*. Leicester, UK: InterVarsity, 2000.

Allen, Holly Catterton. "Bringing the Generations Together: Support from Learning Theory." *Christian Education Journal* 2 (2005) 319–33.

Allen, Holly Catterton, and Christine Lawton Ross. *Intergenerational Christian Formation: Bringing the Whole Church Together in Ministry, Community and Worship*. Downers Grove: InterVarsity, 2012.

Beagles, Kathleen. "Growing Disciples in Community." *Christian Education Journal* 9 (2012) 148–64.

Cannister, Mark. "Thinking Ecclesiologically: Teenagers Becoming Part of the Church." In *Adoptive Youth Ministry: Integrating Emerging Generations into the Family of Faith*, edited by Chap Clark, 136–49. Grand Rapids: Baker Academic, 2016.

Carson, Don A. *Christ and Culture Revisited*. Nottingham, UK: InterVarsity, 2008.

Clark, Chap. *Adoptive Church: Creating an Environment Where Emerging Generations Belong*. Grand Rapids: Baker Academic, 2018.

———. "The Adoption View of Youth Ministry." In *Youth Ministry in the 21st Century*, 73–90.

———. *Hurt 2.0: Inside the World of Today's Teenagers*. Grand Rapids: Baker Academic, 2011.

———, ed. *Youth Ministry in the 21st Century: Five Views*. Grand Rapids: Baker Academic, 2015.

Crispin, Gareth. "Intergenerational Communities and a Theology of Accommodation." In *InterGenerate: Transforming Churches through Intergenerational Ministry*, edited by Holly Catterton Allen, 51–61. Abilene, TX: Abilene Christian University Press, 2018.

Csinos, David M. *Children's Ministry That Fits: Beyond One-Size-Fits-All Approaches to Nurturing Children's Spirituality*. Eugene, OR: Wipf & Stock, 2011.

Dean, Kenda Creasy. *Almost Christian: What the Faith of Our Teenagers Is Telling the American Church*. New York: Oxford University Press, 2010.

DeVries, Mark. *Family-Based Youth Ministry*. 2nd ed. Downers Grove: InterVarsity, 2004.

70. Crispin, "Intergenerational Communities," 59–60.

Diaz, April L. "A Call to Adoption." In *Adoptive Youth Ministry: Integrating Emerging Generations into the Family of Faith*, edited by Chap Clark, 335–46. Grand Rapids: Baker Academic, 2016.

Erikson, Erik H. *Childhood and Society*. Middlesex, UK: Penguin, 1950.

Glassford, Darwin, and Lynn Barger-Elliot. "Toward Intergenerational Ministry in a Post-Christian Era." *Christian Education Journal* 8 (2011) 364–78.

Hamilton, James M., Jr. "That the Coming Generation Might Praise the Lord: Family Discipleship in the Old Testament." In *Trained in the Fear of God: Family Ministry in Theological, Historical, and Practical Perspective*, edited by Randy Stinson and Timothy Paul Jones, 33–43. Grand Rapids: Kregel, 2011.

Harkness, Allan, G. "Intergenerational Christian Education: Reclaiming a Significant Educational Strategy in Christian Faith Communities." PhD diss., Murdoch University, 1996.

———. "Intergenerational Education for an Intergenerational Church?" *Religious Education* 93 (1998) 431–47.

Hellerman, Joseph, H. *When the Church Was a Family: Recapturing Jesus's Vision for Authentic Christian Community*. Nashville: Broadman & Holman, 2009.

Hill-Perry, Jackie. *Gay Girl, Good God: A Story of Who I Was and Who God Has Always Been*. Nashville: Broadman & Holman, 2018.

Jackson, Allen. "Thinking Critically about Families and Youth Ministry." In *Adoptive Youth Ministry: Integrating Emerging Generations into the Family of Faith*, edited by Chap Clark, 150–64. Grand Rapids: Baker Academic, 2016.

Joiner, Reggie. *Think Orange: Imagine the Impact When Church and Family Collide*. Colorado Springs: Cook, 2009.

Jones, Timothy Paul, ed. *Family Ministry Field Guide: How Your Church Can Equip Parents to Make Disciples*. Fishers, IN: Wesleyan, 2011.

———. *Perspectives on Family Ministry: 3 Views*. Nashville: Broadman & Holman, 2009.

Lytch, Carol E. *Choosing Church: What Makes a Difference for Teens*. Louisville: Westminster John Knox, 2003.

Ortlund, Ray. "Marriage." In *New Dictionary of Biblical Theology*, edited by T. Desmond Alexander and Brian Rosner, 654–57. Leicester, UK: InterVarsity, 2000.

Pazmino, Robert, W., and Steve Kang. "Generational Fragmentations and Christian Education." *Christian Education Journal* 8 (2011) 379–94.

Plummer, Robert, L. "Bring Them Up in the Discipleship and Instruction of the Lord: Family Discipleship among the First Christians." In Stinson and Jones, *Trained in the Fear of God*, 45–59.

Powell, Kara, and Chap Clark. *Sticky Faith: Everyday Ideas to Build Lasting Faith in Your Kids*. Grand Rapids: Zondervan, 2011.

Renfro, Paul. "Family-Integrated Ministry: Family Driven Faith." In Jones, *Perspectives on Family Ministry*, 54–78.

Rienow, Rob. *Limited Church: Unlimited Kingdom; Uniting Church and Family in the Great Commission*. Nashville: Randall House, 2013.

Rosner, Brian. "Biblical Theology." In *New Dictionary of Biblical Theology*, edited by T. Desmond Alexander and Brian S. Rosner. Leicester: IVP, 2000.

Shields, Brandon. "Family-Integrated Ministry: Response by Brandon Shields." In Jones, *Perspectives on Family Ministry*, 79–84.

Snailum, Brenda. "Implementing Intergenerational Youth Ministry within Existing Evangelical Church Congregations: What Have We Learned?" *Christian Education Journal* 9 (2012) 165–81.

———. "Integrating Intergenerational Ministry Strategies into Existing Youth Ministries: What Can a Hybrid Approach Be Expected to Accomplish?" *Journal of Youth Ministry* 11 (2013) 7–28.

Stanton, Graham. *Families: A Forgotten Factor?* Cambridge, UK: Grove Y25, 2011.

Stinson, Randy, and Timothy Paul Jones, eds. *Trained in the Fear of God: Family Ministry in Theological, Historical and Practical Perspective.* Grand Rapids: Kregel, 2011.

Questions for Reflection and Discussion

1. Crispin surveys a broad range of approaches to how the relationship between church and family is understood. Which of these most closely corresponds to the approach being employed—whether intentionally or implicitly—within your context? How would you assess the strengths and weaknesses of how your church currently conceives of this relationship?
2. Which biblical insights explored in this chapter do you find most intriguing or compelling? Why?
3. To what extent is your church proactively resourcing and equipping parents as essential partners in ministering to children and youth?
4. Crispin concludes his chapter by advocating for "an integrated, dynamic approach" to the relationship between church and family. What is your response to what he proposes?

5

Generative Catechesis

Teaching the Faith to the Next Generation

Ed Mackenzie

§

EDITOR'S INTRODUCTION: In my opening chapter, I argue that generative churches "strive to impart to their children and youth a vital tradition." I describe the need for the church to provide a setting "in which successive generations might be incorporated into the Christian tradition." Ed Mackenzie builds on this strand of the generative church discussion by focusing upon what he describes as "generative catechesis." The goal of generative catechesis, he argues, is helping people to become formed in the faith. Mackenzie asserts that maintaining a vital practice of catechesis is challenging in our contemporary context; in fact, he chronicles the recent decline of catechesis and a "growing ignorance of Christian teaching and the Christian way of life." He helps us consider the cultural and philosophical currents that have contributed to this situation. He then argues for the importance of the "content" of historic orthodoxy and the need for each person to be "inducted" into this rich heritage so that they can truly understanding and live in light of it. He endorses the value of "teaching as a form of generativity" but also advocates for a holistic understanding of catechesis that encompasses the life of the faith community and engages both one's *knowing* and one's *living*. This chapter makes a valuable contribution to our discussion of the generative church by inviting us to consider the vital role that catechetical renewal can play in helping the church live out its generative calling.

§

Introduction

Catechesis is an ancient means for forming people in the faith. With roots in the New Testament, the process of catechesis developed in the first few hundred years of the church into an intentional process of faith formation. As the church moved into the Gentile world, catechesis socialized pagans into a Christian way of life radically different from the surrounding culture.[1] It involved a systematic and structured initiation into Christianity, helping seekers and converts to learn what to believe, how to pray, and how to live as followers of Jesus.[2] Later in the Reformation era, catechesis helped baptized Christians to grow more deeply in the faith.

As Christians increasingly find themselves as a minority in formerly Christian societies, there is a pressing need to discover ways of catechesis that can help coming generations within the church remain faithful to Christ.[3] In this chapter, I argue that such catechesis needs to be "generative," expressing care for the next generation and relevant to their quest for identity.[4]

I begin by exploring reasons for the decline in catechesis. While historically important in church life, catechesis has declined over the past one

1. For catechesis in the early church, see Kreider, *Change of Conversion*, 21–32; Gavrilyuk, "Healing Power of Initiation," 21–40.

2. For this reason, the Lord's Prayer, the Ten Commandments, and the Apostles' Creed have often been central in catechesis, and especially in the post-Reformation era; Packer and Parrett, *Grounded in the Gospel*, 62–66.

3. The evidence that young people are falling away from churches is well documented; Powell and Clark, *Sticky Faith*, 13–15; Shepherd, *Faith Generation*, 9–30. While catechesis has an important role for all within the church, then, our focus in this chapter will be on catechesis and young people.

4. On Erikson's approach to generativity, see Erikson and Erikson, *Life Cycle Completed*, extended version, 67–70. For a useful summary, see Fowler, *Becoming Adult, Becoming Christian*, 14–22. For a helpful exploration of Erikson's significance for ministry, and particularly for the value of intergenerational relationships, see Myers, "Erik H. Erikson," 60–70.

hundred fifty years, with three key reasons contributing to its demise.[5] Such reasons continue to fuel resistance to the idea of teaching the faith, and so I will also include short responses to them. I next explore the positive case for catechesis, arguing that biblical, historical, and sociological reasons point to its value for the church's ministry among youth. I also point to helpful signs of renewal in this area, including resources designed to help churches in this ministry.

Finally, I sketch out a generative approach to catechesis for today. Such an approach is embodied in community, recognizing that faith is nurtured within a network of rich and diverse relationships. It is holistically orientated, focusing on the transformation of minds, hearts, and actions. It is biblically faithful, rooted in the orthodoxy and orthopraxy of the historic church. And it is contextually relevant, willing to engage with pressing issues in today's social context, such as sexual ethics, pluralism, and consumerism. Such a generative catechesis can equip children and youth—and all within the church—to grow in the knowledge and love of God.

The Decline of Catechesis

While the early church valued the ministry of catechesis for forming people in the faith, catechesis began to decline with the rise of Christendom.[6] With babies baptized into the church, and in a society where the majority confessed Jesus as Lord, there seemed little need to initiate people into the faith. Although there were sporadic attempts to renew catechesis, its revival came with the Reformation. The Reformers pursued catechesis as a response to widespread ignorance of the Bible and to help Christians learn the fundamental features of the Protestant faith.[7] Key figures such as Luther, Calvin, and Zwingli promoted its use, and catechesis—and catechisms—continued to be significant within Protestantism until the early twentieth century.[8]

5. My focus will be on broader Protestantism, since the history of catechism within the Roman Catholic Church has developed a little differently. For an overview of catechesis in Roman Catholicism, see Kelly, *Catechesis Revisited*.

6. Alan Kreider traces the changes in catechesis within the first few centuries, including its eventual eclipse within Christendom; *Change of Conversion*, esp. 86–107.

7. The focus on catechesis also reflected the special place that the Reformers gave to childhood; Osmer, "Christian Education of Children."

8. For a brief historical overview, see Osmer, "Case for Catechism." Osmer notes, however, that catechetical instruction was considerably weakened during the nineteenth century, while Packer and Parrett argue that catechesis waned following the Puritan era, *Grounded in the Gospel*, 66–68.

Since that period, the practice of catechesis has sharply declined within Protestantism. The Roman Catholic catechism—and the rite of catechism within Catholicism[9]—led many Protestants to see it as a "Catholic" practice, and the rise of the Sunday School movement offered a different model of helping young people learn the faith.[10] While a variety of other reasons for the decline of catechesis can also be identified,[11] three reasons are particularly significant, and each of these continues to fuel skepticism toward catechesis today.

The first reason for the decline of catechesis is that such an approach was and is seen as incompatible with new approaches to religious education. As Richard Osmer has argued, the early twentieth century saw the rise of pedagogical theories that gave far more emphasis to conversational and relational learning, and such approaches rejected the kinds of didactic teaching associated with catechesis.[12] Rather than teaching the faith to children, there was a shift to focusing on the process of engagement and the personal experience of the child.[13] Many Christian educators came to prefer environments where young people could construct their own understanding of faith based on the common stories of Scripture.

One example of such an approach is found in Csinos and Beckwith's work, *Children's Ministry in the Way of Jesus*.[14] While Csinos and Beckwith offer helpful insights for engaging children, and while they rightly see spiritual formation as the goal of children's ministry, they tend to contrast a participative approach with those that are focused on passing on doctrines. Helping children to gain knowledge, they argue, involves "top-down assumptions and beliefs," and undermines the spirituality of children.[15] Children should instead be seen as the church's "lead theologians,"[16] and churches should create space for children to explore for themselves what

9. For a useful guide to catechesis in the Roman Catholic Church, including a history of catechesis and the development of the RCIA (Rite of Christian Initiation of Adults), see Kelly, *Catechesis Revisited*.

10. Packer and Parrett, *Grounded in the Gospel*, 71–72, Osmer, "Case for Catechism"; Glassford, "Future Is Behind Us," 172–79, 174.

11. For six such reasons, see Packer and Parrett, *Grounded in the Gospel*, 68–73.

12. Osmer, "Case for Catechism."

13. Religious educators were particularly influenced by the educational philosophy of John Dewey, including his focus on process over content; See Osmer, "Christian Education," 514–15; Massey, "Christian Education Developments," 411–22; and Bendroth, *Growing up Protestant*, 61–80.

14. Csinos and Beckwith, *Children's Ministry*.

15. Csinos and Beckwith, *Children's Ministry*, 54–55.

16. Csinos and Beckwith, *Children's Ministry*, 73.

faith means.[17] Knowing about God differs from knowing God, and churches need to focus on the latter rather than the former.[18]

While focusing on the process of education can be helpful, catechesis rightly recognizes that helping children engage with the content of faith is equally important. Education entails modes of instruction and explanation, as well as modes of participation.[19] Since the church confesses a faith with content, passing on the faith will require teaching young people to understand truths that may not immediately resonate with their experience.[20] This is part of the task of educating people into the faith, as much as is helping young people learn to pray and to live as followers of Jesus. As David Martin has argued, people need to be inducted into a tradition before they can really understand it or live it out.[21]

A second reason for the decline in catechesis is the growth of "expressive individualism" throughout the twentieth century.[22] Such an approach to the self sees truth and meaning residing deep within each individual, so that to be authentic to one's self means expressing one's unique identity within the world.[23] In forming the faith of the next generation, the emphasis can shift from passing on a tradition to finding out what parts of the tradition resonate and speak to young people.[24] Unsurprisingly, expressive

17. Csinos and Beckwith also appeal to the language of children "constructing" their faith (Csinos and Beckwith, *Children's Ministry*, 58). For the extent to which "constructivism" can be bundled together with unhelpful philosophical assumptions, see Henze, "Demystifying 'Constructivism,'" 87–111.

18. There is probably also a reaction against what Westerhoff classically describes as the "schooling instructional" approach to faith formation; Westerhoff, *Will Our Children Have Faith*, 1–20. Catechesis, however, need not and should not be associated with this particular paradigm, even if instruction does take place as part of it.

19. See Westerhoff's helpful discussion of the importance of formation, education, and instruction in Westerhoff, "Formation, Education, Instruction," 578–91; however, as Blevins notes, Westerhoff's work tends to focus on formation within this triad; Blevins, "Worship: Formation and Discernment," 11–27.

20. This does not mean simply downloading content into the heads of young people! As Henze notes, a pedagogical constructivism can affirm the insights of Vygotsky and others without yielding to metaphysical and epistemological constructivism (Henze, "Demystifying 'Constructivism,'" 99–100).

21. See Martin's chapter "Alternative Visions and Constraints."

22. On expressive individualism, see Taylor, *Secular Age*, 473–95. Drawing on Taylor, Root also describes some of the impact of expressive individualism on youth work (Root, *Faith Formation in a Secular Age*, 3–16).

23. On the impact of this perspective in post-religious spirituality, see Mackenzie "Following Jesus in a Spiritual Age," 137–50, 139–41.

24. Bergler argues that a focus on the needs and dreams of young people contributes to what he calls the juvenalization of American Christianity, in which the focus shifts to adolescent desires rather than the more difficult task of spiritual formation

individualism is one of the key contributors to what Christian Smith describes as "moralistic therapeutic deism" (MTD), a view of life in which a distant God wants us to be happy and good to others.[25]

One example of an approach to faith formation that prioritizes the individual is developed by Jeff Keuss, who proposes that young people are best seen as "sacredly mobile adolescents."[26] Keuss's approach welcomes the individualism of today's youth, suggesting that God is present in the midst of their own sacred quests.[27] As Keuss notes, "The reality is that God has deposited rich ore in each and every youth we encounter, and they begin with all the resources they need to find faith."[28] Rather than teaching young people the faith, churches should help them discover the presence of God already within them.[29] Such an approach is also reflected in other models of youth ministry which emphasize the importance of young people constructing a faith for themselves.[30]

Encouraging young people to draw from a faith tradition the elements that help them in their individual sacred quests can lead to a style of faith that one sociologist describes as "bricolage."[31] In such an approach, individuals appropriate faith traditions in a way that suits them.[32] What is important is their own authenticity and sense of connection to God. The problem with such an approach is that it breaks apart the mosaic of truth found within the Christian vision, a vision that unites truths and practices. Such an approach to faith fails to fully pass on the "whole purpose of God"

(Bergler, *Juvenilization of American Christianity*, 1–18). From a different angle, Root also narrates the twentieth-century church's obsession with youthfulness (Root, *Faith Formation in a Secular Age*, 3–30).

25. Smith and Denton, *Soul Searching*, 118–71. On the role of individualism within the lives of teens, see esp. 143–47; 172–75. For an accessible discussion of MTD, see Dean, *Almost Christian*, 3–24.

26. See Keuss, *Blur*, 86–112. Keuss offers this approach partly in contrast to the more negative associations generated by Smith's description of Moralistic Therapeutic Deism as the default faith of American teenagers.

27. Keuss, *Blur*, 21–37.

28. Keuss, *Blur*, 117.

29. For such reasons, Keuss welcomes a blurriness between who is and who is not "in Christ"; *Blur*, 39–56.

30. On the problematic assumptions of various forms of constructivism, see Henze, "Demystifying 'Constructivism.'"

31. Wuthnow applies this to American young adults, who he also describes as "tinkerers" (Wuthnow *After the Baby Boomers*, 13–16, 135).

32. As Bergler notes, "The problem is that by glorifying the process of individual choice and by constantly trying to please young people and attract them to religious faith, youth ministries have formed generations of Americans who believe it is their privilege to pick and choose what to believe" (Bergler, *Juvenalization*, 223).

(Acts 20:27), and so can leave young people with a faith that is fragmented and unintegrated, rather than one which will help them stay faithful to God for the years ahead.

A third reason for the decline of catechesis is a focus in churches on experience and practice over doctrine. While this has roots within the Pietist movement of the post-Reformation era,[33] it also dovetails with the stress on authenticity and personal experience in today's world. If faith is essentially about encountering Christ, then catechesis should be rejected in favor of giving space to experience and encounter. Rather than addressing issues of doctrine—a key dimension of catechesis—churches focus instead on experiences of living out the faith.

Andrew Root's work is one example of this trend.[34] Root constantly draws a dichotomy between faith as "encounter" and faith as "belief." Churches interested in faith formation should not simply focus on beliefs and what Christians think, but should instead create spaces for encounter with the other within which Christ is found.[35] Faith is about experiencing the presence of the risen Christ through ministry with another, and not about beliefs and religious affiliation.[36] While Root agrees that doctrine is important, he subordinates it to a stress on the action of God and the ability of young people to name God's presence within their lives.[37] Similar dichotomies are also found in liberal and evangelical traditions, whether in promoting a gospel of social justice or in celebrating a personal relationship with Jesus disconnected from the church.[38]

33. Packer and Parrett, *Grounded in the Gospel*, 68–69.

34. This perspective is reflected in a number of Root's recent works, including *Faith Formation in a Secular Age* and *Taking Theology to Youth Ministry*.

35. Root draws on the work of Michael Gorman to claim that faith is far more about participation in the event of Christ (an encounter) rather than belief (*Faith Formation*, esp. 119–30). This union is expressed in ministry through which we share in the arc of Christ's death and resurrection (Root, *Faith Formation*, 146–52). Root's reading of faith here is consistent with his notion of ministry as "participating in God's action" (Root, *Taking Theology*, 37–52).

36. Root, *Faith Formation*, 108.

37. Root, *Taking Theology*, 60–62. While Root identifies youth ministry's problem as an overemphasis on knowledge, the movement *away* from catechesis in the twentieth century and toward experience means that a stress on knowing doctrines is rarely a focus in youth groups. As Smith shows, most American teens, and especially mainline Protestant teens, have a poor understanding of their own faith traditions (Smith, *Soul Searching*, 131.)

38. Bergler shows that both these tendencies characterized much of twentieth-century youth ministry, with the 1960s being a key period when they came to the fore (Bergler, *Juvenalization*, 176–207).

Experience and doctrine, however, should be integrated rather than separated, and it is precisely this integration that forms of catechesis can provide. Catechesis brings together what some would choose to separate. As Walker and Parry note, "The church has historically appreciated the indivisibility of right belief, right worship, and right living."[39] Catechesis unites these three facets of faithful Christian living.[40]

The Need for Catechesis

I have traced three key reasons for the decline in catechesis, shown that these remain influential in youth ministry today, and offered some initial responses. There are, however, also significant and positive reasons for recovering forms of catechesis today.

First of all, Scripture points to the need for intentionally instructing people to learn and live out the faith.[41] The verb *katecheo*, from which "catechesis" derives, occurs eight times, with the majority of its instances stressing the importance of teaching the faith.[42] More significant than these verses, there is a range of other verbs that stress teaching the faith. The verb "to teach" (*didaskō*) for instance, occurs ninety-seven times, with the majority of occurrences denoting Jesus's teaching in the gospels and the teaching of his earliest followers in Acts.[43] Paul also speaks of "passing on" (*paradídōmi*) the faith (Rom 1:16; 1 Cor 11:2, 23), "proclaiming the gospel" (*euangelízō*) (Rom 1:15; 15:20; 1 Cor 1:7; 2 Cor 10:16), and "instructing" (*parangelía*) his converts (1 Cor 7:10; 1 Thess 4:11; 2 Thess 3:6). Such verbs point to the importance of intentionally teaching converts the way of Christ.

The New Testament also points to a body of teaching that is passed down to the church, and which Christians are encouraged to embrace and transmit. In 1 Corinthians 15, Paul refers to a tradition that he received and that he was now passing on to those in the faith (1 Cor 15:3–9). In the Pastoral Epistles, Paul encourages Timothy to be faithful to the word that he has been taught (1 Tim 4:11–16; 2 Tim 2:14–15; 4:1–2). And in Hebrews, the author encourages his readers/hearers to hold fast to the truth

39. Walker and Parry, *Deep Church Rising*, 66.

40. Walker and Parry, *Deep Church Rising*, 130–44.

41. As well as the short summary here, see Packer and Parrett, *Grounded in the Gospel*, 33–50, and—focusing on Paul—Osmer, *Teaching Ministry of Congregations*, 26–56.

42. For these uses, see Luke 1:4; Acts 18:25; 1 Cor 14:19; Gal 6:6; while Rom 2:18 speaks of being "taught" out of the law. The verb can also denote "informing" or "telling," as in Acts 21:21, 24.

43. Note too the significance of Matt 28:18–20, in which Jesus's commissions his disciples to teach those baptized all that he had taught.

they have received (Heb 13:7–9). The importance of retaining key elements of the apostolic teaching is also reflected in the emergence of a "rule of faith" among the early church fathers. The rule of faith was a kind of summary of the Christian story and a basic interpretation of it and served to distinguish truthful Christian teaching from its detractors in antiquity.[44]

The New Testament description of teaching the faith, however, is not simply about knowing doctrines, but also about living and being a disciple of Christ. Faith, in other words, is never really learned unless it is lived. Jesus called his disciples not just to know the truth but to live in obedience to it (Matt 7:24–27). In fact, only by living the way of truth could you really know it (John 8:31–32). A similar theme runs throughout the New Testament. 1 John, for instance, calls both for orthodox belief in Jesus *and* a love that expresses itself in deeds and not simply words (1 John 2:18–28; 3:11–22). Similarly, James explains that faith without action is dead; Christians should feed the hungry rather than simply offering them a blessing (Jas 2:14–17).

A second reason for the need for catechesis is that history shows that it was an important means for passing on the faith. While the circumstances of today differ widely from other periods of Christian history, the growing ignorance of Christian teaching and the Christian way of life outside the church and within it suggest that it is worth exploring again this approach today. Teaching in all its forms remains an important way of building up the body of Christ (Eph 4:11–13).

In the early church, the emergence of catechesis was an acknowledgment that the kingdom of God differed from the kingdom of the world and that learning the ways of the former required training! Early catechesis helped people prepare for their baptism, enabling them to understand what it meant to confess Jesus as Lord. Rather than teaching converts about the faith *after* their baptism, catechesis helped people prepare for the deeper countercultural way of life that would follow it.[45] As Webber has argued, the early church approach to catechesis offers a model for developing programs of evangelism and discipleship today, including for young people.[46]

While the Reformers dealt with a society in which the majority of people were baptized, the need to help people understand the gospel and live it out led the Reformers to prepare catechisms for Christians within

44. For the significance of the rule of faith and the ecumenical creeds that later emerged, see Walker and Parry, *Deep Church*, 69–96.

45. As Jenson notes, "Life in the church was just too different from life out of the church, for people to tolerate the transfer without some preparation" (Jenson, "Catechesis for Our Time," 138–39).

46. Webber, *Ancient-Future Evangelism*. See also Arnold, "Early Church Catechesis"; Atkins, "From Darkness to Light."

churches, and especially to help children grasp the faith into which they were born. Luther developed his catechism after noting the ignorance about faith in rural churches, while Calvin developed a catechism to guide the church in Geneva.[47] Churches today can similarly draw on the Reformation insistence that growing in knowledge of faith can help one engage more deeply with God.

Finally, learning the faith is something taught and not simply caught, or—as Tertullian has put it—"Christians are made, not born!"[48] Catechesis recognizes that formation happens all the time, and without teaching our faith, children and young people will be catechized by the wider culture. As Smith shows, young people who are not taught about their faith are more likely to be shaped by moralistic therapeutic deism, while those churches that do teach their young people the faith are more likely to resist its deformation.[49]

Teaching the faith requires helping young people understand both beliefs and practices, as well as seeking ways to enable them to inhabit them. As Gschwandtner has shown, the earliest churches saw doctrine as intimately linked to practice. In fact, doctrine was seen as "absolutely essential for holy living," and the early catechists understood that "a repeated vigilant attention to thorough theological instruction and careful explication must be part of any Christian's growth in holiness."[50] A similar perspective was expressed by the work of Calvin, and later John Ames who described theology as "the doctrine of living to God."[51] The tendency to loosen the link between doctrine and practice in today's church often means that churches prioritize the latter without relating it to the former or recognizing its importance.

A helpful way of reflecting on the relationship of doctrine to holy living is found in the work of Kevin Vanhoozer. In developing what he calls a "canonical-linguistic approach" to doctrine, Vanhoozer notes that doctrine has a definite practical bent. Doctrines, Vanhoozer argues, are "not simply truths to be stored, shelved, and stacked, but indications and directions to

47. On Calvin's Catechism, see Vanhoozer, *Faith Speaking Understanding*, 144–45.

48. Sider, *Christian and Pagan*, 38. This is not to deny the efficacy of God's grace in infant baptism, nor is it to deny that Christians do experience a kind of birth when entering the kingdom (John 3:3), but Tertullian's point is that Christians are formed and trained for the kingdom. Paul makes a similar point in 1 Tim 4:7–8.

49. Smith and Denton, *Soul Searching*, 267.

50. Gschwandtner "Pious Doctrines," 36–57, 45. Jenson similarly argues that the catechumen's initiation into a specific theology also initiated catechumens into a relationship with God (Jenson, "Catechesis," 140).

51. Cited in Vanhoozer, *Faith Speaking Understanding*, xiii.

be followed, practiced, and enacted."[52] Doctrine helps Christians play their role in the theatre of God's divine plan.[53] As Matthew Mason has argued, Vanhoozer's work offers a helpful way of thinking of catechesis.[54] If performing the faith, loving God and neighbor, requires familiarity with the "script" of Scripture, then catechesis is the process through which churches help people gain that familiarity.

Given these reasons for the importance of catechesis, it is encouraging to see signs of its renewal within the wider church. A number of writers have called for its renewal, including practical theologians, systematicians, and biblical scholars.[55] Others have begun to produce new resources for catechesis, such as the New Church Catechism or the Church of England Pilgrim resource.[56] While these are all helpful, it is important to situate such resources within a broader process that engages holistically with each individual.[57]

A Generative Catechesis

If catechesis is an important treasure of the church, then, how might we think of it through the lens of generative church? Such an approach needs to avoid the weaknesses of previous approaches, while also seeking to recover the benefits of a catechetical approach that can form people in the faith.[58]

52. Vanhoozer, *Faith Speaking Understanding*, xiv.

53. Vanhoozer, *Faith Speaking Understanding*, 114–29.

54. Mason, "Back to (Theo-drama) School." Mason published his article prior to Vanhoozer's *Faith Speaking Understanding*, but this work of Vanhoozer's also seeks to unpack how to apply his theology in a church context.

55. To list a few examples, see Arnold, "Early Church Catechesis"; Atkins, "From Darkness to Light"; Dean, *Almost Christian*, 109–30; Gavrilyuk, "Healing Power"; Glassford, "Future Is Behind Us"; Kreider, "Baptism and Catechesis"; Mason "Back to (Theo-drama) School"; Jenson "Catechesis for Our Time"; Packer and Parrett, *Grounded in the Gospel*; Walker and Parry, *Deep Church*, 130–44.

56. For the New Church Catechism, see http://newcitycatechism.com. For Pilgrim, see www.pilgrimcourse.org.

57. Catechesis, in other words, is not simply about having the ability to recite the correct answers! Packer and Parrett note that at times catechesis has become "mere memorization of the questions and answers in the printed catechism," but this is something which the Reformers worked against (*Grounded in the Gospel*, 70).

58. De Kock's description of catechetical approaches distinguishes between deductive approaches (teaching doctrines), inductive approaches (focusing on the individuality of the youth), and abductive approaches (helping young people participate in religious practice) (De Kock, "Promising Approaches to Catechesis," 176–96). While De Kock favors the latter approach, which he also links to an apprenticeship model of catechesis, the generative approach to catechesis I sketch out below includes elements

Generative catechesis will, first of all, be embedded within a community of love and grace.[59] As Steve Emery-Wright and I have argued, young people grow in faith as they are situated in an interlocking number of networks, each of which help young people learn and grow closer to God.[60] Such a community expresses the loving care of the church for young people and its commitment to see them thrive.[61] A generative church, like a generative individual, will express love and care for the next generation.[62]

While individuals within the church may play a key role in catechesis[63]—acting as formal mentors in the faith[64]—catechesis also takes place in the midst of other formative networks.[65] Young people, for instance, may learn about prayer in the midst of family worship in the home, live out a call to service through volunteering at the food bank, and grasp a key element of Jesus's identity through a Bible Study with friends. These too are catechetical experiences. Catechesis in the early church similarly took place in the midst of a range of different relationships.[66]

As well as recognizing the significance of different networks, generative catechesis recognizes the particularly crucial role played by parents in

---

from each approach. De Kock's fuller typology of catechetical approaches helpfully shows the range of approaches, though—as De Kock notes—catechesis often mixes these ideal types (De Kock, "Typology of Catechetical Environments," 264–86).

59. Westerhoff, *Living the Faith Community*, 13–24.

60. Emery-Wright and Mackenzie, *Networks for Faith Formation*. See also the discussion of a "sticky web of relationships" in Powell and Clark, *Sticky Faith*, 93–122, and the importance of a "warm community" in Powell et al., *Growing Young*, 163–95.

61. Lytch notes that a "sense of belonging" is key for helping teenagers remain within the church (Lytch, *Choosing Church*, 35–46).

62. As Erikson notes, care for the next generation is the key virtue emerging from generativity, *Life Cycle Completed*, 67. On the ways in which Erikson's work supports the importance of intergenerational relationships in church, see Myers, "Erik H. Erikson," 69–70.

63. Approaches to catechesis can at times assume a single catechist, such as in De Kock, "typology." In a later article, however, De Kock notes that catechesis can take place in a number of settings, and points to the importance of partnership between the church and the home; De Kock et al., "Comeback of Parents," 155–71.

64. On the role of mentors, see Emery-Wright and Mackenzie, *Networks for Faith Formation*, 58–70; Dean and Foster, *Godbearing Life*, 83–84. De Kock's apprenticeship model of catechesis emphasizes the key role of a mentor (De Kock, "Promising," 191–92).

65. Emery-Wright and Mackenzie, *Networks for Faith Formation*, 25–34; Foster, *From Generation to Generation*, 37–46, 128–30; Smith and Denton, *Soul Searching*, 261.

66. As Kreider points out, catechesis in the early church involved not just teachings sessions, but also practical actions and mentoring relationships; Kreider, "Baptism and Catechesis."

the household of faith.[67] As Bengtson notes, churches often ignore the role of parents in faith formation, and yet parents play a crucial role in passing on the faith.[68] Luther's *Small Catechism* was written as a guide for parents to use within the household,[69] while later forms of catechesis similarly emphasized the importance of teaching faith within the home. Parents are called to work alongside others within the church community to catechize children, helping them to know the fundamentals of what it means to believe and live as a Christian.[70]

Second, generative catechesis will be holistic. Learning the faith will involve shaping hearts, guiding hands, and instructing heads.[71] Beliefs, practices of worship, and living the faith are all included.[72] Such an emphasis recovers an approach to catechesis in which the whole person is trained to be a follower of Christ.[73] It embraces the notion of Christianity as a way of life (Acts 9:2), a way that includes understanding as well as love and practice.[74]

Such an approach rejects overly cerebral approaches to catechesis in which the emphasis is on learning the truth over living in obedience to it.[75]

67. The significance of parents for forming the faith of youth is widely recognized today. See, for instance, Bengtson et al., *Families and Faith*, esp. 184–206; Emery-Wright and Mackenzie, *Networks for Faith Formation*, 35–46; Dean and Foster, *Godbearing Life*, 77–80; De Kock et al., "Comeback of Parents." For a helpful summary of research on the role of parents in faith formation, see Mark, *Passing on Faith*.

68. Bengtson, *Families and Faith*, 202. See also Lytch, *Choosing Church*, 141–89; De Kock et al., "Comback of Parents."

69. Dean, *Almost Christian*, 110–12.

70. Dean's treatment of catechesis highlights the role of parents as "translators" of the faith to their children (*Almost Christian*, 109–30.)

71. Vanhoozer uses the same image in explaining that doctrine "instructs the head, orients the heart, and guides the hand" (*Faith Speaking Understanding*, 26). See also De Kock's description of different learning goals in catechesis, many of which generative catechesis would embrace (De Kock, "Typology," 269–76).

72. While Osmer associates catechesis in the New Testament with passing on Israel's Scripture and Christian traditions, and so distinguishes it from exhortation and discernment (Osmer, *Teaching Ministry*, 26–56), my approach followers Westerhoff in treating catechesis as a broader category (Westerhoff, *Living the Faith Community*, 79–100; "Formation, Education, Instruction").

73. For this holistic approach in historic catechesis, see Gschwandtner, "Pious Doctrines," and Packer and Parrett, *Grounded in the Gospel*, 62–66.

74. In the context of youth ministry, White similarly writes of loving God with the heart (ortho-pathos), the mind (ortho-optomai), the soul (ortho-doxy) and the strength (ortho-praxis) (White, *Practicing Discernment with Youth*).

75. Smith similarly critiques approaches to faith formation that focus on beliefs, critiquing models of the human as thinker and as believer (Smith *Desiring the Kingdom*, 41–46).

But at the same time, it rejects approaches that overemphasize experience or participation to the detriment of learning what it is that Christians actually believe.[76] Generative catechesis brings together what is at times kept separate.

This means that learning the faith will be integrated with reshaping the heart. As James K. A. Smith has persuasively argued, we are moved by our loves and not just by our thoughts, and so attending to the way that we love is significant.[77] A holistic approach to teaching will bring together learning the faith with learning to worship, recognizing that worship transforms our desires and is also a means of grace through which God shapes us.[78] Similarly, generative catechesis will recognize the formative power of service and mission as ways to learn the faith.[79] Learning the faith also involves moral formation,[80] helping young people live a Jesus-shaped way of life.[81]

Third, a generative catechesis will be faithful to Scripture, seeking to inculcate a posture of receptive humility before the truth that God has given.[82] Catechesis will help young people read Scripture, but also be read by Scripture as they hear God speaking into their lives.[83] While Scripture itself

76. For the emphasis on experience in youth ministry, see Bergler, *Juvenalization*, 220.

77. Smith, *Desiring the Kingdom*, 39–73, 133–43; Smith, *Imagining the Kingdom*, 103–50. See also Smith's more accessible development of this theme in Smith, *You Are What You Love*, 1–25.

78. Dean and Foster, *Godbearing Life*; 195–205; Smith, *Desiring the Kingdom*, 133–54; *Imagining the Kingdom*, 151–91; *You Are What You Love*, 57–110; Blevins, "Worship"; Westerhoff, *Living the Faith Community*, 37–49. For a more extended treatment, see Murphy *Teaching That Transforms*, esp. 9–25. For a work that explores worship as a resource for youth ministry, see Edie *Book, Bath, Table, and Time*.

79. So Emery-Wright and Mackenzie, *Networks for Faith Formation*, 93–105; Dean, *Almost Christian*, 85–106; Powell and Clark, *Sticky Faith*, 123–48; Powell et al., *Growing Young*, 234–70.

80. Jenson notes more broadly the need for moral conversion for those entering the church, such that "their moral structure must be disassembled and reassembled on a new pattern," (Jenson, "Catechesis," 146). On the importance of moral exhortation in Paul's letters, see Osmer, *Teaching Ministry*, 32–43; and, in Ephesians, see Mackenzie, "Following Jesus," 146–48.

81. On the importance of early catechesis in shaping people to be like Jesus, see Kreider, *Change of Conversion*, 21–32; Arnold, "Early Church Catechesis," 49.

82. On Paul's vision of submitting to this truth, see Mackenzie, "Following Jesus," 148–49. This might suggest an approach to catechesis that, in De Kock's assessment, is deductive and which adopts a behavioral model of instruction (De Kock, "Promising Approaches"). The commitment to pass on certain truths of the Christian tradition, however, need not commit one to a particular form of pedagogical process, as De Kock's fuller typology recognizes (De Kock, "Typology," 282).

83. For the importance of knowing the "script" of Scripture, see Mason, "Back to

is the primary script for faithful living, generative catechesis will frame its teaching on Scripture within the three primary treasures that catechesis has used within its history; the Lord's Prayer, the Apostles' Creed, and the Ten Commandments.[84] It is these three that can orientate Christians today in thinking through their worship, their beliefs, and their practices.[85] It will also seek to point Christians to the reality of the person of Jesus and to root them deeply in his teaching.[86]

Faith formation often fails to initiate young people into a faith with "thick" beliefs,[87] and so this is a focus that many churches need to recover.[88] By learning these particular texts, young people will be situated within the historic orthodoxy of the church, shaped by the truths that Christians across the ages have held in common.[89] But such texts should also be linked with immersing young people in the world of Scripture, helping them to understand its big story and to explore ways of reading it that can allow the Spirit to speak.[90] Such an approach rejects individualized approaches

---

(Theo-Drama) School," 214–17. Vanhoozer argues that the script of Scripture is not simply a "detailed template for speech and action," but rather a "collection of authoritative scenarios that serve as lessons, positive and negative, for us (1 Cor 10:5–11)" (Vanhoozer, *Faith Speaking Understanding*, 246).

84. Packer and Parrett point to the way in which these three texts highlight three core facets of the faith—learning, worship, and action/ethics—but also sketch out other ways in which these three facets might be explored (Packer and Parrett, *Grounded in the Gospel*, 117–36).

85. Dean calls for catechesis to shift from an emphasis on "religious information to a trust born of love" (Dean, *Almost Christian*, 119). Rather than contrasting the "formation of beliefs'" with trusting Jesus, it is more helpful in my view to think of how the formation of beliefs leads toward greater trust of Jesus, a movement that is reflected in Paul's prayer in Eph 1:15–22.

86. Catechesis, then, is not an alternative to encountering Christ but rather, alongside worship and other means of grace, is a means of such of encounter. Jesus's teaching has at times been underplayed in catechesis, but recovering it is key for engaging young people today (Powell et al., *Growing Young*, 126–62).

87. For the lack of biblical and theological understanding among young people in the church, see Kinnaman, *You Lost Me*, 115–17. As Murphy also notes, "much of what constitutes the discipline of Christian education, both historically and at present, is lacking in serious, thoughtful engagement with the theological traditions of the church" (Murphy, *Teaching That Transforms*, 20–21).

88. Wrestling with doctrine is a key way to address questions of meaning, a key element in attracting young people to church (Lytch, *Choosing Church*, 37).

89. For the importance of theological instruction in early Christian formation, see Gschwandtner, "Pious Doctrines," 42–45.

90. For a range of ways of helping young people grow in biblical literacy, see Edie, *Book, Bath, Table, and Time*, 93–125.

to faith and aims instead to help young people grasp the coherence of the Christian story.

Where and how these texts are taught will depend on the congregation, but seeking ways to embed them in multiple networks makes it more likely that they will be held by young people seeking to be Christians. A series of sermons on the Apostles' Creed, for example, could be run intergenerationally, with opportunities for the young as well as the old for thinking through the faith. The confession that "we believe in God our Father, Creator of all" might be linked to a youth group study on compassion for others. And parents could be encouraged to talk about the Spirit's presence with them at the family table. The object of immersing young people in such orthodoxy is not simply that they can recite texts by rote, but rather so they discover the beauty of God's truth, a truth that compels us all to worship and live for him.

Finally, a generative catechesis will be contextually relevant.[91] While remaining faithful to the tradition, it also needs to show how the faith once delivered to the saints continues to address the specific demands of the faith. In today's context, three issues should be addressed as part of catechesis; sexuality, pluralism, and consumerism.

As numerous commentators note, we live in a highly sexualized age, one in which identity is closely linked with sexual orientation and expression.[92] Culture in the West inducts young people into a worldview in which fulfillment comes through sexual union or experimentation, and the popularity of dating apps and a hook-up culture means that sex is more readily available than ever before.[93] The view that sexual union is humanity's "highest good" has also filtered into the church, as is evident in the conviction that God has created a soul mate for each person or that God will reward those who remain sexually pure with mind-bending sex in marriage.[94]

Generative catechesis will address a sexualized culture by telling a "better story" about God's view of sexuality.[95] While cultivating a Christian worldview on sex, on its own, is insufficient for shaping God's people, it is nonetheless an important ingredient in helping young people think about sex. As Regnerus has shown, young Christians often struggle to connect

91. On the importance of a contextually relevant approach to faith formation, see Foster, *Generation to Generation*, 133–37.

92. For two excellent treatments of helping Christians engage with sexuality in this context, see Grant, *Divine Sex*, and Harrison, *Better Story*.

93. On the role that technology and consumerism play in contemporary sexuality, see Grant, *Divine Sex*, 73–95. On changing notions of sexuality, see Taylor, *Secular Age*, 399–452.

94. Grant, *Divine Sex*, 47–49, 70–71.

95. The phrase is taken from Harrison, *Better Story*, esp. 125–34.

their faith with views on sexuality, and even the best taught Christians often find it hard to articulate their views on sexuality beyond the need to wait for marriage.[96] Churches need to do a lot better in helping young Christians think through a biblical vision of sex,[97] particularly in a context where traditional Christian views on the subject are become more and more countercultural.[98]

Alongside a Christian vision of sexuality, generative catechesis will encourage practices and habits of the heart that can shape young people in faithful discipleship. One such practice is that of including single people—young and old—within the wider life of the church, ensuring that unmarried Christians know themselves as full and valued members of the church.[99] Rather than simply inviting other families to their homes, those who are married need to intentionally invite single people too. Similarly, pursuing life together within the church without the "dating agenda" can be an important way of denying that the goal of life is sexual and marital union with another.[100]

Generative catechesis will also help young people wrestle with the reality of living in a pluralistic society. As Christians increasingly become a minority, they need strong plausibility structures, nurtured by supportive Christian relationships,[101] and wisdom in negotiating with religious and nonreligious others. This is important both in keeping their faith in a pluralistic society and witnessing to others in gracious and life-giving ways.

In response to pluralism, catechesis should attend to the apologetic dimensions of the faith. Rather than seeing it as simply for the enthusiasts, young people should be equipped to know how they might respond to common questions about following Jesus. The aim is not to encourage trite

96. Regnerus, *Forbidden Fruit*, 207.

97. On the need for churches to speak helpfully and practically on sexual ethics, see Regnerus, *Forbidden Fruit*, 213–14; Kinnaman, *You Lost Me*, 162–65. For a helpful discussion of the Christian vision of sexuality, see Grant, *Divine Sex*, 136–64; Harrison, *Better Story*, 125–88.

98. The traditional Christian teaching on chastity, for instance, runs counter to a culture that stresses individualism and authenticity (Grant, *Divine Sex*, 29–53).

99. On the value of singleness within the church, and ways of affirming the single life, see Grant, *Divine Sex*, 156–59, 229–30. This is an issue for emerging adults more than for younger people, but the church needs to model a community life that speaks of God's call on the lives of all, whatever their relationship status.

100. At the same time, Grant suggests that the church also provides a "healthy courting environment" (Grant, *Divine sex*, 230–32)!

101. Shepherd argues that youth groups can act as plausibility structures that can help young people make the "implausible choice" to follow Jesus (Shepherd, *Faith Generation*, 56–78).

answers, but to help Christians wrestle deeply with the reasons for faith. This helps young people grapple with their own questions and doubts,[102] but also gives them confidence in sharing their faith with others.[103]

At the same time, living well with others outside the faith should also be part of catechetical progress. What might it mean to love a Muslim neighbor, an atheist teacher, or a friend who identifies as nonbinary? Rather than expressing intolerance to such neighbors or playing down their own faith to avoid offence,[104] catechesis needs to help Christians act with "gentleness and reverence" among those they meet (1 Pet 3:15–16). Young Christians already believe in integrating evangelism with action,[105] and so catechesis can build on this in helping their witness today.

Generative catechesis will also need to address the consumerism and materialism that tempt all Christians in First World countries today. Such consumerism is a major part of what catechizes young people—and us all—today, with advertisements, celebrities, and popular culture all pointing to gaining possessions as the ultimate goal of life.[106] As Smith brilliantly shows, even visiting a mall shapes us as consumers, offering us an implicit liturgy that associates the good life with acquisition.[107] Such consumerism can also function as an idol for Christians, and this in house temptation makes it important to counter in our efforts at faith formation.

102. As Shepherd notes, passing on faith within a youth group context—what he calls "collaborative catechesis"—often allows for "questioning and wrestling" (Shepherd, *Faith Generation*, 135). Kinnaman also notes the importance of churches helping young people process their doubts (Kinneman, *You Lost Me*, 185–98).

103. For one helpful guide in engaging young people with apologetics, see McDowell, *Apologetics for a New Generation.*

104. Apologetics is also a way of helping young Christians recognize the way in which their own faith is similar to and different from the worldviews of others. Christian Smith's work has demonstrated that many teenagers are shaped by an individualistic worldview that resists the idea of seeking to persuade others of the viability of one's own faith (Smith, *Soul Searching*, 143–47). The same attitude was also present in the emerging adults studied several years later (Smith and Snell, *Souls in Transition*, 49). This "radical American religious individualism"—present in the UK too—can helpfully be challenged through exploring apologetics.

105. Kinnaman, *You Lost Me*, 177.

106. For the impact of such cultural forces on young people, see White, *Practicing Discernment*, 35–62; Turpin, *Branded*, 11–28.

107. Smith, *Desiring the Kingdom*, 93–103; *You Are What You Love*, 38–53. Consumerism also shapes approach to faith (Smith, *Soul Searching*, 176–77) and sexuality (Grant, *Divine Sex*, 73–95). Challenging consumerism, then, is not just about opposing materialistic acquisition, but also about critiquing the frame of mind that approaches life and faith in consumeristic terms.

Catechesis will help young people explore how the Christian faith challenges a consumeristic mindset. Through what one scholar calls "practices of awakening," young people can be brought to recognize the many ways in which North American and European culture shapes us as consumers.[108] Seeing through the false promises offered by advertisers and promises of the good life is one important way to resist de-formation by the market. Catechesis can also provide opportunities for young people to take what Smith calls a "liturgical audit" of their lives, encouraging them to identify the many ways in which their habits are unhelpfully shaped by a consumer gospel.[109]

Responding to consumerism may also mean helping young people adopt practices that resist its influence on their lives. These could include periods of abstaining from media consumption and phone use,[110] engaging in service of others, and adopting simpler ways of living.[111] In this area too, it is important that adults and families in the church model ways of resisting consumerism. This is a challenge for the church as whole, but it is one that takes seriously Jesus's words on the impossibility of serving God and wealth (Matt 6:24).

Conclusion

A church that seeks to be generative for future generations will ignore catechesis at its peril.[112] In Luther's view, catechesis is a mark of the church,[113] and it remains a means for drawing young and old into following Jesus. Exploring catechesis through the lens of "generative church" helps us think about what it means to pass on the faith in a way that is both faithful to God and relevant to the young.

Catechesis embraces a variety of ways in which Christians are formed. Learning to be a Christian involves knowing the shape of the faith we confess, but also how to worship God rightly and how to live for God in the

108. Turpin, *Branded*, 83–108. Turpin suggests that such practices could include field trips around town, studying the consumer culture, and mission trips. See also White's description of helping young people *listen* in the midst of a world where their attention is constantly targeted by advertisers (White, *Practicing Discernment*, 89–113).

109. Smith, *You Are What You Love*, 53–55.

110. Turpin identifies such a strategy as a form of "dehabituation" (Turpin, *Branded*, 120–26).

111. Turpin, *Branded*, 126–28.

112. As Shepherd notes, "Without intentional work to stem generational decline the Church will not be in a position to grow" (Shepherd, *Faith Generation*, 150).

113. Jenson, "Catechesis for Our Time."

midst of a changing world. While it has a particular value for those new to faith, catechesis is a lifelong journey. We never stop growing in the knowledge and love of God.

My argument for generative catechesis offers broad principles rather than a specific model. Indeed, one characteristic of a generative catechesis will be that it may vary in different settings even if the key elements remain the same. Context matters, and churches will need to consider how best to catechize the young people in their midst.

For churches seeking to engage intentionally in catechesis, a good place to start is by auditing catechetical opportunities that are already taking place within the church. If beliefs, worship, and actions are the three broad areas of catechetical endeavor, where and how is teaching in such areas taking place? Take time to celebrate and honor the good that is happening while also exploring ways to address areas that might be missing.[114]

Churches need to remember that catechesis takes place in the home as well as the church, and in other contexts too. There are numerous opportunities for teaching and learning the faith each day,[115] even if the church also employs more formal occasions to teach. While the minister or youth pastor will not be the sole catechist, they are particularly well placed to discern where and how young people are being catechized and can also supplement such catechesis in their own relationships with young people.[116]

God is the one who saves, but God also calls us to teach and pass on the faith to the young. Recovering the call to catechize is essential as we seek to serve coming generations. As we plant the seeds of the gospel deeply in the lives of young people, we can pray and trust that that the Spirit will bring forth growth, helping young and old together become like Jesus.

Bibliography

Arnold, Clinton E. "Early Church Catechesis and New Christians' Classes in Contemporary Evangelicalism." *Journal of the Evangelical Theological Society* 47 (2004) 39–54.

114. For some excellent ideas for incorporating catechesis within church, see Packer and Parrett, *Grounded in the Gospel*, esp. 75–94, 181–202.

115. A simple example might be the practice of saying grace at table. Saying grace, in my view, is part of what it means to worship, and also to witness through gratitude to the goodness of God in the midst of the world. It is at home that saying grace is often best learned.

116. In Mason's view, catechesis should be pastor led, a view with strong historical precedents; Mason, "Back to (Theo-Drama) School," 221. Although pastors may not be the sole catechists of young people, they do have an important role in ensuring that it takes place for all within the church.

Atkins, Martyn. "From Darkness to Light: Lessons in Disciple-Making from Our Great-Grandfathers in Christ." In *Let My People Grow: Making Disciples Who Make a Difference in Today's World*, edited by Mark Greene and Tracy Cotterell, 57–69. London: Authentic, 2006.

Bendroth, Margaret Lamberts. *Growing Up Protestant: Parents, Children, and Mainstream Churches*. New Brunswick, NJ: Rutgers University Press, 2002.

Bengtson, Vern L., et al. *Families and Faith: How Religion Is Passed Down across Generations*. Oxford: Oxford University Press, 2013.

Bergler, Thomas E. *The Juvenilization of American Christianity*. Grand Rapids: Eerdmans, 2012.

Blevins, Dean. "Worship: Formation and Discernment; A Wesleyan Dialogue between Worship and Christian Education." *Wesleyan Theological Journal* 33 (1998) 11–27.

Csinos, David M., and Ivy Beckwith. *Children's Ministry in the Way of Jesus*. Downers Grove: InterVarsity, 2013.

Dean, Kenda Creasy. *Almost Christian: What the Faith of Our Teenagers Is Telling the American Church*. Oxford: Oxford University Press, 2010.

Dean, Kenda Creasy, and Ron Foster. *The Godbearing Life: The Art of Soul Tending for Youth Ministry*. Nashville: Upper Room, 1998.

De Kock, A. (Jos). "Promising Approaches to Catechesis in Church Communities: Towards a Research Framework." *International Journal of Practical Theology* 16 (2012) 176–96.

———. "A Typology of Catechetical Environments." *International Journal of Practical Theology* 18 (2014) 264–86.

De Kock, Jos, et al. "The Comeback of Parents in Catechesis Practices." *Journal of Youth and Theology* 14 (2015) 155–71.

Edie, Fred P. *Book, Bath, Table, and Time: Christian Worship as Source and Resource for Youth Ministry*. Youth Ministry Alternatives. Cleveland: Pilgrim, 2007.

Emery-Wright, Steve, and Ed Mackenzie. *Networks for Faith Formation: Relational Bonds and the Spiritual Growth of Youth*. Eugene, OR: Wipf & Stock, 2017.

Erikson, Erik H., and Joan Erikson. *The Life Cycle Completed*. Extended ed. New York: Norton, 1997.

Foster, Charles R. *From Generation to Generation: The Adaptive Challenge of Mainline Protestant Education in Forming Faith*. Eugene, OR: Cascade, 2012.

Fowler, James W. *Becoming Adult, Becoming Christian: Adult Development and Christian Faith*. San Francisco: Jossey-Bass, 2000.

Gavrilyuk, Paul L. "The Healing Power of Initiation: Toward the Retrieval of Patristic Catechumante." In *Immersed in the Life of God: The Healing Resources of the Christian Faith; Essays in Honor of William J. Abraham*, ed. Paul L. Gavrilyuk et al., 21–40. Grand Rapids: Eerdmans, 2008.

Glassford, Darwin K. "The Future Is Behind Us: Catechesis and Educational Ministries." *Christian Education Journal* 3 (2012) 172–79.

Grant, Jonathan. *Divine Sex: A Compelling Vision for Christian Relationships in a Hypersexualized Age*. Grand Rapids: Brazos, 2015.

Gschwandtner, Christina M. "'Pious Doctrines and Virtuous Actions': The Relation between Theology and Practice in Early Catechetical Instruction." *Wesleyan Theological Journal* 40 (2005) 36–57.

Harrison, Glynn. *A Better Story: God, Sex and Human Relationships*. London: InterVarsity, 2016.

Henze, Mark E. "Demystifying 'Constructivism': Teasing Unnecessary Baggage from Useful Pedagogy." *Christian Education Journal*, 3rd ser., 5 (2008) 87–111.

Jenson, Robert W. "Catechesis for Our Time." In *Marks of the Body of Christ*, edited by Carl E. Braaten and Robert W. Jenson, 137–49. Grand Rapids: Eerdmans, 1999.

Kelly, Liam. *Catechesis Revisited: Handing on Faith Today*. London: Darton, Longman & Todd, 2000.

Keuss, Jeff. *Blur: A New Paradigm for Understanding Youth Ministry*. Grand Rapids: Zondervan, 2014.

Kinnaman, David. *You Lost Me: Why Young Christians Are Leaving Church . . . and Rethinking Faith*. Grand Rapids: Baker, 2011.

Kreider, Alan. "Baptism and Catechesis as Spiritual Formation." In *Remembering Our Future: Explorations in Deep Church*, edited by Andrew Walker and Luke Bretherton, 170–206. London: Paternoster, 2007.

———. *The Change of Conversion and the Origin of Christendom*. Harrisburg, PA: Trinity, 1999.

Lytch, Carol Eichling. *Choosing Church: What Makes a Difference for Teens*. Louisville: Westminster John Knox, 2004.

Mackenzie, Ed. "Following Jesus in a Spiritual Age: Post-Religious Spirituality and the Letter to the Ephesians." *Evangelical Quarterly: An International Review of Bible and Theology* 82 (2015) 137–50.

Mark, Olwyn. *Passing on Faith*. London: Theos, 2016.

Martin, David. *Christian Language and Its Mutations: Essays in Sociological Understanding, Theology and Religion in Interdisciplinary Perspective*. Hants: Ashgate, 2002.

Mason, Matthew. "Back to (Theo-drama) School: The Place of Catechesis in the Local Church." *Scottish Bulletin of Evangelical Theology* 30 (2012) 206–22.

Massey, Karen G. "Christian Education Developments in the 20th Century." *Review and Expositor* 96 (1999) 411–22.

McDowell, Sean, ed. *Apologetics for a New Generation: A Biblical and Culturally Relevant Approach to Talking about God*. Eugene, OR: Harvest House, 2009.

Murphy, Debra Dean. *Teaching That Transforms: Worship at the Heart of Christian Education*. Grand Rapids: Brazos, 2004.

Myers, William R. "Erik H. Erikson and the Deep Context of Ministry." *Theology Today* 73 (2016) 60–70.

Osmer, Richard R. "The Case for Catechism." *Christian Century*, April 1997, 408–12.

———. "The Christian Education of Children in the Protestant Tradition." *Theology Today* 56 (2000) 506–23.

———. *The Teaching Ministry of Congregations*. Louisville: Westminster John Knox, 2005.

Packer, James I., and Gary A. Parrett. *Grounded in the Gospel: Building Believers the Old-Fashioned Way*. Grand Rapids: Baker, 2010.

Powell, Kara, et al. *Growing Young: Six Essential Strategies to Help Young People Discover and Love Your Church*. Grand Rapids: Baker, 2016.

Powell, Kara E., and Chap Clark. *Sticky Faith: Everyday Ideas to Build Lasting Faith in Your Kids*. Grand Rapids: Zondervan, 2011.

Regnerus, Mark D. *Forbidden Fruit: Sex and Religion in the Lives of American Teenagers*. Oxford: Oxford University Press, 2007.

Root, Andrew. *Faith Formation in a Secular Age: Responding to the Church's Obsession with Youthfulness*. Grand Rapids: Baker Academic, 2017.

———. *Taking Theology to Youth Ministry: A Theological Journey through Youth Ministry*. Grand Rapids: Zondervan, 2012.

Shepherd, Nick. *Faith Generation: Retaining Young People and Growing the Church*. London: SPCK, 2016.

Sider, Robert D., ed. *Christian and Pagan in the Roman Empire: The Witness of Tertullian*. Washington, DC: Catholic University of America Press, 2001.

Smith, Christian, and Melinda Lundquist Denton. *Soul Searching: The Religious and Spiritual Lives of American Teenagers*. Oxford: Oxford University Press, 2005.

Smith, Christian, and Patricia Snell. *Souls in Transition: The Religious and Spiritual Lives of Emerging Adults*. Oxford: Oxford University Press, 2009.

Smith, James K. A. *Desiring the Kingdom: Worship, Worldview, and Cultural Formation*. Cultural Liturgies 1. Grand Rapids: Baker Academic, 2009.

———. *Imagining the Kingdom: How Worship Works*. Cultural Liturgies 2. Grand Rapids: Baker Academic, 2013.

———. *You Are What You Love: The Spiritual Power of Habit*. Grand Rapids: Brazos, 2016.

Taylor, Charles. *A Secular Age*. Cambridge: Belknap of Harvard University Press, 2007.

Turpin, Katherine. *Branded: Adolescents Converting from Consumer Faith*. Cleveland: Pilgrim, 2006.

Vanhoozer, Kevin J. *Faith Speaking Understanding: Performing the Drama of Doctrine*. Louisville: Westminster John Knox, 2014.

Walker, Andrew G., and Robin A. Parry. *Deep Church Rising: The Third Schism and the Recovery of Christian Orthodoxy*. Eugene, OR: Cascade, 2014.

Webber, Robert E. *Ancient-Future Evangelism: Making Your Church a Faith-Forming Community*. Grand Rapids: Baker, 2003.

Westerhoff, John H., III. "Formation, Education, Instruction." *Religious Education* 82 (1987) 578–91.

———. *Living the Faith Community*. New York: Seabury, 2004.

———. *Will Our Children Have Faith*. Rev. ed. Toronto: Morehouse, 2000.

White, David F. *Practicing Discernment with Youth: A Transformative Youth Ministry Approach*. Cleveland: Pilgrim, 2005.

Wuthnow, Robert. *After the Baby Boomers: How Twenty- and Thirty-Somethings Are Shaping the Future of American Religion*. Princeton: Princeton University Press, 2007.

Questions for Reflection and Discussion

1. Mackenzie sees evidence of a catechetical crisis within the church today. How would you respond to his appraisal and the underlying factors he identifies? How would you evaluate your own church context in relation to what he describes?
2. What resources, processes, and experiences have factored most significantly in how your tradition historically has approached helping people become formed in the faith? What resources, processes, and experiences currently factor most prominently in your church's efforts?
3. Mackenzie outlines what he sees as several crucial dimensions of "generative catechesis." What is your assessment of the points he raises in this section of the chapter? Is there anything Mackenzie does not mention that you deem to be an essential component of "generative catechesis" in your current context?

Part Two

Contextual Conversations

6

The Relationship between a Generative Church and Denominational Growth

A Reflection on the Baptist Union of Southern Africa

GARTH AZIZ

§

EDITOR'S INTRODUCTION: This book is devoted to a vision of congregational generativity that enables youth to become enfolded into—and empowered to contribute meaningfully to—the life of the church; this vision is rooted in the hope that the church can be a place in which they can find supportive, sustainable ties. Aziz shares these hopes. He describes some of the confusion within churches of his denomination regarding *how* best to minister among youth and *whose* responsibility this is; amid these realities, he sees evidence that youth ministry's influence is declining. Aziz then advances a proposal intended to help stem the tide of this decline. While centered in the life of his own denomination, his insights are applicable to churches from a broad range of traditions. Like several other authors in this volume, he emphasizes the importance of the intergenerational church as a setting for members of younger generations to be formed in the faith. These faith communities can provide a powerful context for young people to develop *social capital*, a core ingredient in Aziz's proposal. Aziz argues that participating actively in the church's cherished rituals is a valuable avenue for social capital to be developed. This chapter enables us to consider how generative churches can marshal the relational and ritual dimensions of church life to aid younger people in developing enduring ties to their faith communities.

§

Introduction

In this chapter, I wish to address the relationship between a generative church and an intergenerational church and the role of liturgy in creating social capital. I aim to investigate how an intergenerational church can create social capital, specifically through bonding, which can ensure denominational sustainability. This chapter relates to the Baptist Union of Southern Africa (BUSA); in it I reflect briefly on a recent research project that raised concern about the youth as a missing generation in the BUSA, as well as the possible implications of this missing generation.

In my doctoral studies, I reflected on the state of affairs within the Baptist Union of Southern Africa (BUSA) regarding the theological nature of the youth pastor role.[1] In the study, I utilized a qualitative research design that involved qualitative interviewing. The research sample comprised fourteen respondents, all senior or lead pastors of churches. Seven of the respondents were at churches where they employed a full-time youth pastor and seven respondents were at churches where there were only volunteer youth workers. The findings that are relevant for this chapter focused on three areas, namely the need for an intergenerational church, the role of the youth pastor and significant adults in the lives of the youth, and the role that youth ministry can contribute to the growth and sustainability of the local church and the denomination.

Among respondents, there was a great emphasis on the need for, and the nature of, an intergenerational ministry in the church. The expectation was that the successful creation of an intergenerational ministry fell within the domain of the youth pastor and that it was almost exclusively their responsibility. There was clear evidence that youth ministry was declining, and this was mainly because youth pastors were unable to relate adequately and effectively to the youth and their culture. In the churches where there

1. Aziz, "Practical Theological Reflection."

was no full-time youth pastor, the discussion around intergenerational ministry was almost nonexistent. Furthermore, there was a limited understanding of what an intergenerational ministry entails.

Most of the respondents argued that, when the youth pastor grows too old, his/her ability to relate with and minister effectively to the youth also diminishes, perhaps even becoming nonexistent. This reflects a misunderstanding of the role of adults in the lives of the youth. It also feeds the assumption that in order to have an effective and meaningful relationship with the youth, you have to be young, culturally savvy, and "on the same level" as the youth. As a result, more mature adults are believed to have little or no place in the lives of the youth. This could also be a reason why most of the churches with full-time youth pastors have separate worship venues for the adults and the youth. Yet, it is in this vital area of worship that intergenerational relationships can contribute positively to the creation of religious social capital.

Furthermore, the respondents raised a concern about the state of youth ministry in the local church, as well as at the national denominational level. Their prime concern was an ineffective and dying youth ministry. The ministers assumed that this state of affairs was mainly due to a lack of understanding of and support for the youth. The respondents felt that, if the youth ministry were not revived, it would eventually lead to the decline of the local church and the denomination. Thus, the current and future state of the youth ministry would directly affect the well-being of the church and the denomination.

The outcomes of my doctoral study demonstrated a limited understanding of intergenerational ministry and the role of significant adults in creating religious social capital in the lives of youth. Yet the respondents did make a valid point when they linked the growth and sustainability of the church and denomination with the status and well-being of its youth. It would be valuable to investigate the connection between these two themes. In short, a greater level of understanding and intentional involvement by significant adults in intergenerational ministry is exactly what is required for churches to be generative.

While there is a growing body of literature on the study of youth ministry and the intergenerational church, there is limited research on the relationship between the intergenerational church and denominational growth. Therefore, I believe that it is prudent to consider the connection between the role of an intergenerational church in the formation of religious social capital and denominational growth. In other words, does a generative church—through an intentional intergenerational ministry—create enough social capital with the youth to foster denominational growth?

In this chapter, I will attempt to investigate the role of generative churches by focusing on the concepts of intentional intergenerational ministry, religious social capital, and denominational growth.

Surveying the Landscape

Amid a recent increase in literature on intergenerational ministry, the role of intergenerational churches in creating social capital—as well as its efficacy in contributing to denominational growth—remains under-researched. This brief literature review will examine the intergenerational church and religious social capital, which are the primary focus areas of this study.

The Intergenerational Church

There has been a growing body of literature published on intergenerational churches and the need for intergenerational ministry in churches in recent years. The emphasis of the various sources includes a biblical understanding of and motivation for intergenerational ministry, the need to integrate the different generations intentionally (because the separation of families according to age and life stages has a direct impact on the passing on of the faith between the generations), and pragmatic ways of implementing an intergenerational ministry. I will briefly review some of the literature to provide a theoretical background to intergenerational ministry.

Certain scholars address the need for an intergenerational church community within a South African context.[2] While these authors focus on the person and agency of children, they nonetheless stress that an intergenerational ministry not only empowers children to be part of the community, but also to be collaborators and co-researchers in the community. This implies that there should be intentional recognition for children in such communities. They argue that an intergenerational ministry allows the faith and its traditions to be passed from one generation to the next. In fact, children will be active agents in changing and shaping the spaces where they are actively involved.

Various scholars examine the situation of specific generations within the church.[3] For example, Seibel and Nel pay special attention to the absence of Gen X from church life. They argue that the absence of Gen X is influenced significantly by the lack of intergenerational ministry. A key

2. Weber and De Beer, "Erratum."

3. Seibel and Nel, "Generation X."

function of the church, they argue, is to "perpetuat[e] its faith tradition from one generation to the next."[4] They further claim that the intergenerational church has always been an important aspect of the local church's existence.[5] The intergenerational church has the important task of passing on the "faith tradition" through the generations, which involves change as an inherent characteristic and result. Citing Lytch's *Choosing Church*, they argue that "constant religious socialisation and meaningful religious experiences" are factors that promote "loyalty of young people to a particular religious tradition."[6] Furthermore, each generation should be empowered to "make their distinctive mark upon the shape of that tradition." This involves two important tasks: first, the church should engage in "reshaping the faith" in ways that would be meaningful to the current and emerging generations; second, the current and emerging generations should be empowered "to impact the shape of the tradition." This would require those who are in leadership positions to involve the current and emerging generations intentionally in leadership roles but also a willingness to release their hold on authority and the safeguarding of traditions to the emerging generations.

In addition to these examples, other scholars have engaged in extensive research devoted to conceptualizing intergenerational ministry.[7] Some of these researchers have attempted to differentiate between multigenerational and intergenerational ministries by recognizing the importance of intentionality on the part of the intergenerational church. Many have also attempted to be pragmatic in recommending ways for the church to be intergenerational.

This expanding body of literature reflects a growing interest in the intergenerational church. It has attempted to provide biblical support for the intergenerational church, to conceptualize the intergenerational church, and to show how such a ministry can be implemented. Furthermore, there is increasing interest in the South African context regarding the intergenerational church. Throughout the above-mentioned literature surveys, there is a distinct focus on the intergenerational church being instrumental in passing the faith and its traditions on to the following generations. However, the role of the intergenerational church in creating social capital is absent from this literature.

4. Seibel and Nel, "Generation X."

5. Seibel and Nel, "Generation X."

6. Seibel and Nel, "Generation X."

7. Allen, "Qualitative Study"; Allen, "Nurturing Children's Spirituality," 266–83; Allen, "Bringing the Generations Together," 319–33; Allen, "Bringing the Generations Back Together," 101–4; Allen and Ross, *Intergenerational Christian Formation*; Allen and Ross, "Why Churches Tend to Separate," 8–14.

Religious Social Capital

Swart provides an impressive article on the need for social capital formation—especially in the South African context—based on empirical research conducted in this context.[8] He goes to great lengths to address both the strengths and weaknesses of the concept of social capital. He also focuses on the three different types of religious social capital, namely "bonding," "bridging," and "linking." Furthermore, he shows how these are important because social capital is focused on relationships. He develops the concept of religious social capital and shows how ritual is an important but missing link in religious social capital. While the focus of the article is not on the benefits of social capital in the church, it clearly shows how the church has been instrumental in generating social capital to address certain needs in society.

Francis and Lankshear also conducted empirical research on social capital in religious communities, more specifically, the Anglican Church.[9] Their discussion focuses on five types of social capital, namely "bonding," "bridging," "linking," "social trust," and the "congregational bonding social capital index."[10] Their specific focus in this research was on the last of these. They conceptualize bonding social capital as "a dense layering of norms and trust that is found in homogenous groups and which tends to reinforce the group's homogeneity. This kind of social capital 'undergirds reciprocity and mobilizes solidarity' and acts as a 'kind of sociological superglue' in maintaining strong in-groups loyalty and promoting robust identity."[11] While the lowest level of congregational bonding existed among the younger generations in the church, namely those in their twenties and thirties, the results of Francis and Lankshear's study stress that bonding social capital is positively generated through frequent church attendance and congregational activity.

Leonard and Bellamy, writing in an Australian context, conducted empirical research on social capital in churches across Australia.[12] They refer to bonding as "social capital that may be developed within a congregation."[13] They identify four aspects of social bonding in churches, namely participation

8. Swart, "Social Capital," 221–49.

9. Francis and Lankshear, "Introducing the Congregational Bonding Social Capital Scale," 224–30.

10. Francis and Lankshear, "Introducing the Congregational Bonding Social Capital Scale," 224–30.

11. Francis and Lankshear, "Introducing the Congregational Bonding Social Capital Scale," 224–30.

12. Leonard and Bellamy, "Dimensions of Bonding," 1046–65.

13. Leonard and Bellamy, "Dimensions of Bonding," 1046–65.

in activities, personal connections and relationships, collective agency, and unity and homogeneity.[14] They argue that this topic is important because, ultimately, the activity or involvement of church members has a direct impact on the survival of the church.

This brief survey of the literature on social capital and the church has indicated that the church has been instrumental in providing social capital for the well-being of society. Furthermore, the literature reveals that social capital—especially "bonding" as social capital—is instrumental in the well-being of the church through the creation of relationships. However, there seems to be a gap in identifying the role of social capital in denominational relationships and sustainability.

The Relationship between a Generative Church and an Intergenerational Church

Generativity generally refers to the roles that one generation plays in passing on traditions to the emerging generation. Generativity can be defined as "the concern in establishing and guiding the next generation" and is linked to personal meaning and social responsibility.[15] It "represents the individual expression of an internalized cultural demand to care for others and an inner desire to demonstrate acts and attitudes consistent with benefiting those who are to follow."[16] Furthermore, generativity is also "a selfless concern for the welfare of future generations and for the world at large that may be expressed in diverse ways, including teaching and mentoring, communal, political, and environmental activism, or through more privatized creative activities."[17] It also has been argued that "many generative acts are a manifestation of a deeply felt need for interpersonal givingness and caring, and the desire to attain fusion with others, characteristics that are the hallmark of communion . . . [and] seen as demonstrating a sense of basic trust in the world and in other human beings."[18]

Recent empirical research demonstrates a positive relationship between intrinsic religiosity and generativity.[19] Religiosity "represents attitudes and behaviors that connect an individual to specific organized faith practices."[20]

14. Leonard and Bellamy, "Dimensions of Bonding," 1046–65.
15. Sandage et al., "Generativity, Relational Spirituality," 1–16.
16. Brady and Hapenny, "Giving Back," 162–67.
17. Dillon et al., "Is Spirituality Detrimental," 427–42.
18. Dillon et al., "Is Spirituality Detrimental," 427–42.
19. Dillon et al., "Is Spirituality Detrimental," 427–42.
20. Dillon et al., "Is Spirituality Detrimental," 427–42.

Consistent with this definition, by reflecting on previous studies, we can see a particular emphasis on the relationship between participation in church activities and generativity.[21] The empirical finding "supports the 'religious capital' model by demonstrating that investment in religious practices yields a long-term benefit toward the cultivation and enactment of generativity."[22]

Therefore, generativity implies that the generative generation is one that has already been established in the faith and the receiving generation is one that has yet to begin or has recently begun its faith journey. Interestingly, generativity is not limited to the older generation, but it is also possible for it to be cultivated in and by the younger generations.[23] However, being generative involves more than merely passing on traditions. It implies that the older generation must acknowledge the need to pass on the tradition to the emerging generation, but also that this emerging generation should be empowered not only to inherit the tradition handed down to it, but also to influence and possibly change it. Therefore, there should be an intrinsic trust in the next generation. A generative church exists when adults in a church choose to be intentional in passing on traditions, empower generations to take and shape those traditions, and demonstrate a willingness to accept change when it appears.

A generative church, therefore, is a church where there are multiple generations engaged together in intentional acts. It also assumes that there are intentional and meaningful relationships between the different generations. It implies that there is the intentional empowerment of the emerging generations rooted in an intrinsic trust among the members of the generative generation. Therefore, a generative church clearly must be an intergenerational church.

An intergenerational church exists when there are "two or more different age groups of people in a religious community together learning/growing/living in faith through in-common-experiences, parallel-learning, contributive-occasions, and interactive-sharing."[24] Thus, it is more than just being together; it is an intentional being together, whereby similar care and concern "brings the generations together in mutual serving, sharing or learning within the core activities of the church in order to live out being the

21. Dillon et al., "Is Spirituality Detrimental," 427–42.

22. Dillon et al., "Is Spirituality Detrimental," 427–42.

23. Brady and Hapenny, "Giving Back," 162–67; Dillon et al., "Is Spirituality Detrimental," 427–42; Sandage et al., "Generativity, Relational Spirituality," 1–16.

24. Allen, "Bringing the Generations Together," 319–33.

body of Christ to each other and the greater community."[25] The intergenerational church should have all the characteristics of generativity.

Building Social Capital through Bonding

I have already mentioned that mutual activities are a means of passing traditions from one generation to the next. In addition to this, there are countless other benefits of being an intergenerational church, namely the fostering of unity and meaningful relationships across all generations, greater faith formation and perseverance, and fostering leadership development. As Allen expresses,

> The general idea . . . is that children, teenagers, and adults (young, middle, and older adults, both single and married) gather in settings where all members give and receive from each other. All ages can participate actively in prayer and worship, and, in some settings, share spiritual insights, read Scripture, and minister to one other. Another current phrase that describes this concept in general is James Gambone's (1998) "intentional intergenerational ministry" or IIM.[26]

An intergenerational ministry increases social capital.[27] However, "Christians do not in the first place live the Christian life to produce social capital, but instead that 'increased social capital is a longterm, secondary consequence of Christian life.'"[28]

Arguably, it is chiefly through intentional mutual activities that social capital is generated. As demonstrated above, a positive relationship has been documented between social capital and participation in religion. However, there has not been any research to show that creating social capital through bonding—by participating in mutual activities in an intergenerational church through acts of generativity—is a means of sustaining and promoting positive behavior toward the local church, as well as church traditions or denominations.

25. Allen and Ross, *Intergenerational Christian Formation*, 17.
26. Allen, "Bringing the Generations Together," 319–33.
27. Snailum, "Integrating Intergenerational Ministry Strategies," 7–28.
28. Swart, "Social Capital," 221–49.

Conceptualizing Social Capital

While this term has already been introduced above, it is good for us to explore exactly what is meant by *social capital* and how it benefits the church. To answer that question, we need to conceptualize social capital. Fortunately, because of the abundance of theoretical research and empirical data that has been generated in this area, much has been written about social capital and its complexity.[29]

The most basic definition of social capital is a network of relationships that serves as a resource, referring "to the norms and networks that enable people to act collectively."[30] Social capital among youth, therefore, can be understood as "interactive, trustworthy, and mutual relationships with parents, friends, and adults."[31] Furthermore, "social capital provides a conceptual model of how positive outcomes are mediated in a social context through interpersonal, associational, and cultural social ties, recognizing that benefits are socially embedded."[32] Therefore, social capital is a complex phenomenon that requires us "to adopt and apply a more dynamic understanding of social capital: one in which a distinction could be made between different types, levels or dimensions of social capital; different performance outcomes associated with different combinations of the various dimensions; and different sets of conditions that support or weaken the different combinations."[33]

Conventional understanding of social capital has evolved over time to what is commonly accepted today as a threefold typology of social capital, namely *bonding*, *bridging* and *linking*.[34] The following lengthy excerpt provides a useful summary of the threefold typology and how it might relate to social capital and the church:

> Bonding social capital is seen as a dense layering of norms and trust that is found in homogenous groups and which tends to reinforce the group's homogeneity. This kind of social capital "undergirds reciprocity and mobilises solidarity" and acts as a "kind of sociological superglue" in maintaining strong in-groups loyalty and promoting robust identity (Putnam 2000, 25). Bridging social capital occurs when individuals or groups form linkages

29. Leonard and Bellamy, "Dimensions of Bonding," 1046–65.
30. Swart, "Social Capital," 221–49.
31. Gast et al., "We Only Speak English Here," 94–121.
32. King, "Adolescent Spirituality," 227–42.
33. Swart, "Social Capital," 221–49.
34. Swart, "Social Capital," 221–49.

> with others different from themselves (heterogeneous relationships), and so create new spaces where power, information, and communication can be shared. Putnam sees this kind of social capital as a "kind of sociological WD40" (25). Linking social capital specifically addresses the power differentials within society and allows more marginal groups to link with the resources of more powerful groups "as a way of beginning to address the asymmetrical nature of power and influence in civil society."
>
> Using social capital theory employing these distinctions, research has discussed and identified the ways in which faith communities contribute to the development of social networks and social well-being among their members (bonding social capital); to the development of social life and interpersonal networks extending into local and wider communities (bridging social capital); and to the development of connections between individuals and networks operating within different strata of society (linking social capital).[35]

Therefore, social capital—comprised of a network of human capital—should ultimately be directed toward using available resources (e.g., skills) to serve the wider community. But it is also possible to link and limit social capital to the church, as opposed to the community at large, by focusing on bonding social capital, which involves "dense, multiplex networks, long-term reciprocity, thick trust, shared norms and less instrumentality (that is, not specifically developed for personal or group advantage). . . . Bonding will refer to the social capital that may be developed within a congregation."[36] The following aspects of bonding may be identified in relation to the church: participation in activities; personal connections and relationships; collective agency; unity; and homogeneity.[37] Interestingly, collective agency and personal connections are the largest contributors to bonding social capital, rather than participation in activities.[38] "Collective agency" is defined as "bonding [that] can occur between the members of a group or community around a common set of goals and objectives," whereas "personal connections" can refer to "bonding [that] can be about friends and acquaintances and the way people connect with each other informally."[39] Bonding through activities such as voluntary service for charity works and even involvement in rituals and church activities, such as the

35. Leonard and Bellamy, "Dimensions of Bonding," 1046–65.
36. Leonard and Bellamy, "Dimensions of Bonding," 1046–65.
37. Leonard and Bellamy, "Dimensions of Bonding," 1046–65.
38. Leonard and Bellamy, "Dimensions of Bonding," 1046–65.
39. Leonard and Bellamy, "Dimensions of Bonding," 1046–65.

choir or various other departments, are "activities that increase opportunities for social networking that should increase social capital."[40] However, the absence of participation in activities might be due to a committed group of people already having enough contacts and networks and, therefore, not seeing the need for church activities to create social capital.[41]

Bonding social capital serves not only to provide opportunities for creating relationships and social networks but also to solidify and enhance relationships that already exist within the social setting of the church. It should be noted that the aim of bonding is to benefit not only the individual but also the present and future realities of the church as a community. Bonding, therefore, is vital to sustaining the local church, passing on faith traditions and cultivating new ones, and empowering the generational succession of leadership and vision.

Building Social Capital through Shared Rituals

The generations present within the church must intentionally engage in shared activities or rituals.[42] Many evangelical traditions tend not to think of themselves as having rituals or liturgy. However, rituals are common practices or activities that are agreed upon by all participants and performed repeatedly to express individual and collective devotion. All churches have them.

Rituals must be recognized as a "critical component of religion that defines the sacred within any community through the symbols and practices that it actualizes." Ritual is the language of religion. "It becomes impossible to conceive of religion without rituals." It is useful to consider the following definition of ritual by Swenson: "Ritual is repeated consecrated (sacred) behaviour that is a symbolic expression of the moods and motivations of religious participants and unseen powers. Ritual forms a bond of friendship, community, and unity with the believer and her/his god. Finally, ritual transports the participant into another world (the world above) wherein there are peace and harmony."[43]

Liturgy, comprised of rituals, provides the substance of Christian worship, which "is governed by norms, draws on a tradition, includes bodily rituals or routines, and involves formative practices." Liturgy, in this sense, stresses formative practices where different spiritual meanings are expressed

40. Leonard and Bellamy, "Dimensions of Bonding," 1046–65.

41. Leonard and Bellamy, "Dimensions of Bonding," 1046–65.

42. Allen, "Bringing the Generations Back Together," 101–4.

43. Swart, "Social Capital," 221–49.

and experienced in the actions of the individuals through various elements of Christian worship. This understanding of liturgy is shared across various denominations and theological traditions. Ultimately, liturgy is about forming and shaping the identity to be more Christlike. As Smith expresses, liturgy is a "certain species of practice"; practices, he further explains, "are material, embodied routines that we do over and over again; they are usually aimed at a specific end, or goal; and their repetition and practice has the effect of making them more and more automatic such that they become part of the very fiber of our character, wired into our second nature."[44] Liturgy, ultimately, is concerned with capturing the very desires at the heart of who we are as people.

Ritual, therefore, is basically routine; it is the repeated behavior determined by the faith community to be sacred. Ritual has benefits for both the individual and community by creating friendships and attachment. "Liturgies—whether 'sacred' or 'secular'—shape and constitute our identities by forming our most fundamental desires and our most basic attunement to the world. In short, liturgies make us certain kinds of people, and what defines us is what we love."[45] Ritual, therefore, could be anything from singing to fellowship, as long as the behavior and interaction between the members is deemed sacred and continual.

Often, active involvement in ritual is not forced but results from an intergenerational ministry. As an example of this, one study found that "intergenerational relationships fostered intrinsic religious motivation which led to increased participation in religious practices and spiritual disciplines, as well as influenced how youth committed to and served their faith community."[46]

Religious ritual is a missing element in the current conversation about religious social capital, and it could serve as a significant contributor to generating religious social capital. Religious ritual has a role to play in creating social capital because there is a substance expressed in ritual language that could greatly aid the creation of social capital:[47]

- Ritual as "remembering": the way in which ritual reminds both individuals and social groups about their heritage and past;

44. Smith, *Desiring the Kingdom*, 86.
45. Smith, *Desiring the Kingdom*, 25.
46. Snailum, "Integrating Intergenerational Ministry Strategies," 7–28.
47. Swart, "Social Capital," 221–49.

- Ritual as "social bonding": the way in which ritual functions to bond persons together, increase levels of social cohesion and strengthen group solidarity;
- Ritual as "regulating moral behavior": the way in which ritual regulates the behavior of societal members and in the process maintains moral order;
- Ritual as "socialization and changes in social status": the way in which ritual enables the transition of an individual from one status to another (for example, marriage);
- Ritual as "psychological development": the way in which ritual facilitates a sense of psychological well-being among individuals and groups;
- Ritual as "empowerment": the way in which ritual assists individuals and whole groups in feeling stronger, less disaffected, and readier to serve others.

Furthermore, involvement in rituals and shared activities must involve more than just participation. The older generations must be intentional in creating meaningful opportunities and experiences whereby the younger generations are able to journey along with the older generations and thus be empowered to inform practice and even policy in the church.[48] Ritual, therefore, should be a mutually agreed-upon activity whereby meaning is derived from all generations present.

Establishing Ties and Ensuring Support between Local Church and Denomination through Bonding

It now is important that we return to the question of the connection between an intergenerational church and denominational succession. A denomination that takes its future seriously needs to take its current and future generations seriously. Church growth strategies that include age-segregated ministries as a drawcard to attract people are shortsighted.[49] An intergenerational church, comprising at least three generations, is vital for a growing and sustainable church. In the same way, a denomination's future is dependent on the active presence of many generations. If a church

48. Weber and De Beer, "Erratum," a3572.

49. Merhaut, "Intergenerational Faith Formation," 28–37.

or denomination is not intergenerational, it will die.[50] Each generation is responsible for the "passing of the baton of leadership to a successive generation."

It therefore becomes the responsibility of the leadership not only to pass on the faith traditions and hand over the leadership reigns to future generations, but also to encourage the various generations to be active together in the leadership structures of the church. The inclusion of the future generations in the church leadership structures challenges the notion that the youth are the leaders of tomorrow. Instead, the youth should be regarded as leaders of today and should be empowered to assume leadership positions. There are many opinions on why the youth leave the church. However, it is possible that, by empowering them through intentional intergenerational ministries, this exodus of youth from the church can be minimized. The exodus of the youth not only threatens the future of the local church, but also indirectly affects the future of its denomination. If the local church cannot be sustained, it is obvious that this will have a direct effect on the well-being of the denomination. Youth, as collaborators and co-researchers, are able to "shape spaces and conversations . . . and are able to influence the adults."[51] As a result, as the faith of the youth matures and becomes sustainable, they are more likely to commit actively to their faith and faith traditions and to enjoy a prolonged stay at the church.[52]

Clearly, there is a strong case to be made for the relationship between a generative church and denominational growth. The question, then, is how to foster an intergenerational church in which the youth become the instruments for the future sustainability of the local church and the denomination. I propose the following three means as a way forward: first, harnessing the role of ritual in creating social capital; second, embracing intentionality in creating and growing relationships between the various generations; and third, redistributing power and ownership by reshaping traditions.

A Way Forward

The creation of social capital should not be the focus of denominational sustainability, as the development of social capital is a natural product of a generative church. Therefore, the challenge is not creating social capital, but rather the creation of a truly generative church. At this point, I wish to suggest the following as an aid to the creation of a generative church,

50. Whitesel and Hunter, *House Divided*.

51. Weber and De Beer, "Erratum," a3572.

52. Snailum, "Integrating Intergenerational Ministry Strategies," 7–28.

bearing in mind that a generative church is essential for the survival of a denomination.

It is my contention that the creation of opportunities for the younger generations to participate fully in the life of the church should not be imposed by those in power, who are usually the older generations. Such a unilateral imposition assumes that the younger generations are not aware of what they want or do not have the necessary abilities and wisdom to suggest possibilities of what may be beneficial. In this chapter, I have argued that the younger generations should be co-researchers who inform policy and practice—not merely passive bystanders. This also implies that the current rituals should be evaluated to see if they are conducive for use within an intergenerational church. Participation in rituals should entail more than the youth's simply following the current rituals in the hope that it will engender some form of commitment on their part. There must be an intentional exchange of power to allow the next generation to shape the rituals. An intergenerational ministry enables people of all ages to be involved and engaged in shared activities, including worship, fellowship, study, decision-making, mission, outreach, and service.[53] Rituals should be practices that are mutually agreed upon and informed by all the generations present. This allows for shared ownership of the space and rituals, as well as a willingness to see the rituals evolve through constant dialogue between the various generations.

A truly intergenerational church is one where there is a sharing of power, ownership, and trust and a recognition that even very young persons have the right to make a significant difference in the life of the church.

Conclusion

In this chapter, I have examined the relationship between a generative church and an intergenerational church, and I have argued that an intergenerational church *is* a generative church. I have also argued that liturgy is key in the creation of social capital, but that social capital is an automatic result of a generative church. Liturgy, therefore, should be a priority in our consideration of intergenerational ministry. Moreover, the liturgy of an intergenerational church should be agreed upon mutually by all the generations present. A generative church not only allows the older generations to pass on their traditions and faith to the youth but also allows the youth to reshape traditions through liturgy.

53. Allen, "Bringing the Generations Back Together," 101–4.

While the BUSA can boast 144 years of existence, it must acknowledge that its future is directly dependent upon its youth. However, this dependence does not entail merely the presence of the youth in the local church but rather their active involvement in it, through which they can be empowered to shape new traditions through various forms of liturgy.

Bibliography

Allen, Holly Catterton. "Bringing the Generations Together: Support from Learning Theory." *Christian Education Journal*, 3rd ser., 2 (2005) 319–33.

———. "Bringing the Generations Back Together: Introduction to Intergenerationality." Guest editorial. *Christian Education Journal*, 3rd ser., 9 (2012) 101–4.

———. "Nurturing Children's Spirituality in Intergenerational Christian Settings." In *Children's Spirituality: Christian Perspectives, Research, and Applications*, edited by Donald Ratcliff, 266–83. Eugene, OR: Cascade, 2004.

———. "A Qualitative Study Exploring the Similarities and Differences of the Spirituality of Children in Intergenerational and Non-intergenerational Christian Contexts." PhD diss., Biola University, 2002.

Allen, Holly Catterton, and Christine Lawton Ross. *Intergenerational Christian Formation: Bringing the Whole Church Together in Ministry, Community and Worship*. Downers Grove: IVP Academic, 2012.

———. "Why Churches Tend to Separate the Generations." *Journal of Discipleship and Family Ministry* 3 (2013) 8–14.

Aziz, Garth. "A Practical Theological Reflection of the Office of the Career Youth Pastor." PhD thesis, University of Pretoria, 2016.

Brady Loretta C., and Amanda Happeny. "Giving Back and Growing in Service: Investigating Spirituality, Religiosity, and Generativity in Young Adults." *Journal of Adult Development* 17 (2010) 162–67. https://doi.org/10.1007/s10804-010-9094-7.

Calhoun-Brown, Allision. "Be Fruitful and Multiply? Church Size and the Generation of Social Capital." Paper prepared for the American Political Science Association annual meeting, Washington, DC, September 1–4, 2005.

Cloete, Anita. "Spiritual Formation as Focus of Youth Ministry." *Dutch Reformed Theological Journal* 53 (2012) 70–77. http://dx.doi.org/10.5952/53-3-4-250.

Dillon, Michele M., et al. "Is Spirituality Detrimental to Generativity?" *Journal for the Scientific Study of Religion* 42 (2003) 427–42.

Francis, Leslie J., and David W. Lankshear. "Introducing the Congregational Bonding Social Capital Scale: A Study among Anglican Churchgoers in South London." *Journal of Beliefs and Values* 36 (2015) 224–30. http://dx.doi.org/10.1080/13617672.2015.1041786.

Gast, Melanie Jones, et al. "'We Only Speak English Here': English Dominance in Language Diverse, Immigrant After-School Programs." *Journal of Adolescent Research* 32 (2017) 94–121. https://doi.org/10.1177/0743558416674562.

King, Pamela Ebstyne. "Adolescent Spirituality and Positive Youth Development: A Look at Religion, Social Capital, and Moral Functioning." In *Approaches to Positive*

Youth Development, edited by Rainer K. Silbereisen and Richard M. Lerner, 227–42. London: Sage, 2007.
Maselko, Joanna, et al. "Religious Social Capital: Its Measurement and Utility in the Study of the Social Determinants of Health." *Social Science and Medicine* 73 (2011) 759–67. doi:10.1016/j.socscimed.2011.06.019.
Sandage, Steven J., et al. "Generativity, Relational Spirituality, Gratitude, and Mental Health: Relationships and Pathways." *International Journal for the Psychology of Religion* 21 (2011) 1–16. https://doi.org/10.1080/10508619.2011.532439.
Seibel, Cory L., and Malan Nel. "Generation X, Intergenerational Justice and the Renewal of the Traditioning Process." *HTS Teologiese Studies / Theological Studies* 66 (2010) Art. #876, 7 pp. DOI: 10.4102/hts.v66i2.876.
Smith, James K. A. *Desiring the Kingdom: Worship, Worldview, and Cultural Formation*. Grand Rapids: Baker Academic, 2009.
Snailum, Brenda. "Integrating Intergenerational Ministry Strategies into Existing Youth Ministries: What Can a Hybrid Approach Be Expected to Accomplish?" *Journal of Youth Ministry* 11 (2013) 7–28.
Swart, Ignatius. "Social Capital, Religious Social Capital and the Missing Element of Religious Ritual." *Religion and Theology* 24 (2017) 221–49. https://doi.org/10.1163/15743012-02403008.
Weber, Shantelle, and Stephan De Beer. "Erratum: Doing Theology with Children in a South African Context: Children as Collaborators in Intergenerational Ministry." *HTS Teologiese Studies / Theological Studies* 72 (2017) a3572. https://doi.org/10.4102/hts. v72i1.3572-01.
Woolcock, Michael. "Social Capital and Economic Development: Towards a Theoretical Synthesis and Policy Framework." *Theory and Society* 27 (1998) 188.

Questions for Reflection and Discussion

1. Aziz describes some of the confusion he encountered within Baptist churches in his country in the course of his research. As you think about your own congregational context, what seems to be the prevailing assumption about whose responsibility it is to invest in the members of emerging generations? How are these assumptions being expressed practically within the life of your church?
2. How would you characterize your church's track record in helping adolescents develop social capital? What rituals, if any, have proven most helpful in facilitating *bonding*, *bridging*, and *linking* in the lives of young people?
3. Aziz argues that the members of younger generations should be treated as "co-researchers who inform policy and practice—not merely passive bystanders." To what extent is this the case within your church at present? What factors have given shape to the current reality in this regard?

7

Grow Together

The US Church and the Witness of the Global South

MICHAEL DROEGE

§

EDITOR'S INTRODUCTION: North American society has been described as suffering from a "crisis of generativity."[1] Michael Droege provides a similar assessment of mainline denominations in the United States today; these churches, by his account, are suffering from an acute crisis of generativity. In fact, he suggests, vast numbers of these churches have fallen into a state of stagnation. In this chapter, he urges us to join him in exploring the factors that have contributed to this crisis. He is convinced that those trying to diagnose the situation from within mainline churches all too commonly misidentify its root causes. While a lack of intentionality may be a factor, Droege argues that a significant problem lies with the unforeseen consequences of choices that churches have made quite intentionally over the course of several decades. Droege desires to see young people develop a vital sense of connectedness to mainline congregations and their rich faith traditions. What is most needed, he concludes, is a renewed theological vision

1. K. Brynolf Lyon, "Aging and the Conflict of Generations," in *Pastoral Care and Social Conflict*, edited by Pamela D. Couture and Rodney J. Hunter (Nashville: Abingdon, 1999), 92.

of the church. He proposes that US mainline churches would be aided in reconnecting with this vision by looking beyond themselves and learning from the legacies of generativity modeled by churches in other cultures. This chapter challenges us to consider the relationship between our desire to be generative and the theological, philosophical, and structural paradigms that influence our ministries among youth in our own contexts.

§

Introduction

As I sat down to write this chapter, I received a call from a former student of mine who I had not spoken to in twenty years. He wanted to talk to me because he found himself at a crossroads in his faith journey and, as he remembers, I was "cool" and had been kind to him during his awkward teenage years. He had not been practicing faith since high school. At that time, his life became uprooted when he moved from the area and the church I was serving at the time. The intervening years found him unable to reconcile the progressivism of his emerging adult years with the faith community and beliefs of his family. As a result, he had left Christian faith and practice behind. We talked for hours, and I was able to address some of his questions about theology and how the church relates to the social issues that concern him and his generation. Yet while we were speaking, I couldn't help but reflect on how many former students of mine were in the same place in their faith. As they grew up, they had a great time participating in programming focused on them and their developmental stage; but as childhood transitioned to adulthood, they no longer found the church a community in which to continue growing or that seemed relevant to what they were discovering in their world. Simply put, too many of our kids are not staying with the church.

I do want to clarify that I am not questioning whether these young adults "are good people" or necessarily whether "they still believe in God." Many people who leave the church live with a strong moral compass; only a small minority ever self-identify as atheist or agnostic. Rather, my concern is why these kids into whom we have poured countless resources have not continued as engaged members of a local faith community. Those of us who serve in the mainline church in the United States, if are honest with ourselves, are far too familiar with this trend. The majority of the kids who have passed through our youth ministries emerge with a fondness for their time with us and memories of the experiences to which we introduced them, but only a very slim minority develop the kind of deep roots that allow them to remain with the church and to continue growing in their faith.

The people of the United States have had a long history of believing themselves to be the "missionaries" of the world. Our economic resources have made us the world's leading consumers, tourists, police force, source of aid, and—it has also been believed—the world's primary exemplars of Christianity. The United States seldom sees itself as among the ones needing help. We are the innovators, the inventors, and the senders. To those who see themselves as possessing the bulk of the resources, it is hard to be open to learning from others. Yet, we must acknowledge that the mainline church in the United States (more specifically, the predominantly Caucasian, historical denominations) is in trouble. The answer to this crisis lies in taking a good, hard look at how we are doing ministry.

Theologian Richard Osmer suggests that the work of practical theology is to identify *what is going on, why is it going on, what ought to be going on,* and *how we might respond.*[2] This is the framework I will use to explore the state of faith formation among young people from mainline backgrounds in the United States.

What Is Going On?

- In 1972, 28 percent of Americans identified themselves as belonging to a mainline congregation, according to the General Social Survey (GSS). That number had dropped to 12.2 percent by 2014. That is a more than 50 percent decline in just over forty years.[3] Fortunately, the most recent Gallup poll shows this drastic decline stabilizing in the last five years.[4]
- While also evidencing a slowing of the drastic shift that occurred around the turn of the millennium, a 2017 report by the Presbyterian Church, USA, shows a continued trend of decline in what is termed "other losses," those not attributed to death or membership transfer. In 2017, members who were simply removed from the rolls total 74,129.[5]

2. Osmer, *Practical Theology.*
3. Stetzer, "State of the Church in America."
4. Gallup, "Religion."
5. Van Marter, "PC(USA) Membership," 2.

- According to statistics reported by the United Methodist Church's General Council on Finance and Administration, for the last ten years, worship attendance in the United States has decreased an average of 52,383 per year.[6]
- United Church of Christ statistics indicate an average of one congregational closure per week in the years between 2008 and 2015.[7]
- The Roman Catholic Church is also showing losses in local parishes. Peter Steinfels, codirector of Fordham's Center on Religion and Culture, noted that if all the Catholics who have left the church decided to form a single church, they would constitute the second largest denomination in the nation.[8]

Clearly, the mainline church is experiencing a crisis of attrition. It is important to stress again that these figures only represent mainline and, as mentioned above, predominantly white, churches.[9] When I began my research into what is happening within mainline denominations, I was intrigued by the prospect that declining participation of young adults might not be a universal reality; perhaps I would discover that there are denominations and specific cultural expressions of Christianity that are not experiencing this crisis.

I spent my first decade in youth ministry in communities that were predominantly African American. I do not recall struggling with numbers at youth meetings or seeing a desperate generational gap. The research seems to back this up. By and large, historically black congregations have been relatively immune from the level of membership decline witnessed in their white counterparts. When attendance statistics are broken down culturally, the population of the African American and Hispanic church remains largely unchanged.[10] If we look beyond the United States, we find statistics about the growth rate of the church in the Global South that are staggering.[11] While congregations in Europe are experiencing a far more

6. May, "Economist," 4.

7. UCC Center for Analytics, Research, and Data, "A Statistical Profile," 3.

8. Steinfels, "Further Adrift."

9. When figures are broken down by demographic or denomination, research shows that historically African American congregations and evangelical Protestant congregations have exhibited no statistical change positively or negatively (Smith et al., "America's Changing Religious Landscape," 8, 9.)

10. Smith, et al., "America's Changing Religious Landscape," 14.

11. In terms of definition, "the Global South" refers to the post-colonial developing world that comprises the more southern portion of the globe. Less defined geographically than economically/culturally, the South includes countries in Latin America,

severe decline, one only needs look to the Global South to see a church whose population is growing explosively. In 1910, the Global South only accounted for 17.8 percent of the population of Christians worldwide. The figure for that region of the world as of 2010 shows that the majority of Christians now are concentrated there. While some of the growth early in the Global South can be attributed to Western evangelism, it is clear that Christianity in the southern hemisphere is largely unaffected by the trends occurring within churches in the global north.[12] As the center of Christianity continues to move to the southern hemisphere, study after study indicates that the shrinking numbers spoken of are largely a European and North American problem.[13]

The "crisis" then is not that Christianity as a religion is losing ground, but that mainline congregations in the United States and other Western countries are not effectively passing along their values or effectively retaining young members. This is clearly an area of concern for established congregations. As with any family that desires its children to carry on the values and name of the family of origin, the mainline church is struggling to transfer its message to the next generation. When coupled with the stylistic elements of multimedia and more contemporary music being offered outside the traditional mainline church order of worship, the message simply comes off as out of touch and ground is lost. However, as we will explore later in this chapter, while contemporary worship and theological conservatism are often used as criteria to critique the traditional mainline church, I would like to suggest that the church's decline is a symptom of poor faith formation praxis rather than a systemic problem with its theology or liturgical practices.

Africa, and South Asia.

12. It should be noted that these statistics do not have the same denominational distinctives that the US statistics indicated. Evangelical Protestantism, especially Pentecostalism, accounts for a large part of Christian expression in this part of the world. The arguments made here are not denominational or theological in nature but gaining clues about sustainability from how faith is transferred from one generation to the next, something historical US churches are struggling to achieve. Also, by way of definition, when we speak of the Global North, we are speaking of the primarily euro-centric church that finds its roots in historic Catholicism and European Protestantism, later developed in the United States through various historical stages of religious growth such as the Great Awakening, Azusa Street, and Evangelicalism.

13. Granberg-Michaelson, "Think Christianity Is Dying?"

So, Why Is This Going On?

Booksellers are well stocked with titles attempting to diagnose why the church is struggling or to prescribe the latest answer for church growth. Outside critiques of the mainline church usually focus either on its progressive theology and corresponding social ethics or its approach to worship, suggesting it is the antiquated worship forms employed by mainline churches that disconnect the young. While theology and liturgy are important issues, for this chapter I want to focus on what is heard most often from within the mainline church itself—a misdiagnosis that places the focus chiefly on external, rather than internal, contributors to decline.

If I had to rank the most common gripe about the shrinking numbers of youth from the elder members of congregations I have served, it is that sports and other extracurricular activities for kids have now invaded Sunday mornings. Researcher Steve McMullin studied sixteen mainline congregations in decline and found that many clergy and congregants cited the secularization of Sunday morning, manifested specifically in kid sports and members' openness to work, as the reason for decline. McMullin admits surprise at these results. People offered many different reasons for the church's decline, but most answers focused upon external factors. As McMullin summarizes,

> Although survey respondents identified other possible factors, no other factors were mentioned as frequently. The general busyness of life was blamed by 17.9 percent, while 13.4 percent believe people do not attend church because of specifically religious reasons ("People don't believe they need God in their lives"; "They are not saved"; "Do not have a personal relationship with Jesus Christ"; "They have lost focus on God"; "Fear of being confronted with their sins"). Only 8.2 percent thought it related to people's negative attitudes toward churches, and even fewer (6.4 percent) thought that people find the church irrelevant. A mere 4.3 percent answered that people do not attend church because the church is not doing what it needs to do, and only 3.3 percent said that it is because church is boring.[14]

While the most noteworthy finding of this survey was that people saw the major causes of decline as external to the congregation and not internal, this perspective was not shared by every pastor polled. McMullin sought out two growing churches, both of which had experienced severe decline but were now in a season of growth, to test if growth had any bearing on how

14. McMullin, "Secularization of Sunday," 43–59.

a congregation answers the question. The pastors of the growing churches responded with a far more internally focused perspective, citing the church's inability to change outdated practices in response to the modern needs of culture as a major cause of decline. It seems that these growing churches were willing to take a look at how they were doing church instead of searching for a scapegoat by pointing to what was going on around them.

Older members of declining congregations often wax nostalgic for the "good old days" when the sanctuary was full but have a very difficult time connecting declining membership with church practice. Understandably, it is a challenge to accept that something internal is a cause for decline when the forms of worship presently practiced and programs presently offered were what worked when the church was full. One can see how pastors and congregants are tempted to conclude that there must be external factors for decline since the internal forms once proved effective in the past. This perspective raises a caution flag for presently growing churches that attribute their success to the ability to present their message in relevant forms. At one time, churches now in decline would have said the same thing. The answer must go beyond the style of morning worship if the church is to avoid following a cycle of grown, decline, and death, with each generation creating new congregations. While these new congregations are free to develop relevant ministry without the restraints of tradition, the tradeoff is that new ministries can lack the history and cultivated perspective found in longstanding congregations. There is a richness of wisdom that comes with time. I suggest that without considering a new paradigm, there is a danger of simply repeating cycles that force choices between "tradition" and "relevance." Can historic congregations embrace new faith formation practices that cultivate relevance by appropriating the wealth of the wisdom gained with time?

What Is Going On?

The discovery of the state of the church beyond my limited context caused me to search for theologians from the Global South working in the field of youth ministry. If our current praxis was not doing the job we intended it to do, perhaps a writer from that part of the world would help me reshape my thoughts. Some of the best work I found came out of South Africa, which provides a unique perspective as an African nation with clear cultural ties to Europe. This led me to the work of Malan Nel, now Extraordinary Professor of Practical Theology at the University of Pretoria.

What I had forgotten was that I was first introduced to Nel's work fifteen years earlier through a book called *Four Views of Youth Ministry and the Church*. In this volume, edited by Mark H. Senter III, four scholars each present their perspectives on youth ministry and then respond to one another's positions. At the time I read *Four Views*, I was firmly entrenched in what Senter's book identifies as the Missional Model, which sees teens and teen culture like a foreign land and youth workers as missionaries. As a youth "missionary," I went to where the kids were, practicing an "incarnational" style of ministry that proved effective in enabling me to develop relationships with students; in turn, this provided me a platform to engage them with the message of Christianity. I observed the cultural dissonance between the world of adults and the world of teenagers yet lived with the belief that an effective ministry immersed in the teenage world would eventually grow the church.

At that time, I would have been counted among those who criticized the "Inclusive Congregational Approach" Nel introduced in *Four Views*. While his view emphasized the importance of the relationship between the church and youth, I found this approach untenable. I was convinced that, if relevant and transformative ministry was going to happen, it could not be done within the traditional church structure. Nel's approach felt quite foreign, which—I was later to discover—was quite literally the case. With time, I began to see his understanding of youth ministry differently and to recognize its potential to aid churches in my American context.

Nel's argument begins from a theological perspective, specifically by focusing upon the biblical theme of covenant.[15] In Nel's view, God's redemptive mission is expressed through God's promise to God's community, or *corpus*, of which youth are a part.[16] Following from this theological grounding, Nel explains, where the church has gone wrong is in exchanging the redemptive context of the corpus—the church as a whole—with modern pedagogical frameworks that placed youth as the center of attention within a parallel ministry. The church is the *macro* expression of this redemptive covenant community, while the family is its *micro* expression. Within the family, dynamics change with the passage of time and the life stages of each member, but the goal of growing together as a family remains. Ideally, a family grows together and not apart, which requires change and growth in all members. A parent cannot use the same parenting techniques with a child of two years old as with a child of nineteen, but a healthy family grows and adjusts with the life stages of each member. The central importance of

15. Nel, *Youth Ministry*, 13.

16. Nel, *Youth Ministry*, 17.

the family remains, but change is experienced as the family grows together. The change in the child requires change in the parent and among siblings. Unhealthy families often cannot adapt to change. These families are marked by conflict, which can lead to separation and estrangement. Similar dynamics are often recognizable in the church, as well.

According to Nel, in the church, God has provided a community composed of people who, through the Spirit of God, are experiencing growth and change.[17] Elder members of this community play an important role as anchor-points as the whole community grows and develops together. Nel's theological starting point is key to understanding the practical approach to youth ministry he develops.

Nel's theological vision stands in stark contrast from the vision that predominates in much of modern youth ministry. Other approaches find their roots in the creation of youth subculture. Prior to the industrial revolution and the rise of the distinct life phase that came to be called adolescence, the church mostly grew together as a cohesive community. They celebrated new births, went through social changes together, wrestled with theological challenges together, and then, often at death, mourned together. Prior to the end of the nineteenth century, most people moved from childhood to adulthood somewhere in their early teens.[18] Children grew to marrying age, took their place in the family farm or business, or began an apprenticeship. The economics of the industrial revolution forced these young workers from the job market and created an idle class that, due to child labor laws, were not allowed to work. Within a few decades, this allowed for the creation of a distinct youth culture as "teenagers" had more time on their hands.

Ultimately this period came to be characterized by an "in-between" experience of being physically ready for adulthood but being told to wait until eighteen or twenty-one or beyond to step into adult life. In this social environment, teens are left to establish their own subculture, having left childhood while still awaiting adulthood. Over time, this has given teens many options for how to spend their time and raised questions of how they relate to the adult world as they create their own cultural mores, thereby deepening the distance from the adult world. Thus, adolescence is more a created social phenomenon than a physiological stage of aging.

17. Nel, *Youth Ministry*, 22.

18. It is important to note that adolescence is a created social class, not a physiological stage of aging. There are a host of factors that led to the creation of this class, and ensure its maintenance, such as the economics of the industrialized world, the furtherance of higher education, and family planning. For further study, see Arnett, *Emerging Adulthood*. Another great work on this subject is Chinn's *Inventing Modern Adolescence*.

The education system stepped in as an answer to the problem of adolescence as it became more common for people to continue their education through high school. Youth ministry as it is commonly understood today began to emerge in this new adolescent environment as church practices followed culture change. The first youth ministries can trace their roots back to "intra-church" organizations like Christian Endeavor, but our modern youth ministry models stem from the emergence of the "para-church" movement in the post-WWII era. Popular movements sprung up with names like Youth for Christ, Young Life, and Word of Life. They all focused on creating religious spaces for the new segment of society known as "teens." Rallies, camps, radio programming, and "clubs"[19] found great success in attracting adolescents to a place where they could hear gospel preaching with people their own age. The church quickly recognized the success of this phenomena and even partnered with leaders from these movements by encouraging their young people to participate. A generation later, the church adopted a similar model within the church itself with the emergence of the youth pastor and the church youth group. In turn, a multi-million-dollar resource and entertainment industry was developed to support these efforts.

While American culture led to the creation of the adolescent subculture, the church furthered the division by creating a Christian youth subculture within the already established adolescent subculture. The youth group was effective at creating a small community for teenagers, but it also caused them to experience growing isolation from the greater church body. Teens were given a "wait until you are older" signal, despite the fact that many were confirmed into the whole church in their early teenage years. To address the challenges posed by this "not yet" generation of people, age-specific approaches to ministry were developed that focused primarily on Christian education, living ethically, and acts of service, all steeped in youth culture. Nel argues that this focus on adolescent development began to distance the church from its core mission of whole-church faith formation.

Nel urges us to return to the understanding that the theological purpose of youth ministry is the building up of the church. While this may seem like an elementary principle, it does call into question the departure points of other views. While other approaches to youth ministry can be done within the church and can aid it in fulfilling its mission, Nel desires us to consider whether they truly embody the church's prime directive.

19. The word "club" while not exclusively used, was coined by Jim Rayburn, founder of Young Life, to reflect the club culture of the high school and met in homes because Rayburn decided that was the most effective setting for this new work (see https://www.younglife.org/About/Pages/History.aspx).

When Nel describes God's work of building up the local church, he sees youth as needing to be a part of the whole. Their involvement is an important dimension of how the church grows. What Nel is calling for is a basic understanding of the oneness of the church and the work of God to grow and direct the corpus as a whole. Thus, for Nel, youth ministry is a ministry of participation in congregational life. If the church is the visible demonstration of the kingdom of God where all people gather as one to learn how to love one another, we must commit to living life together.

This makes youth ministry the responsibility of the whole congregation (and thus necessarily intergenerational), a key component of Nel's inclusive congregational approach. The ministries of the church are ministries to the whole church, which means youth are both being ministered to and doing ministry in every corner of congregational life. Central to Nel's perspective is that youth ministry too often has been one ministry of the church instead of every ministry considering where youth might fit. This does not mean that we should ignore the differentiated nature of adolescent development; it does mean we must recognize the uniqueness of the age cohorts represented in our congregations and make sure our preaching, worship, teaching, pastoral care, leadership, etc., are inclusive of each member. As Nel points out, individualization happens naturally; our responsibility is to help form Christian community.

This approach is intended to foster growth as a corpus and not merely as individuals. The challenge in adopting this model is recognizing how it conflicts with American ideals of individualism and the lower value placed on community as a whole. While America's dominant white culture has often seen itself in an idealistic fashion, I have found that there is a great contribution to be found in the socialization practices of minority cultures that provide insight into the problem of church attrition. These practices are much closer to the vision for which Nel advocates. I will briefly reflect on a few examples here.

Ken Crane, in his book *Latino Churches: Faith, Family, and Ethnicity in the Second Generation*, argues that the Latino church serves as a "community of memory" in which language, culture, and family traditions are maintained. Through Christian practice and tradition, families can avoid what Crane calls "dissonant acculturation." Dissonant acculturation can be seen across immigrant cultures in which the second generation becomes more "American." Even in the case of immigrant families in the United States characterized by a diversity of religious affiliations (older members maintain strict Catholic traditions while younger members are drawn to Protestant expressions), Christian traditions and the common language of faith are still shared generationally. In the Latino culture, religious festivals, home altars, blessings, and even the rite of quinceañeras are all ways of keeping young people connected to their cultural identities.

Cognitive Belief vs. Corporate Belonging

To a Western thinker, this sense of family or communal faith may raise red flags. In modern Western thought, religion is largely understood as an expression of cognitive belief. Christian practice thus is an affirmation of one's belief. The expectation is that propositionally based education will lead to religious participation. When we look outside of the dominant American culture, we find cultures for whom belonging is a more central value. The goal is belonging to one another rather than adherence to propositional truths. This does not mean they ignore theology. Quite to the contrary, theirs is a lived theology of the community not merely individual belief or piety.

Wallace Charles Smith asserts that the historically black church was born from West African concepts of extended family and kinship. Smith sees the church growing and evolving as a "new family for those constantly being uprooted from their original families."[20] The historically black church in the United States strives to maintain these bonds of kinship that define the African American church experience.

Myers describes the youth ministry model of the historically black church in terms of a kinship model "centering on intergenerational, communal worship, and the empowerment of adolescents."[21] It is not uncommon to walk into a historically black congregation and see youth serving as musicians, worship leaders, dancers, ushers, or readers. Myers notes in his study that, while there were age-specific ministries in the church, they all somehow supported the larger church experience, with every member of the ministerial staff somehow involved in "youth ministry." Some recent studies are suggesting that as historically black communities become less homogenous, African American congregations are starting to see some of the earmarks of generational dissonance.[22] Yet there remains much to be learned from African American church traditions.

20. Smith, *Church in the Life of the Black Family*, 22.

21. Myers, *Black and White Styles of Youth Ministry*, 109.

22. For further study on this, I suggest Mitchell, *Black Millennials and the Church*.

Where Do We Go from Here?

When I began my own journey of research and discovery, I had serious questions not only about the state of my profession, but about the viability of the Christian church itself. Is this movement, this faith to which I have given the entirety of my adult life, a thing of our primitive past? Was it time to learn a new trade? Digging for the answers to explain a dying church has far more than professional implications for someone who has been in active engagement with his religion for over forty-five years. It brought me a great deal of joy and relief to find the work of Nel, who sparked a flame of hope that we may have simply been thinking about youth ministry the wrong way.

Mainline church attrition is a stark reality and, regardless of the creative and determined minds that have attempted to tackle the question, little more is ever accomplished than a slowing of attrition; but there is never a moment where the tide is turned. I personally have followed the conventional wisdom of my Caucasian, suburban cultural context that a highly skilled youth worker and an engaging and creative youth program were the keys to patch the proverbial hole in the boat but found myself in the same sinking vessel. The church from which I came has been doing a particular brand of youth ministry for over seventy-five years. This style was hip, relevant, and promised to be the answer to win a generation for Christ. Teenagers were welcomed into youth rooms, camps, and concert halls, with fun and relevant programming designed just for them. While we celebrated our successful ministries, they would exit by the back door, many never to return.

Following modern learning theory and sociological perspectives seemed like wisdom, yet we did not take the time to ask ourselves if we shared the same goals as the surrounding culture. Christianity has always engaged in dialogue with the cultures in which it resides, but if a culture's values are adopted without criticism, the church runs the risk of becoming complicit in agendas for human development and community building that are decidedly not Christian.

Our educational system and developmental processes often seem focused on preparing children for productive work that makes a "good living" and a comfortable retirement. In the context of the communities that are predominantly white and economically affluent, this consumeristic individualism has deeply infected family life and how church involvement is understood. When this same framework is adopted by the church, we run the risk of losing the theological call of *ekklesia* for which Nel advocates and should not be surprised that our communities continue to fragment.

Clues to living out Nel's vision of youth ministry have been found outside the dominant US culture as we recognize that people groups who successfully maintain a sense of "kinship" tend to have greater success in passing the faith down to younger generations. In these communities, there is a sense of family and "us-ness" that holds generational faith, even if there are changes in the expression of that faith. It is far less about the theology or the modernity of the worship experience and more about the creation and nurture of an intergenerational family where young and old have a sense of belonging and purpose.

Since its publication in the early 2000s, the National Study of Youth and Religion (NYSR) led by sociologist Christian Smith has opened the eyes of the American church to the relationship of youth to their church of origin and the personal beliefs that they hold. Like many youth practitioners, I was not surprised by the research telling us that the beliefs of teenagers tend to change over time, that they are not emerging from youth ministry with the beliefs of their family or church of origin, or that they are disappearing from churches. It is a reality that youth workers face every day. However, there is a tacit perspective in the NSYR that is important to note: its focus on beliefs and behavior to the neglect of belonging. Christian Smith does note, however, that many of the teens who are experiencing positive outcomes are experiencing healthy socialization in two spheres: individual family households and multigenerational religious congregations.[23] If this is the case, it is sobering that the majority of the work we do in youth groups has to do with belief and behavior when the leading factor of retention is helping young people gain a feeling of belonging to the church family.

While there is hope, there is a great deal of work to be done as we change the paradigm of ministry. Many in the churches we serve remember their youth ministry experience fondly and believe it was youth group that made the difference. However, further dialogue reveals that it was actually the connectivity experienced with an adult leader and subsequent "getting involved" that helped to solidify their longevity in the faith. As a practitioner, I am committed to creating spaces for the young to "be themselves" and find their voices within the church. But if their voices are not engaged by the congregation as a whole as they develop, they are sure to find other contexts in which to express them.

Indeed, there are voices that require our attention: the voice of the young, the voice of the Global South and minority American churches that are growing as one body; the voice of Malan Nel and a growing number of others who are calling us to reevaluate our youth ministry paradigms; the

23. Smith and Denton, *Soul Searching*.

voice of the Spirit calling us to unity; and the voice of time that is calling us to recognize that dividing ourselves has harmed us, but not irreversibly. The call to the mainline church in the United States is to develop an intergenerational community that truly allows us to grow together.

Bibliography

Crane, Ken R. *Latino Churches: Faith, Family, and Ethnicity in the Second Generation.* New York: LFB Scholarly, 2003.

Gallup. "Religion." In Depth: Topics A to Z. https://news.gallup.com/poll/1690/Religion.aspx#1.

Granberg-Michaelson, Wes. "Think Christianity Is Dying? No, Christianity Is Shifting Dramatically." *Washington Post*, May 20, 2015. https://www.washingtonpost.com/news/acts-of-faith/wp/2015/05/20/think-christianity-is-dying-no-christianity-is-shifting-dramatically/?utm_term=.3b5f7d87280f.

May, Heather Hahn. "Economist: Church in Crisis but Hope Remains." *United Methodist News Service*, May 20, 2015.

Mitchell, Joshua. *Black Millennials and the Church: Meet Me Where I Am.* Valley Forge, PA: Judson, 2018.

Myers, William. *Black and White Styles of Youth Ministry: Two Congregations in America.* Eugene, OR: Wipf & Stock, 2009.

Nel, Malan. *Youth Ministry: An Inclusive Congregational Approach.* Pretoria: Design, 2000.

Osmer, Richard Robert. *Practical Theology: An Introduction.* Grand Rapids: Eerdmans, 2011.

Senter, Mark, ed. *Four Views of Youth Ministry and the Church: Inclusive Congregational, Preparatory, Missional, Strategic.* Grand Rapids: Zondervan, 2010.

Smith, Christian, and Melinda Lundquist Denton. *Soul Searching: The Religious and Spiritual Lives of American Teenagers.* New York: Oxford University Press. 2005.

Smith, Gregory, et al. "America's Changing Religious Landscape." Pew Research Center, May 12, 2015. https://www.pewforum.org/wp-content/uploads/sites/7/2015/05/RLS-08-26-full-report.pdf.

Smith, Wallace C. *The Church in the Life of the Black Family.* Valley Forge, PA: Judson, 1985.

Steinfels, Peter. "Further Adrift: The American Church's Crisis of Attrition." *Commonweal Magazine*, October 18, 2010. https://www.commonwealmagazine.org/further-adrift.

United Church of Christ Center for Analytics, Research, and Data. "Fall 2016: The United Church of Christ; A Statistical Profile." Cleveland: United Church of Christ, 2016. http://www.uccfiles.com/pdf/Fall-2016-UCC-Statistical-Profile.pdf.

Van Marter, Jerry. "PC(USA) Membership Decline Slows, but Does Not Stop" Louisville: PCUSA Office of the General Assembly, 2017. https://www.pcusa.org/news/2018/6/4/pcusa-membership-decline-slows-does-not-stop/.

Questions for Reflection and Discussion

1. Droege chronicles evidence of struggle within mainline churches that he has encountered at both the large-scale, denominational level and the deeply personal level—in what he has watched occur among the young adults in whose lives he has invested. These challenges are not unique to US mainline churches. Where have you observed evidence of the church struggling to retain young adults today?
2. In your own thinking about the current trend of young people leaving the church, what factors have you assumed to be behind their departure?
3. Droege provides a historical account of how youth ministry has undergone a philosophical and structural evolution over several decades time. What key philosophical and programmatic decisions have shaped how youth ministry is currently approached in your church?
4. Droege introduces us to the theological vision of youth ministry championed by Malan Nel. As you contemplate what it might look like practically to implement this vision, what do you find most interesting or inspiring about it? Droege recalls initially dismissing Nel's ideas as foreign and impractical. Are there aspects of his theological vision that cause you to respond similarly? If so, why?

Part Three

Pastoral Conversations

8

Who Is This For?

WENDELL LOEWEN

§

EDITOR'S INTRODUCTION: In his treatment of generativity, Donald Capps suggests that some adults experience a crisis when their "need to be needed by one or more members of the younger generation is not reciprocated by those who are younger."[1] Adult leaders within some churches today wonder if perhaps they are trapped in a similar situation. They are guided by a desire to make generative investments in the lives of the adolescents with whom they come into contact, yet they do not always experience the sort of reciprocation for which they hope; or, as Loewen exposes in this chapter, the youth in whose lives they are striving to have influence may simply *feign* reciprocity. As Malan Nel expresses in the preface to this volume, "To argue that we have 'lost the youth' is so often not true: we never had them." Loewen draws our attention to a critical consideration in the discussion of generativity: to what extent are the spaces we have created for engagement with adolescents truly generative. Like many of us, Loewen yearns for youth to be provided a context in which they can wrestle authentically with Christ's invitation to the life of faith. While every generative church must exercise intentionality in investing in the members of rising generations, this chapter challenges us to recognize that even our best intentions must continuously be subject to reflection and revision.

1. Capps, *Decades of Life*, 127.

§

YEARS ago, during the final evening session of our denomination's national youth convention, the speaker issued a couple of very passionate and quite typical faith invitations. As one of the event's organizers, I was invested and eager to see who and how many young people would respond. The first invitation was for students to accept Christ for the first time. Among the crowd of about 1,200 young people, I recall estimating about thirty, maybe forty students who stood to say "yes" to Jesus! I know the angels in heaven rejoiced over those life-changing decisions. My joy quickly turned to curiosity when the speaker issued a second faith invitation—for students to rededicate their lives to Christ. What happened next was mystifying. At once, as if on command, and without hesitation, hundreds of teens stood to announce their recommitment to Jesus! So massive was the response, I could almost feel the updraft stirred by their collective vertical momentum. From where I stood, I did not see a single young person still seated in their chairs. What puzzled me, however, was that I had seen this movie before—dozens of times in fact. Conference after conference, camp after camp, retreat after retreat, the vast majority of the teens in attendance rise in unison to recommit their lives to Christ as if the moment was somehow choreographed. But, by now I started connecting some dots.

Some of my recent study was suggesting that today's adolescents experience a sense of abandonment and betrayal from the adults around them.[2] Furthermore, they feel a kind of hostility from adult systems—defined as any institution, organization or relationship that is for and about the adults in charge.[3] Adult "systems" can include school, sports, work, family—even church. In fact, if you were to interview them, most adolescents might disclose that the adults in their world are not really "for" them and would go on to acknowledge that almost all those adults have some sort of "agenda" for them.

So, let's get back to the youth convention. If those adolescents at the conference intuitively perceived (correctly or incorrectly) that they found themselves in a hostile adult system (despite being called a "youth" convention) how might one think they would respond to the invitation to recommit their lives to Jesus? What would be the "safest" thing to do?

Well, let's first think about what would be the most "dangerous" response. To remain seated! To stay in one's chair would mean that the adults

2. See Clark, *Hurt 2.0*.

3. Clark, *Hurt 2.0*, 30.

in the area might corner them after the session to have a conversation about life and spiritual things. Most adolescents would rather endure a root canal! So, the safest thing to do is what they think the adults want them to do—stand. That way the awkward conversations with their sponsors can be avoided.

I know this sounds like an incredibly cynical, and unspiritual, perspective. Honestly, I wish all these mass responses were total God-moments. But I've seen them over and over again for the past twenty years. Sadly, something else is going on.

After that event, I began recalling additional student responses in other youth ministry settings. This is why, when asked, "How can I pray for you?" my small group almost always responded with something having to do with homework or some other innocuous issue. I know their entire lives are not consumed with school, but it's safe.

I also remembered that when I would urge my students to "bring their friends" to an upcoming youth event, they almost never did. Why? Well, for one, if they were unsure about the event's quality, they didn't want to embarrass themselves. But more significantly, if they could detect that the event had any whiff of "agenda," such as evangelism, they would almost never subject their friends to such animosity.

Have you ever wondered why students—even student leaders—act like super saints in youth group but live very different lives at school? Or why their social media presence in no way lines up with who they appear to be when they're on the mission trip? Have you wondered why students never really want to dive in and dig deep on important spiritual and life issues? Could it be that they perceive the youth program as a hostile adult system and that the adults in the youth ministry are unsafe?

I believe this is the unvarnished truth about where many, if not most, of the students in our youth ministries and churches are. And these are the issues I have attempted to tackle head-on for over a decade. So, let's take a brief look inside the world of adolescence, discover where this sense of hostility comes from and, most importantly, what we can do about it.

Abandonment and Hostility

When it was released in 2004, the movie *Napoleon Dynamite*, though widely panned by critics, was overwhelmingly embraced by teens. Why? Well, one reason was that it portrayed an unpopular misfit who found wider acceptance while staying true to himself. But at a deeper level, we might notice something else. Where are the adults? There is no mention of Napoleon's parents. He and his brother Kip live with their grandma. But she's out chasing her own dreams on the sand dunes until she breaks her tailbone in a dune buggy accident. The boys' Uncle Rico, who ends up staying with them, only wants to make money and recruits Kip as an accomplice in his money-making schemes. The school's principal doesn't want to see Napoleon and his friend Pedro succeed in the school's election. In the movie, there are no adults who are really for the teens. Mostly, adults are depicted as absent or even hostile. I believe teens embraced the movie because it portrayed their adult-less adolescence so accurately. This abandonment has become the defining issue for today's adolescents.[4]

Now, abandonment carries a range of meanings. What I'm describing here, however, is psychosocial abandonment. This refers to a society-wide slide in the nurture and care for the next generation. Adults and adult systems have abandoned their role in supporting young people and walking alongside them into adulthood.

Imagine this all-too-familiar scenario. Amanda is an excellent student and a very good soccer player. She has a huge chemistry test coming up on Thursday and needs to find time to study in her uber-busy schedule. Her parents have told her, in no uncertain terms, that if she doesn't ace this test, she has no shot at a 4.0 grade-point average. Without the 4.0, she won't be the school's valedictorian. Therefore, she'll lose out on that great scholarship to that prestigious university. And without that scholarship, Amanda can say "good-bye" to the high-paying career she (and her parents) have been pursuing all these years. She feels as though her entire future rests on this exam! So, Amanda asks her soccer coach if it would be okay for her to skip soccer practice on Wednesday to study for Thursday's test. The coach barks, "We've got a big game against Central on Friday night! I need you to be 'all in'! You know the rules—if you don't practice, you don't play!" What is Amanda to do in this situation? She's at the mercy of adults with competing agendas and none of them are really considering what's best for her.

So, when adolescents feel pressure from parents to perform, or when they feel the heat from coaches to win, or they get the sense that teachers just want to receive the positive evaluations that get them promoted, or they get the "guilt" vibe from their youth leaders because they missed the Bible study, skipped the service project or lock-in, it's hard not to feel a sense of hostility from adults and adult systems.

Now, you may be skeptical. Surely this isn't the narrative for all adolescents! Abandonment may not be the defining issue for every adolescent in

4. This is the premise on which Clark's work is based. Also, see Clark, *When Kids Hurt.*

North America. We are doing a 30,000-foot bird's-eye view of culture and there are always exceptions. The research, however, is showing that abandonment describes the reality of a surprising majority of young people.[5]

You may also feel a bit resentful. You might believe that your "agendas" for students are, in fact, what's best for them and that they feel hostility because they're young, naïve and don't know what's best for them. I understand that sentiment. I felt it for years. But in some ways, it doesn't matter. The adolescent perception of hostility is, in fact, their reality whether we like it or not.

Consider this experience. Some years ago, I served as a consultant for a local high school in the aftermath of a teen suicide. A talented, popular, seemingly well-adjusted twelfth grader took his own life for reasons not completely known. But, nonetheless the school, its teacher, administrators and students were confused and in shock. I was asked to meet with all three groups, concluding with a student assembly in the school's auditorium. When I first began to speak, I got the vibe that the students were thinking, "What does this old man have to say to us?" I could read the body language—arms crossed, hoodies up, heads down, and eyes rolling. But as I began talking in terms they could understand about abandonment, hostile adult systems and agendas, I got a different read from the room. Students started perking up and paying attention. As they glanced at each other in bewilderment, I got the sense that they were wondering how I got into their heads or infiltrated their hidden teenage world. Was I some kind of mole? I had their attention to say the least! Now, it was time to turn the corner. So, I concluded with a plea for the students to find a teacher or an adult who cares—because I really believe that! I know that safe, caring adults who want to come alongside students are out there! They do exist! Well, in that moment, as if a switch had been flipped, the mood and the feedback shifted again—back to the passive-aggressive body language with their protective shields on activation alert. Sadly, I was just another condescending grownup trying to convince them that the adult world is really not that antagonistic—but they knew better.

You see, it takes more than just words, and more than just a clever speech, and more than just a moment, to become a safe person. It will take time, energy, and creativity—and lots of all three. So, what is the church to do in the midst of today's youth culture and adolescent mindset? Here are some practical ideas.

5. If you need more convincing, ask some youth professionals such as school counselors, youth pastors, or youth development volunteers about systemic abandonment. Perhaps the sheer volume of stories might be persuasive.

It Starts with Ecclesiology

I teach a course called The Church and Its Mission. The course is about the identity and purpose of the church, primarily in its local expression. Essentially, what we believe about what the church is (its identity) will inform what the church does (its purpose). Increasingly I am coming to the conclusion that the church is, in part, a counter-, or contrast culture. While some aspects of our culture can be affirmed, and other elements can be redeemed, other facets must be challenged or rejected. The Apostle Paul reminds us that we are not to be conformed to the pattern of this world (Rom 12:1–2), and much of Jesus's ministry and teaching was, in many ways, countercultural.

If we were to understand the church as a kind of contrast culture, how then do we respond to adolescents in our congregations that are experiencing a world of abandonment and hostility?

Markers

In a world that has erased much of the significance and value in any number of developmental markers, the church can restore meaning to such markers. This communicates that their teens are growing toward healthy adulthood. For example, when adolescents receive their driver's license, congregations can recapture it as a rite of passage, conferring on them the responsibilities that come with new freedoms. As a part of the church's liturgy, markers could be as simple as a blessing when teens reach a particular age. They could also come in the form of weekend retreats in which young women and men are affirmed and invited to participate more fully in adult roles, responsibilities, and decisions. These markers can reinfuse certain achievements with meaning.

Scaffolding

In a context in which adolescents feel forced to navigate life on their own, the church is a place where abandonment and isolation should not exist. Adults in the church can move toward forming relationships with teens. It could include seeking out young people before or after worship gatherings; it also might entail affirming them through handwritten notes, text messages, or via social media. Adults can make sure they are present at important school events and the church could recruit a greater number of adult volunteers in the youth ministry. Simply with their words and their time, adults can provide a congruent message of love, caring, and hope. In doing these things, adults begin to frame a support system around adolescents. It's a process called scaffolding.

Be Authentic

The adolescent search for authenticity should not only be encouraged but also reflected in the local church's ministry practices. Many teens perceive adults and adult systems as phony or pursuing their own interests. Congregations should shift from being relevant to being real. Teens know that life is complex and sometimes heartbreaking. They are wary of, and may label as false, any gospel that sells Jesus as a step toward personal success and fulfillment. Our worship services and youth programming should not avoid life's tough issues. What does it mean to forgive an abusive parent? How can we find a way to live for Christ and still have serious questions about God's power in the world? How do we cope with the anguish and guilt of addiction? These are real life issues. If we don't deal with them, who will? And, we can address them in the context of faith and loving community.

Recapture Community

Today's adolescents are driven to community for answers and their sense of abandonment has only deepened that desire. Fortunately, it is in the context of the wider community that truth and life are experienced. Local congregations have an opportunity to embrace teens as an integral part of the faith community—a unique expression of the people of God. Together, we all navigate the storms of life. Together, we help create meaning, identity and a sense of purpose as we invite others to journey through life in community. Churches and youth ministries can model the communal nature of God by forming interpretive communities that help teens reflect on the world around them. This can be accomplished as a multitude of adults surround teens in a variety of ways. Small groups can be retooled to practice accountability and to emphasize being Jesus to friends, rather than focusing mainly on intellectual content. Intergenerational activities and mentoring relationships can help adults and teens hear each other's stories, fears, and dreams.

Solidify Meaning and Identity

In a culture that seems devoid of real meaning and true identity, we can significantly shape adolescents' sense of who they are. One way is to place a renewed emphasis on calling. It's important for adults in the church to communicate that God is in the business of calling and that each student is, in fact, called by God, to God, and for God. We are called to love God, love others, follow Jesus, and be God's blessing in the world. That is our primary calling. Our secondary calling involves our career. It is the expression of our primary calling.[6] The church's task is to help adolescents pay attention to God and to how God is calling them. Students can explore the three P's—people, passions, and passages. We can encourage them to spend time reflecting on: (1) the "people" that have been positive influences on their lives, or those they want to emulate; (2) their "passions" or what makes them come alive; and (3) Scripture "passages" that are particularly meaningful to them. With some time, students can begin to connect the dots and find the initial clues to God's call on their lives, or their call story. As the story emerges, adolescents soon realize that they are an important part of God's people who have been chosen and sent by God to be agents of God's reign in the world. Simply by understanding that they are a people who belong to God, offering an alternative reality to the world, they can begin to develop a more coherent sense of self.

Create Sacred Space

The busyness and clutter produced by popular culture's mass and social media requires so much of teens' time and offers so many distractions that it creates conflicts with adult demands and generates excessive stress. The rush and rhythm of today's culture makes it very difficult for adolescents to tune in to God, develop their true identity, and be formed in their faith.

In the context of community, congregations can help teens recreate and rediscover "sacred space." Finding ways to help students slow down, reflect and unclutter is a powerful practice. Spiritual disciplines such as fasting, silence, solitude, and frugality enable teens to reduce the distractions of their world in order to reflect on who they are as children of God and contributors to their spiritual family. This might mean taking students to a remote mountain retreat or a quiet lake without a planned agenda or schedule. There, for a short time, they can replace the hectic rhythms of everyday life with moments of keen awareness of God. Youth ministries should also find ways to integrate these practices into their programming. Without conscious efforts to create sacred space, our adolescents may drift aimlessly on the currents of an all too destructive culture instead of deliberately choosing to live out their unique identity in Christ.

6. Os Guinness's book *The Call* provides a foundation for my theology of calling.

Share Stories

In some respects, the church has almost no way of competing with our popular culture's media machine. The images and messages are everywhere, and they are powerful! One subversive practice that can counter the cultural narrative is to share stories. I know, this sounds far too simple, yet the effects can be powerful. The church can create ways to gather adults and students together and share stories. These can be life stories, call stories, or most embarrassing stories. Teens can ask the adults how they first fell in love. The adults can ask students what makes them come alive. Or both generations can talk about a time when they got in trouble!

The purpose is not only to break down generational barriers, but to demonstrate to adolescents that the adults in their world are real people with goals, dreams, successes, and weaknesses. It can also show the adults that teenagers are still developing, growing, and learning. By sharing stories, adults and adolescents get to know each other better and learn to grant each other some grace.

Understanding

The hostility that adolescents feel from the adult world stems, to some degree, from the sense that adults somehow know what it's like to be a teenager today and can therefore assume they speak into adolescents' lives with authority. But, perhaps outside of parents, there is a credibility gap. Contemporary adolescence is qualitatively different than that of previous generations. The pressures and stresses are unique and complex. Teens have to navigate very different cultural waters today. Adults who refuse to recognize that come off as condescending. Trust, or lack thereof, is a significant issue. A way that adults can address this is to work hard at understanding. Congregations should hold listening meetings with students when it's time to hire a new pastor or reshape the youth or children's program—then, actually listen! Adults should not presume they know what young people are thinking or feeling on certain issues. They should ask lots of questions. One of my favorite questions is to ask, "What's it like to be a teen today?" When adolescents "get" that adults are at least trying to understand, that will earn adults a lot of credibility and build a good deal of trust. Active understanding generates a sense of safety.

Tap Into Longings

Since adolescents tend to adopt an ethic of self-interest and self-protection, they base their decisions on "What's easiest for me, right now." In other words, their choices are largely influenced by the present. So, what they might do, or what they might say, is probably not coming from a deeply held credo or philosophy of life. Even though their actions may be unwise or even hurtful, teens are just living in (or out of) the moment. Adults have a wonderful opportunity to tap into adolescents' longings. It's a way of trying to understand what is really going on. For instance, if a teenage daughter tells her parents, "Leave me alone! It's my life!" she may not be insisting that her parents, in effect, abandon or ignore her. She may be asserting, "I want to be uniquely me!"

Longings such as feeling a sense of belonging, understanding their identity, knowing that they and their choices matter, or being loved unconditionally are deeply held values that are important for adults to help bring to the surface. Not just uncovering but tapping into these deep longings provides adults some perspective on adolescent choices and actions. It also bridges the gap between teen culture and the adult world and helps adolescents in the process of self-understanding. It takes practice, patience, and a good dose of experimentation to develop this skill, but adults who have a knack for tapping into longings are considered "superchill"! In other words, safe.

Work at Becoming a Safe Person

One of the simplest ways to counter the sense of hostility from adult systems is to make it personal—try becoming a safe person. Start simply. Try listening. What I mean is listening outside of your own autobiography. Listen without formulating a quick answer in your head. This is often called empathic or active listening. While it's simple, listening to an adolescent's heart may be the most loving, life-giving, and safe thing one could ever do.

Along with listening, try being appropriately vulnerable. This doesn't mean airing your dirty laundry or letting your skeletons fly out of the closet. There's something misguided, unfair, even wrong, when students are put in a position in which they're asked to minister to the adults. Developmentally, they are not ready for that. Having said all that, there is a place for appropriate vulnerability. It shows that you are real; you make mistakes, and students can identify with that. It also makes you safer.

Finally, celebrate curiosity and honesty. I remember when I was leading a study on the fleeting nature and value of possessions, Becca blurted, "But I like stuff!" What a beautiful interruption! I stopped to praise Becca for her honesty and admitted that I liked stuff too. Students need to know that you are a safe person and that church or youth group are safe spaces to express opinions and ask hard questions.

Avoid "Challenge" Language

This is something that Chap Clark told our doctor of ministry cohort years ago: "Never use the word 'challenge' when speaking to adolescents!" And, I took it to heart.

Years ago, I was the guest speaker at a youth ministry event in Wichita. The youth pastor was out of town and since he was my former student, I was happy to fill in. We studied the story of Peter venturing out onto stormy waters in a daring pursuit of Jesus (Matt 14). But rather than focusing on his lack of faith and subsequent plunge into the sea, my hope was to rehabilitate Peter. He was the only one who stepped out of the safety of the boat! The other disciples lacked Peter's courage and desire to follow Jesus. So, I encouraged the students to "step out of the boat" and follow Jesus, even though it may seem scary or dangerous. I was careful and intentional about using "encourage" and "invitation" language. "So, my invitation to you," I said, "is to step out of the boat! Take a risk! Jesus will catch you if you fall!" As I closed in prayer, I felt like the students were with me. They were leaning in, nodding affirmingly and ready to respond. So, when I turned the evening over to a volunteer, who I think was a tough but loving military veteran, he proceeded to add his own unsolicited opinion. Unfortunately, what he said almost completely undid what I had been trying to carefully communicate for the past twenty minutes. Repeatedly, he used the word *challenge*. "I challenge you to follow hard after Jesus," he said over and over. I watched in disbelief as students began checking out. Their nonverbal message was clear. "We are so done with this."

What does the word "challenge" communicate? It says, "As an adult, I know, and you don't. I've got it right, and you don't." It comes off as hostile language. Instead, it is wise to use words such as "invite" or "encourage" in its place. It doesn't assume that adolescents are not enough or that their life is a mess, but it does give them the opportunity to choose how they want to respond.

Get Adult Systems Working Together

The earlier story about Amanda's struggle to fulfill the competing agendas of the adults in her world perfectly illustrates a significant problem in terms of abandonment. Adolescents are often caught in a tug-of-war, of sorts, being pulled in multiple directions by the clashing motives and desire of the adults in their world. It doesn't take long for young people to recognize that there are few adults that are for them. It's a hostile world that they must survive.

This is a wonderful opportunity for the church! The first step is to stop competing with other adults and their agendas and support the students in your congregation. Here's a great example. On a Wednesday night (or whenever you run your weekly youth meetings) toward the end of a semester when projects and tests loom large, set aside your typical programming and offer time and space for your students to get caught up on their homework or prepare for exams. You can even provide adult tutors. Instead of competing with the schools, find ways to support the students and ease their stress a little. While it's not a long-term solution, it does communicate that you understand and that you are safe.

More significantly, congregations can provide leadership and direction in their local communities in terms of bringing together parents, teachers, school administrators, coaches, and churches to begin brainstorming and implementing partnership strategies. Someone needs to provide this kind of countercultural leadership. Someone must be an advocate for adolescents. Why not the church? It takes persuasion and time to show how this is good, not only for adolescents, but good for their schools and communities. This would require adaptive leadership because competing factions, values, and goals are at play.

Ask Yourself, "Who Is This For?"

Over the years this has been a useful filter for me. If there's a question about ministry strategies or structures as they relate to today's adolescents, I ask myself, "Who is this for?" If I really ask the question, and I'm not afraid of the tough interpretations, often the answer can be quite instructive.

For example, when I feel like I need to have 100 percent participation in the dodgeball game (or worship) prior to my devotional, and I see some of our marginal students sitting it out, I need to ask, "Who is this for?" Is it because I want to feel as though my ministry is effective, or that I'm successful? Then, it's probably for me. If it makes students feel unsafe, insecure, or anxious, then it's not really for them—it's for me.

I also ask the question of parents who have an agenda for their kids and live vicariously through their performance. They persistently yell at the officials when their daughter is on the wrong end of a bad call, or they boorishly confront the coach when their son is not getting enough playing time. Who is this for?

If our deep desire is to authentically connect with and nurture young people in the church, we ought to pay attention to whether our strategies and structures come off as hostile or hospitable—safe or unsafe. Strategies that are perceived as hostile are, in the end, ineffective and counterproductive. If we, through our words and actions, are deemed to be unsafe, the gospel will have a very hard time penetrating the protective shields they form around their hearts.

Conclusion

If we pay attention and look beneath the surface, we will find evidence of abandonment and hostile adult systems almost everywhere—from youth sports to school and even the church. In so many contexts, adolescents feel unsafe. As a result, they're just trying to survive. Where can they go to find safe spaces and adults in their world? Our local congregations have the wonderful opportunity to be a contrast culture. We can create our programming, relationships and ministry structures to provide those safe venues and people so our students can grow in life and develop in faith.

Ridge Burns, one of my longtime youth ministry influences, used to say, "Students must be sociologically comfortable before they can be theologically aware." That ministry axiom applies in any number of ways, and I have used it quite often over the years. But, when it comes to the realities of contemporary adolescents, it has never been truer than it is today.

Bibliography

Capps, Daniel. *The Decades of Life: A Guide to Human Development*. Louisville: Westminster John Knox, 2008.

Clark, Chap. *Hurt 2.0: Inside the World of Today's Teenagers*. Grand Rapids: Baker, 2011.

———. *When Kids Hurt: Help for Adults Navigating the Adolescent Maze*. Grand Rapids: Baker, 2009.

Guinness, Os. *The Call: Finding and Fulfilling the Central Purpose of Your Life*. Nashville: Nelson, 2003.

Questions for Reflection and Discussion

1. Loewen begins this chapter by suggesting that many adolescents experience church youth ministry as a "hostile adult system." What is your response to this assessment? In what ways does this correspond—or not correspond—to your experience?
2. Loewen outlines several important practical ideas to help churches become safe spaces for young people. Which of these ideas do you already see being lived out within your church? Which, if any, are not currently happening in your church? What changes would you like to see happen in response to this chapter?
3. As you look at the youth ministries to which you have been connected—whether as a student, leader, or parent—how would you evaluate them in light of this question: "Who is this for?"

9

On the Brink of Everything

Embracing Generativity with Parker Palmer

DARREN CRONSHAW

§

EDITOR'S INTRODUCTION: Throughout this book, we have maintained a focus upon generativity as a characteristic of the church. We have concerned ourselves with exploring the central question of what it means for generativity to be understood as a corporate virtue expressed in the congregation's shared life. Nonetheless, as I acknowledge in my introductory chapter, institutions do play an important role in the development of generativity as Erikson originally envisioned it—as a virtue within adult persons—by providing the context in which it can be encouraged and expressed. In this chapter, Cronshaw invites us to contemplate the relationship between corporate and individual generativity. He reflects upon how his role as a pastor enables him—as a man advancing through his own middle adult years—to be generative, while at the same time fostering the life of a generative faith community in which others also can grow as generative persons. To help us explore the interplay between corporate and individual generativity, Cronshaw takes us on a guided tour of the legacy of one exemplar of generativity, the renowned American educator Parker Palmer. This chapter provides us an opportunity to reflect upon how the development of generative personhood is bound up with the character of the institutions to which we belong and how nurturing generative communities can be an expression of generativity within the lives of ministry leaders.

A View from the Brink

AGING is often seen as a time of decline and inaction, but Parker J. Palmer insists on reframing it as a passage of discovery and engagement.[1] After eight decades of life, Palmer wrote *On the Brink of Everything: Grace, Gravity and Getting Old*, in which he narrates how he warmly welcomes what has come with his own aging; for example:

> Age brings diminishments, but more than a few come with benefits. I've lost the capacity for multitasking, but I've rediscovered the joy of doing one thing at a time. My thinking has slowed a bit, but experience has made it deeper and richer. I'm done with big and complex projects, but more aware of the loveliness of simple things: a talk with a friend, a walk in the woods, sunsets and sunrises, a night of good sleep.[2]

Part of the gift of the book, moreover, is its appeal to all generations to keep engaging the needs of the world, together. In a world obsessed with effectiveness and short-term results, Palmer appeals to his readers to take on big jobs worth doing, such as fostering justice, peace, and love.[3] His first suggestion for a graduating class was along these lines:

> Be reckless when it comes to affairs of the heart. . . . What I mean is to fall madly in love with life. Be passionate about some part of the natural and/or human worlds, and take risks on its behalf, no matter how vulnerable they make you.
>
> No one ever died saying, "I'm so glad for the self-centered, self-serving, and self-protective life I lived" Offer yourself to the world—your energies, your gifts, your visions, your spirit—with openhearted generosity.[4]

1. Palmer, *On the Brink of Everything*, 8.
2. Palmer, *On the Brink of Everything*, 1.
3. Palmer, *On the Brink of Everything*, 47.
4. Palmer, *On the Brink of Everything*, 45.

These were Palmer's words of encouragement to a group of (presumably mainly young adult) students, but his encouragement to prepare for and live a life of generativity—investing in and leaving a legacy for future generations—applies to people of all ages.

I was born in 1971, so at the time of writing this I am forty-eight, middle aged. That is a little over halfway to Palmer's age. My view on aging feels "from the brink" of being well along on the journey. As with others of my Generation X, my youth and young adulthood are behind me and my elder years are in front of me. This chapter is a reflective review of *On the Brink of Everything* read through my experience of my aging and generativity journey but also in preparation for what is still ahead of me.

Palmer comments that aging is inevitable, but how we navigate it is a choice:

> The laws of nature that dictate sundown dictate our demise. But how we travel that arc towards the sunset of our lives is ours to choose: will it be denial, defiance, or collaboration?[5]

Personally, I am asking in what ways I can collaborate with aging and foster generativity. Vocationally, moreover, I am asking in what ways I can, as pastor and teacher, help others navigate and collaborate with their aging, and thus foster our corporate congregational generativity.

On the Brink of Everything is a beautiful collection of essays collated with poetry and songs. Others who read it may value other themes. As I reread it in the future, there will likely be other lessons of wisdom. But this chapter discusses three themes that I found particularly valuable for me and the congregation I serve: Palmer's writing on vocation, the grace of the word *enough*, and the generativity of investing in and learning from different generations.

Accidental Authoring about Vocation

Born 1939 in Chicago, Palmer is a writer, teacher, and activist who describes his growing edge as "learning how to live an engaged and creative life as an elder on 'the brink of everything.'"[6] *On the Brink of Everything* is his most recent of ten books spanning education, politics, spirituality, and especially vocation. Part of the value of *On the Brink of Everything* is Palmer offering a

5. Palmer, *On the Brink of Everything*, 4.

6. "The Growing Edge with Carrie Newcomer and Parker Palmer," https://www.newcomerpalmer.com/.

long view backward on his books and where they fit into his own vocation and his teaching about vocation from different angles.

Palmer describes himself as "an accidental author." His urge to write started in his early twenties, but his first book was published almost two decades later and then only serendipitously. One of his students sent one of Palmer's lectures on Thomas Merton to the student's uncle, a Merton devotee who worked as an editor, who asked Palmer if he could publish it in a monthly newsletter. Later he asked Palmer for other articles and Palmer sent a dozen pieces. Then he asked Palmer to bring seven or eight of them together in a book. Nine months later Palmer held his first book, *The Promise of Paradox: A Celebration of Contradictions in the Christian Life* (1980).[7]

Like most of his writing, *The Promise of Paradox* reflects on Palmer's experience of identifying and pursuing his vocation, and in this case embracing the mystery and reality of paradoxes in that journey. He makes rich use of Merton, as a kind of patron saint of social activists, who appeals for integrating spirituality with the struggles and mess of life. Palmer learned lessons on how the spiritual life is not orderly and pristine while teaching for a decade at Pendle Hill. He was attracted to Pendle Hill's living-learning community by their alternative approaches to education, which he adopted and developed: learning in shared community, without exam-based competition, celebrating diverse expressions of intelligence rather than just intellectual capacity, and appealing for teachers to be learners and to help students to engage with big questions: "As teachers, we must not only make room for the Spirit to move within us but also cultivate learning situations that will help students open up to that movement."[8]

The same dynamic of fostering a learning community applies to generative churches at their best. Generative church leaders want to create space in which they themselves can experience the Spirit's transforming work, but also to cultivate spaces for conversation and learning that will help church members be open to the Spirit's movement. The best learning in churches, like in Palmer's classroom, happens as teachers grapple themselves with the biggest questions, and invite others to join them in a shared community of exploration and mutual discovery.

Palmer wrote his second book, *The Company of Strangers: Christians and the Renewal of America's Public Life* (1983), to explore how spirituality integrates with a calling to co-create love and justice in the world. This earliest writing showed Palmer always wanted spirituality to be, not narcissistic

7. Palmer, *Promise of Paradox*; discussed in Palmer, *On the Brink of Everything*, 64–68, 88–89, 99–100.

8. Palmer, *Promise of Paradox*, 133.

and preoccupied with interiority, but engaged with the biggest, most challenging problems in the world.[9] He later expanded on this in his fourth book: *The Active Life: A Spirituality of Work, Creativity and Caring* (1990).[10] Palmer felt called first to a vocation of community organizing rather than the classroom, and he has often written out of this experience of public engagement.[11]

Churches committed to generativity also need a commitment to public engagement. Investing in the lives of emerging generations is not just about retaining them as members but helping them, and people of all ages, engage with the biggest issues facing our communities and the world. Palmer has continued to appeal to leaders across different spheres, including the church, to prioritize generativity and invest themselves in what matters in civic life for the sake of coming generations.

Palmer reflected further on the vocation of teaching and his philosophy of education in his third and fifth books: *To Know As We Are Known: Education as a Spiritual Journey* (1983) and *The Courage to Teach: Exploring the Inner Landscape of a Teacher's Life* (1997).[12] He was identifying what called him to teach, how he could help others find and follow their vocations as teachers, and particularly how they could bring the resources of their inner and outer lives, or action and contemplation, into teaching.

Palmer's attentiveness to the inner life of the teacher offers a helpful model for others including church leaders. Leaders in any sphere who are committed to generativity, including those whose vocation is leading the church, must foundationally foster their own identity and integrity. This means, as Palmer encouraged for teachers, for church leaders to reclaim the passion of their vocations, to connect the best of their intellect, emotion and spirit, and to invite others to connect and learn from one another. The best generative churches are the best learning communities—not relying on the hired holy person to teach them but led on a journey of learning from one another.

Palmer's sixth book is his seminal book on vocation, *Let Your Life Speak: Listening for the Voice of Vocation* (2000).[13] He counsels listening to the "voice of vocation" in the ways we are made rather than what we think

9. Palmer, *Company of Strangers*; discussed in Palmer, *On the Brink of Everything*, 100.

10. Palmer, *Active Life*.

11. Palmer, *On the Brink of Everything*, 61.

12. Palmer, *To Know as We Are Known*; Palmer, *Courage to Teach*; discussed in Palmer, *On the Brink of Everything*, 101; also Palmer and Scribner, *Courage to Teach Guide*.

13. Palmer, *Let Your Life Speak*.

we "ought" to be and do, or what expectations others put on us. Palmer often quotes Frederick Buechner to describe vocation as "the place where your deep gladness meets the world's deep need."[14] That is a liberating truth. It does not just say pursue what makes you happy if that makes no difference to others and has no generative impact. But neither does it suggest we "should" respond to any and all needs in the world. For example, Palmer turned his back on educational leadership opportunities for the sake of prioritizing his teaching, with a sense of clear vocation as a master-teacher: "I had never stopped being a teacher. . . . In fact, I could have done no other: teaching, I was coming to understand, is my native way of being in the world. Make me a cleric or a CEO, a poet or a politico, and teaching is what I will do."[15] Through his work with other teachers, but also with those working in law, medicine, ministry, and philanthropy, he has encouraged people to get in touch with and pursue with passion their own vocational foundations and "true self." Helping individuals discern their vocation and uncover their true self is part of the essence of the generative church, as well.

Palmer's interest in *self* began with his own doctoral research and continued in *On the Brink of Everything*.[16] He explains his failure to "listen to my life" led to a time of deep depression. It was listening to what Merton calls the "true self" that wants us to be "who we were born to be" that liberated him beyond his "intellectual self" preoccupied with hovering above life's mess, or the "ethical self" that feels pressured to "live by someone else's 'oughts,'" or a "spiritual self" that aims to "fly nonstop to heaven."[17] Vocation based on understanding "true self" might move beyond what looks like "smart career moves" and rather listens to the inner voice that persistently says, "You can't *not* do this."[18] Palmer retells the old Hassidic tale that reminds us to live into our true self rather than someone else's:

> Before he died, Rabbi Zusya said: "In the world to come they will not ask me, 'Why were you not Moses?' They will ask me, 'Why were you not Zusya?'"[19]

Life is too short to try to be anyone other than what we are made to be. A generative church will help people discern what they are made to be and do. A church that is growing in generativity will find ways to help young

14. Buechner, *Wishful Thinking*, 95; cited in Palmer, *Let Your Life Speak*, 16; discussed in Cronshaw, "Australian Reenvisioning of Theological Education," 227.

15. Palmer, *Let Your Life Speak*, 21.

16. Intrator, "Journey of Questions," xxxii.

17. Palmer, *On the Brink of Everything*, 74–75.

18. Palmer, *On the Brink of Everything*, 63–64.

19. Palmer, *On the Brink of Everything*, 75.

and old to identify and pursue with passion their true selves or vocations—where people's "deep gladness meets the world's deep need."

Palmer articulated a vision of integrating one's inner and outer self in his seventh book, *A Hidden Wholeness: The Journey toward an Undivided Life* (2004).[20] He has developed "circles of trust" as groups that help people live toward greater integrity and wholeness. He outlines principles of space-making and non-advice-giving listening that can help the soul feel safe enough to show up and help people journey toward living "divided no more." Palmer borrowed the term "hidden wholeness" again from Merton, referring to the wholeness that can be seen hidden beneath the surface of broken politics, relationships, or individual hearts.[21] Palmer invites people as individuals to discover their own unique vocation, but he is unapologetic about this discovery happening best in community.

Palmer's frameworks for circles of trust point toward communal generativity. Their principles underline the importance of communities being safe places that help individuals discern and pursue their vocation with passion. It is not enough for a generative church to tell people they should pursue their vocation. Churches need to foster safe places and respectful listening so that people's true self can emerge.

Palmer focused on ways that community, conversation, and contemplative pedagogies can help higher education students find their vocation in his eighth book, *The Heart of Higher Education: A Call to Renewal* (2010), coauthored with Arthur Zajonc and Megan Scribner.[22] They appeal for reshaping higher education to both nurture the inner world of students and address the huge problems of our world. Following Wendell Berry, they assume that good work and good citizenship come from making good human beings. They want to help the next generation not just get qualified to get well-paid jobs but to be prepared—in mind, soul, and spirit—to discover and pursue their vocations. The generative vocation of the teacher, laying behind this vision, is to help students to explore the "big questions and worthy dreams" of their vocations.

The heart of the generative church and the church's hope for renewal, to borrow from Palmer's language, is also to help the next generation explore the "big questions and worthy dreams" of their vocations. Just as Palmer experienced at Pendle Hill, this does not have to be solely in formal educational contexts. The generative church will help its members nurture

20. Palmer, *Hidden Wholeness.*

21. Palmer, *On the Brink of Everything*, 68–71.

22. Palmer et al., *Heart of Higher Education.*

their inner lives as well as engage with the most complex challenges our neighborhoods and world face.

Palmer's ninth book was *Healing the Heart of Democracy: The Courage to Create a Politics Worthy of the Human Spirit* (2011).[23] In the face of divide-and-conquer politics, Palmer appeals for "we the people" to rediscover a vocation of investing in civic life and the common good. Palmer thus returns to familiar themes about vocation and public engagement but updates them to address new issues. Generative churches, moreover, will also invite their people to give themselves to serving and contributing to the common good.

By the time of his tenth book, *On the Brink of Everything: Grace, Gravity and Getting Old* (2018), Palmer is seventy-nine and looks back over his life and writing. He reminds himself that his vocation, through different jobs, has been a teacher-and-learner, and that this has often been expressed in writing.[24] Palmer has a way of elevating the gravitas of important topics, and he does this with writing itself. He says writing is not filling his head with ideas and downloading them onto a page but unfolding what is going on inside him.[25] He writes from a place of being mystified and wanting to learn and understand rather than writing as an expert. He got into problems, he admitted, when he was trying to pretend he was smarter than he was, or tried "writing to impress rather than express."[26] His best writing came from adopting a "beginner's mind" and seeking to understand topics that intrigue and puzzle him—social change, teaching, spirituality, democracy, and how people discover their vocation of contributing in these areas:

> Writing is not about gathering facts, wrapping them in lucid thoughts, then getting them down on the page. It begins with dropping deep into my not-knowing, and dwelling in the dark long enough that my eyes adjust and start to see what's down there. I want to make my own discoveries, think my own thoughts, and feel my own feelings before I learn what the experts say about the subject.[27]

With a song written with Carrie Newcomer, Palmer expresses how, in the midst of writing words, he has learned to hear the sound of the soul, which is what gives anyone clues about their vocation:

23. Palmer, *Healing the Heart of Democracy.*
24. Palmer, *On the Brink of Everything*, 85.
25. Palmer, *On the Brink of Everything*, 4.
26. Palmer, *On the Brink of Everything*, 91.
27. Palmer, *On the Brink of Everything*, 91.

Two Toasts

To Words and How They Live Between Us . . .
Praise be that this thin mark, this sound
Can form the word that takes on flesh
To enter where no flesh can go
To fill each other's emptiness
To the words and how they live between us

To Us and How We Live Between the Words . . .
And in between the sounds of words
I hear your silent, sounding soul
Where One abides in solitude
Who keeps us one when speech shall go
To the words and how they live between us
To us and how we live between the words . . .[28]

Palmer has brought his feeling of bafflement and his gift of words to the topic of aging, realizing it is one of life's mysteries that faces us all. In being true to his experience of aging, he invites readers to listen to their experience.[29] Two themes in Palmer's writing speak particularly to my soul: the grace of the word *enough* and the generative dance of different generations.

The Grace of Enough

Saint Thomas Aquinas commented, "All that I have written seems like straw to me." This was just three months before his death in 1274. He was not sure if he had done "enough" as he wrestled with the question "Does my life have meaning?" Palmer admits he asks the same question, and more often as he grows older. I will never have the fame or impact of Aquinas or Palmer, but I ask the same questions about where my significance lies. This leads me to ask how the church, when it is functioning generatively, can help me and others with the grace of *enough*.

Part of the gift of a generative church to all generations is to affirm our "enoughness" in at least two ways. First, community can help us with framing our lives as enough when it practices encouragement. We can be

28. Parker J. Palmer (words) and Carrie Newcomer (music), "Two Toasts," https://www.newcomerpalmer.com/contact-growing-edge/; Palmer, *On the Brink of Everything*, 184.

29. Palmer, *On the Brink of Everything*, 6.

encouraged through the recognition of our contributions and through notes of appreciation.[30] My church is generous with encouragement and mutual support of me as a pastor. One Sunday, as Tara Reid spoke on inspiration, she finished with some words of encouragement for me and then invited others to add their encouragement. I regularly return to those words in my journal. Leaders need the mutuality of being encouraged even as we encourage others. We all thrive when affirmed and encouraged.

Nevertheless, reassurance from others is insufficient to bring us to a feeling of *enoughness*. Relying on the affirmation of others, or as Palmer says, dwelling on the question of whether our life has meaning, does not necessarily lead in helpful directions. What is liberating, Palmer suggests, is realizing we may not understand where our meaning and influence most lies, but being content to be who we are, as one among many, and not needing to stand out.[31] This second element of community—celebrating that we are a part of a community without needing to compare and contrast ourselves—can also foster a sense of contentment or enoughness. In a cultural context where people are often preoccupied with building their significance by accumulating more, doing more, earning more, buying more, or experiencing more, a generative church can counterculturally remind people that they are enough without having to be more than their neighbors.

The self-therapy of Palmer's poetry points me in generous, gracious, life-giving directions rather than driven, accumulative, life-draining ruts. Palmer wrote these lines after observing a plowed field:

Harrowing

The low has savaged this sweet field
Misshapen clods of earth kicked up
Rocks and twisted roots exposed to view
Last year's growth demolished by the blade.

I have plowed my life this way
Turned over a whole history
Looking for the roots of what went wrong
Until my face is ravaged, furrowed, scarred.

Enough. The job is done.
Whatever's been uprooted, let it be

30. Palmer, *On the Brink of Everything*, 17–18.
31. Palmer, *On the Brink of Everything*, 18–20.

Seedbed for the growing that's to come.
I plowed to unearth last year's reasons—

The farmer plows to plant a greening season.[32]

Of all Palmer's books, poems, and words, he asserts the most important sentence is that one word, "Enough."[33]

"Enough" is a bold word of contentment and sufficiency in the face of expectations. It is a word we need in our aging toolbox as we navigate a materialistic society. One of the questions that baffles Palmer is "Why do so many affluent Americans who have more money and material goods than they need never feel that they have enough?"[34] We assert *enough* against society's pressure to accumulate more. It is also a word we need in our overworked and all too often workaholic culture. This drivenness can emerge for our own internal pressures and/or the expectations of others, including forgotten subconscious narratives learned in childhood such as the message I was often given, "You are a good worker, Darren." Grace says, instead, that you are good not just because of your work ethic. Palmer cites Merton in warning against the contemporary violence of overwork:

> The rush and pressure of modern life are a form, perhaps the most common form, of its innate violence. To allow oneself to be carried away by a multitude of conflicting concerns, to surrender to too many demands, to commit oneself to too many projects, to want to help everyone in everything is to succumb to violence. The frenzy of the activist . . . destroys the fruitfulness . . . because it kills the root of inner wisdom which makes work more fruitful.[35]

We need our work—its nature and focus, and what we expect of it and ourselves—to emerge from the sanctuary of our inner wisdom or essence of our soul and what we are made for. Unfortunately, as Palmer explains, we too often violate the sanctity of our own self or the self of others by seeking to numb the pain of our suffering: "Sometimes we try to numb the pain of suffering in ways that dishonour our souls. We turn to noise, frenzy, nonstop work, and substance abuse as anesthetics that only deepen our suffering."[36]

32. Palmer, *On the Brink of Everything*, 24.

33. Palmer, *On the Brink of Everything*, 24.

34. Palmer, *On the Brink of Everything*, 94.

35. Merton, *Conjectures of a Guilty Bystander*, 81; cited and discussed in Palmer, *On the Brink of Everything*, 139–40.

36. Palmer, *On the Brink of Everything*, 160.

Enough is good news for our soul that we do not have to perform more, or accumulate more, or do more, or be more to be loved by others or to accept ourselves.

The generative church, at its best, can adopt a posture of affirming and celebrating *enoughness* in its emerging generations. As young people grapple with questions of identity and worth, grace is such a critically important message not just to hear preached but to receive and adopt into one's inner soul. There are many voices in society that hammer young people with the message that they are not enough and do not match up—they are not smart enough, beautiful enough, thin enough, hard-working enough, volunteering enough, and even sometimes not old enough. An affirming generative church, in contrast, will be generous with the grace-filled message of enoughness. Moreover, embracing ourselves and the whole of who we are does not have to wait until we are older.[37]

Carrie Newcomer wrote a companion song on perspectives that come with aging. In place of working and worrying, searching, and hurrying, Newcomer describes coming to a new place of forgiveness and wonder. She sings of "all the things that used to matter" not meaning so much; instead by scattering them and letting them be taken away, she finds "there is nothing in my way." Instead of more accumulation being assuring, "less is more" in terms of the grace of enough. The chorus sung three times includes the words:

> This has been too much and little,
> The ache of it bewildering.

Her response in the present moment is "But for now we'll stand together" and then finally "But for now we'll stand in wonder." Reaching "the brink of everything" it suggests there is less of a need to strive and accumulate, and more of a contentment of enoughness and posture of awe:

> **On the Brink of Everything**
>
> Last night I heard a wood thrush calling,
> In the evening like they sing,
> I saw you standing by the water,
> Out on the brink of everything
> On the brink of everything.
>
> Yeah all the things that used to matter,

37. Palmer, *On the Brink of Everything*, 175.

No, they don't mean so much today.
Toss the seeds and let them scatter,
The birds and wind take them away,
'Til there is nothing in my way.

This has been too much and little,
The ache of it bewildering.
But for now we'll stand together.
Here on the brink of everything,
Here on the brink of everything.

I can't see past this horizon,
No, I can't see what's waiting there.
I never sang 'cause I knew something.
I sang because it was a prayer,
The finest one that I could bear.

This has been too much and little,
The ache of it bewildering.
But for now we'll stand together.
Here on the brink of everything,
Here on the brink of everything.

This body has been many things,
It's been rain and snow and earth and dust.
I've worked and worried, searched and hurried.
But now it's just forgiveness.
Now it's just forgiveness.

I'll walk with you as far as I can,
And all we love is all we'll take.
I'll send a postcard when I get there,
Just to say I got there safe,
Just to say I got there safe.

And I won't need no choir of angels,
Just that old song we used to sing.

But for now we'll stand in wonder,
Here on the brink of everything,
Here on the brink of everything.[38]

Palmer acknowledges the presence of mystery and the reality of not knowing everything about anything let alone God: "But for now we'll stand in wonder."

One of Palmer's favorite quotes about not expecting simplicity and easy answers is by Chief Justice Oliver Wendell Holmes: "I wouldn't give a fig for the simplicity on this side of complexity, but for the simplicity on the other side of complexity, I would give my life." One of Palmer's stories is a Celtic story about a monk who died and was buried in the monastery wall. Three days later the other monks heard noises inside the crypt, so they opened it and found their brother resurrected. Amazed, they asked what heaven was like. He replied, "It's nothing at all like the way our theology says it is." Without further talk, they put him back in the wall and resealed it.[39] Palmer comments:

> For me, the constant challenge of both faith and writing is to hold the paradox of the treasure and the earthen vessel with deepest respect. The vessels deserve our respect because they give us a chance to protect the treasure, share it with one another, and pass it along to the next generation. But if a vessel begins to obscure the treasure, we must toss it into history's landfill in favor of one that reveals more than it conceals.[40]

Enough applies to dogmatic theology as well as being an antidote for consumerism or workaholism or other addictions that harm our souls.

Palmer helpfully reminds us that *enough* is the most important word of grace in the face of any obsession:

> That word can safeguard the soul, and saying it comes more easily with age. These days I say "enough" without hesitation to anything that's not life-giving—whether it's frenzy and overwork, a personal prejudice, an unhealthy relationship, a societal cruelty or injustice, the feckless exercise of power in fields form religion to politics, or the racism, sexism, xenophobia, and crypto-fascism sickening the US body politic.[41]

38. Carrie Newcomer, "On The Brink of Everything," https://www.newcomerpalmer.com/contact-growing-edge/; https://www.youtube.com/watch?v=7eUuNCddCFg.

39. Palmer, *On the Brink of Everything*, 104–5.

40. Palmer, *On the Brink of Everything*, 105.

41. Palmer, *On the Brink of Everything*, 25.

Enough thus graciously confronts unhealthy personal choices whether driven by internal compulsion or external expectations, but also boldly stands against injustices and discriminations. The word brings a dose of emotional and spiritual balance and health to individuals, but also fosters generativity by not letting injustice and discrimination go without protest.

Where *enough* is not appropriate, however, is to suggest that old age is a season to dial down efforts to change the world and play things safe. Instead, Palmer suggests that, as we age, we are especially called to boldly speak up for things we care about. One advantage of doing that when we are older is that we have even less need to count the cost.[42] We face the choice, as Erik Erikson suggested, of pursuing generativity, of investing for future generations, or the "stagnation" of age that leads to apathy and despair.[43]

Generativity and the Dance of the Generations

Palmer appeals to people of all generations to invest themselves in things that matter for the future of the world. This is why he urges taking on big jobs worth doing, such as spreading justice, peace, and love.[44] When he told graduates to "be reckless when it comes to affairs of the heart," he reassured the parents he was not seeking to corrupt them, but urging them to follow their passions in adopting an interest in some part of the world that matters. He offers the same advice to older generations and urges them to keep engaging with global issues.[45] He reframes aging as creating more rather than less opportunities for contribution: "Old is just another word for nothing left to lose, a time of life to take bigger risks on behalf of the common good."[46]

Palmer says a healthy response to aging which many older folks adopt is to unload material goods that used to be useful but now only clutters up the home. But we also need to jettison psychological junk, or convictions about what gives life meaning that no longer serves us. Palmer counsels not just asking, "What do I want to let go of, and what do I want to *hang on to?*" but more importantly, "What do I want to let go of, and what do I want to *give myself to?*"[47] This latter question is one of generativity.

42. Palmer, *On the Brink of Everything*, 25.

43. McLeod, "Erikson's Stages of Psychosocial Development," 7; cited in Palmer, *On the Brink of Everything*, 25–26, 176.

44. Palmer, *On the Brink of Everything*, 47.

45. Palmer, *On the Brink of Everything*, 45.

46. Palmer, *On the Brink of Everything*, 2.

47. Palmer, *On the Brink of Everything*, 26–27.

As we have explored elsewhere in this book, generativity, as Erikson originally coined the term, involves "an interest in establishing and guiding the next generation."[48] It is about leaving a legacy for the future. It is about making decisions now with the perspective of how those decisions will invest in and affect future generations.

Palmer expands the concept of generativity beyond offering ourselves to emerging generations to also learning from them.[49] He suggests it is not about "passing the baton" as if older people are then no longer responsible for the race, but—to change the metaphor—about inviting younger people to "join the orchestra" and sit together to learn and play the music. The beauty of this exercise in generative music making is that we can learn from one another—older people can help the younger learn their instruments, and the younger can help the older learn the music of their world.[50] Or to change the metaphor again, learning from one another in mutual mentoring is like an ancient dance that moves our hearts and feet to make the world better, as Palmer wrote previously:

> Mentors and apprentices are partners in an ancient human dance, and one of teaching's great rewards is the daily chance it gives us to get back on the dance floor. It is the dance of the spiraling generations, in which the old empower the young with their experience and the young empower the old with new life, reweaving the fabric of the human community as they touch and turn.[51]

Young and old working together are like the two poles of a battery—when joined, different generations generate energy for transformation in an otherwise age-segregated society.[52] They bring benefit to each other. Younger generations can learn and be given fresh opportunities from mentors. Older generations do not just teach but learn from those who are younger, thus gaining fresh energy and perspectives for changing the world.[53] Erikson calls this *generativity*, an alternative to stagnation that leads to despair.

Palmer models a passion for generativity in the context of his own aging. To use the metaphor of the title of his book, as he stands "on the brink of everything" and closer to the end than the start of life, he particularly welcomes the opportunity of giving himself to others:

48. Erikson, *Identity and the Life Cycle*, 97.
49. Palmer, *On the Brink of Everything*, 25–26.
50. Palmer, *On the Brink of Everything*, 33.
51. Palmer, *Courage to Teach*, 26; cited in Palmer, *On the Brink of Everything*, 38.
52. Palmer, *On the Brink of Everything*, 31.
53. Palmer, *On the Brink of Everything*, 176.

I won't be glad to say goodbye to life, to challenges that help me grow, to gifts freely given, or to everyone and everything I love. But I'll be glad to play a bit part in making new life possible for others. That's a prospect that makes life worth dying for.[54]

Bibliography

Buechner, Frederick. *Wishful Thinking: A Seeker's ABC*. San Francisco: HarperOne, 1993.

Cronshaw, Darren J. "Australian Reenvisioning of Theological Education: In Step with the Spirit?" *Australian eJournal of Theology* 18 (2011) 223–35.

Erikson, Erik H. *Identity and the Life Cycle*. New York: Norton, 1959.

Intrator, Sam M. "A Journey of Questions: The Life and Work of Parker J Palmer." In *Living the Questions: Essays Inspired by the Work and Life of Parker J. Palmer*, edited by Sam M. Intrator, xvii–lix. San Francisco: Jossey-Bass, 2005.

McLeod, Saul. "Erik Erikson's Stages of Psychosocial Development." *Simply Psychology* (2013). https://www.simplypsychology.org/Erik-Erikson.html.

Merton, Thomas. *Conjectures of a Guilty Bystander*. New York: Random House, 1965.

Palmer, Parker. *The Active Life: A Spirituality of Work, Creativity, and Caring*. San Francisco: Jossey-Bass, 1999.

———. *The Company of Strangers: Christians and the Renewal of America's Public Life*. New York: Crossroad, 1981.

———. *The Courage to Teach: Exploring the Inner Landscape of a Teacher's Life*. 20th anniversary ed. San Francisco: Jossey-Bass, 2017.

———. *Healing the Heart of Democracy: The Courage to Create a Politics Worthy of the Human Spirit*. San Francisco: Jossey-Bass, 2011.

———. *A Hidden Wholeness: The Journey toward an Undivided Life*. San Francisco: Jossey-Bass, 2004.

———. *Let Your Life Speak: Listening for the Voice of Vocation*. San Francisco: Jossey-Bass, 2000.

———. *On the Brink of Everything: Grace, Gravity, and Getting Old*. Oakland, CA: Berrett-Koehler, 2018.

———. *The Promise of Paradox: A Celebration of Contradictions in the Christian Life*. Notre Dame: Ave Maria, 1980.

———. *To Know as We Are Known: Education as a Spiritual Journey*. New York: Harper & Row, 1983.

Palmer, Parker, and Megan Scribner. *The Courage to Teach Guide for Reflection and Renewal*. 20th anniversary ed. San Francisco, Jossey-Bass, 2017.

Palmer, Parker, et al. *The Heart of Higher Education: A Call to Renewal*. San Francisco: Jossey-Bass, 2010.

54. Palmer, *On the Brink of Everything*, 181.

Questions for Reflection and Discussion

1. Would you consider your church to be one that encourages, empowers, and equips adults to live generatively? Why or why not?
2. In this chapter, Cronshaw reflects upon Parker Palmer as someone who has exhibited a commitment to live generatively. As you think about the people who have been influential in your life over the years, who would you identify as individuals who have been exceptional models of generativity?
3. As you contemplate your own vocational journey, what are some specific ways that you have been called to invest yourself generatively for the benefit of emerging generations?

Conclusion

The Generative Church

Cory Seibel

David's Problem

King David was advanced in years. Throughout much of his life, this man had been passionate about worshiping God. This passion is evident in the many psalms that he penned and the biblical picture of him exuberantly leading the nation of Israel in worship (2 Sam 6). It also led him to desire to provide a "home" for the Lord. As he expresses in 1 Chronicles 17:1, "Here I am, living in a house of cedar, while the ark of the covenant of the Lord is under a tent." As he approached the end of his life, building the temple became perhaps his supreme aspiration (1 Chr 17:16–27).

Despite possessing this great desire, we are told that David was prevented by the Lord from taking on this project. Because his hands had been polluted by war, this was not to be his role: "But this word of the Lord came to me: 'You have shed much blood and have fought many wars. You are not to build a house for my Name, because you have shed much blood on the earth in my sight'" (1 Chr 22:7). God instead revealed to David that the building of the temple was to be accomplished in the next generation by his son Solomon (1 Chr 22:9–10). How did David choose to respond to this news? With resentment? By washing his hands of this goal? By stating, "Fine, then let Solomon figure it out for himself"?

David's Response

Scholars estimate that Solomon was between fourteen and twenty years old when he assumed the throne; J. Barton Payne argues that he likely was closer to twenty.[1] Upon becoming king, this young man would bear immense responsibility. Recognizing this, David chose to help set the stage for what God intended to accomplish in the next generation. As 1 Chronicles 22:5 records, "David said, 'My son Solomon is young and inexperienced, and the house to be built for the Lord should be of great magnificence and fame and splendor in the sight of all the nations. Therefore I will make preparations for it.' So David made extensive preparations before his death." I will reflect briefly here upon the specific preparations made by this aged ruler.

First, David passed along a compelling *vision* of the project to his son (1 Chr 22:11–13, 17–19). This vision included an account of the LORD's *purpose*, assurance of the LORD's ongoing *presence*, and anticipation of the LORD's *provision*. This provision included not only the resources needed for this grand construction project, but also the "discretion and understanding" Solomon would need in reigning over his people (1 Chr 22:12). As Michael Wilcock reflects, this discretion and understanding would become Solomon's gifts. As he explains, "They are gifts in the sense that Solomon will give them, devote them, to the building of the temple. But they are also gifts to be given to him in the first place. It is the Lord who will declare him to be a man of peace and will grant him discretion and understanding."[2]

Second, David also passed along the *plans* that the Spirit of God had given him, making it clear that it would be Solomon's responsibility to carry it out to completion (1 Chr 28:11–21). David essentially indicated that he had written blueprints of the plan that had been revealed to him (1 Chr 28:19). However, the existence of these plans did not seem to preclude the possibility of Solomon introducing his own ideas into the design. As Wilcock states, "The building became known as 'Solomon's Temple,' and he clearly left on it the imprint of his own imagination; so either the plan handed down to him accorded exactly with what he wanted to do anyway, or else the details laid down left him sufficient freedom to express the exuberant mind which the older history attributes to him (1 Ki. 4:29–34)."[3]

Third, David also gathered the *resources* that would be needed for the accomplishment of this project (1 Chr 29:1–20). He called upon others to do the same (vv. 1–9). From David's perspective, these resources had been

1. Payne, "1, 2 Chronicles," 411.
2. Wilcock, *Message of Chronicles*, 94.
3. Wilcock, *Message of Chronicles*, 110.

provided from God's hand (vv. 10–16); the gathering of such resources for the temple would be merely a matter of stewarding what already belonged to God (v. 16). According to 1 Chronicles 29:6, "the leaders of families, the officers of the tribes of Israel, the commanders of thousands and commanders of hundreds, and the officials in charge of the king's work" joined in contributing resources for the temple project and "gave willingly."

Finally, David set the whole project within an intergenerational context of relationship with God and participation in what God was doing: "Lord, the God of our fathers Abraham, Isaac and Israel, keep these desires and thoughts in the hearts of your people forever, and keep their hearts loyal to you. And give my son Solomon the wholehearted devotion to keep your commands, statutes and decrees and to do everything to build the palatial structure for which I have provided" (1 Chr 29:18–19). This intergenerational focus accorded with the desire David expresses in Psalm 102 that God's renown would endure through all generations (v. 12) and that future generations would praise the LORD (v. 18).

In many respects, David was a flawed figure whose failings are well documented within the pages of the Old Testament; he erred "royally" on several occasions. Yet David's posture toward his son's role in the construction of the temple can be affirmed as something he handled well. In David, we see a model of generative faith, a confidence in God and what God desired to do that moved him to invest in God's work among the next generation. This generative faith helped make possible the continuation of a God-given dream and its realization within the next generation.

Our Situation

Our contemporary world provides another intriguing picture of a grand intergenerational building project. The Basílica de la Sagrada Família in Barcelona is an enormous cathedral designed by the Spanish architect Antoni Gaudí, who died in 1926. Although the structure remains incomplete, it has already been designated as a UNESCO World Heritage Site. Construction of Sagrada Família began in 1882. Gaudí devoted the last years of his life to the project. At the time of his death at age seventy-three, less than a quarter of the project was complete. Sagrada Familia's construction progressed slowly due to its reliance on private donations and the disruption posed by the Spanish Civil War. Work on the structure resumed with intermittent progress in the 1950s. Construction finally passed the midpoint in 2010. The anticipated completion date of this project is 2026, the one-hundred-year anniversary of Gaudí's death. Much like in David's day, the pursuit of this goal has required the sustaining of vision, the passing along of plans, and the gathering of resources across many generations.[4] It has challenged each generation to contend with a sense of incompleteness and to invite the next generation to join them in carrying on the work.

In a very real sense, this intergenerational challenge is not unique to the people of Barcelona. In this book, we have been exploring the reality that we, too, are involved in a "building project" that spans generations. Each succeeding generation within the church is called to participate in the kingdom that God is building in this world.[5] However, this project will never be completed in its entirety until we experience the culmination of all things in Christ. Thus, as has been the case for every generation of Christians that preceded us, we must recognize that it extends beyond us into the generations to come.

Like King David, we must decide how we will choose to respond to this reality. We could act as though it is not necessary to think intergenerationally about our calling. The current generation of leaders could simply choose to assert, "We've got this," thus falling prey to the illusion that we are capable of ushering in the reign of God in its fullness or that the reign of God is somehow synonymous with our generational "building" project. Or existing leaders might determine that the next generation will need to figure things out for themselves in their own good time and dismissively leave them to their own devices.

In Acts 13:36, the Apostle Paul asserts that David was deeply immersed in the project that God desired to accomplish within his generation: "Now when David had served God's purpose in his own generation, he fell asleep; he was buried with his ancestors and his body decayed." While this may be so, David was not exclusively preoccupied with this generational agenda.

4. "History of the Basílica," http://www.sagradafamilia.org/en/history-of-the-temple/.

5. Craig Van Gelder provides an important point of clarification that is worth mentioning here: "It is interesting to listen to the words used to discuss the church's relationship to the kingdom of God. It is not uncommon to hear such concepts as 'the church is responsible to build the kingdom of God,' or 'the church is to extend God's kingdom in the world,' or 'the church must promote the work of the kingdom of God,' or 'the church is to help establish God's kingdom in the world.' These images of build, extend, promote, and establish stand in sharp contrast to the biblical language used to define the relationship of the church to the kingdom of God. The biblical language places emphasis on our response to God's redemptive reign. The words most commonly used are receive, enter, seek, and inherit. . . . The church does not possess God's reign, it is to be possessed by it. This makes the church an agent of the kingdom. Its nature, its very existence, stems from the presence of the kingdom. Its ministry, what it does, is an expression of God's redemptive work in the world" (Van Gelder, *Essence of the Church*, 87–88).

As we have seen, he also took intentional steps to help the next generation fulfill its God-give purpose.

We too surely desire to serve the purposes of God in our own generation. Many of us are deeply engaged in this pursuit in a variety of ways. Like David, however, we are called to exercise generative faith. This is expressed poignantly in Psalm 78:2b–7:

> I will open my mouth with a parable;
> I will utter hidden things, things from of old—
> things we have heard and known,
> things our ancestors have told us.
> We will not hide them from their descendants;
> we will tell the next generation
> the praiseworthy deeds of the Lord,
> his power, and the wonders he has done.
> He decreed statutes for Jacob
> and established the law in Israel,
> which he commanded our ancestors
> to teach their children,
> so the next generation would know them,
> even the children yet to be born,
> and they in turn would tell their children.
> Then they would put their trust in God
> and would not forget his deeds
> but would keep his commands.

As I noted in my introductory chapter, some churches unfortunately lose sight of their calling to remain generatively concerned for rising generations. Fostering the congregational virtue of generativity requires intentionality.[6]

6. In their book, *Generations*, Strauss and Howe provide an intriguing historical anecdote that is relevant to this point. They describe how the first generations of Puritans that arrived in America were so preoccupied with "messianic visions" that their offspring "understood that no one cared much about their welfare" (133). With time, "Puritan parents and leaders raged over the apathy of the younger Cavalier generation who seemed perversely reluctant to join their churches" (127). They add, "Spiritual self-absorption was both the strength and the weakness" of the first generation of Puritans. "It gave the Puritans the confidence to plant the first successful colonies in the American wilderness. Yet it did so by making them think they were building the only perfect society since Adam's Fall. New Jerusalem was a project the next generation would not understand—and would secretly resent." As a result, "their punishment was to see, among the devils attacking Eden, the faces of their firstborn" (128). Clearly, the

Investing Generatively Today

What steps then should we take to invest generative faith in the next generation? The authors who have contributed to this volume have provided many insights that are helpful to us in answering this question. As I conclude our contribution to this discussion, I will seek to offer a few summarizing reflections here in conversation with the story of David and Solomon.

First, like David, a generative church will try to impart to the next generation a compelling *vision* of what God is doing and how God desires to involve them. Much research on today's younger generations demonstrates that they possess a desire to participate in a purpose greater than themselves.[7] We are presented with the opportunity to invite the next generation to discover what God wishes to continue through them. Like David, we can offer them assurance that, just as we have experienced God's faithfulness over the course of our lives, they too will be blessed by the Lord's purpose, presence, and provision. A generative church will possess the confidence that the sovereign God, the One whose "dominion endures through all generations" (Ps 145:13), is already in the process of providing everything the members of rising generations need, including—and especially—spiritual gifts. As Dori Grinenko Baker and Katherine Turpin express, we bear a responsibility to *notice*, *name*, and *nurture* what we see God forming in them.[8]

Second, it is important for us to entrust to the members of rising generations the *plans* for continuing God's work. We must strive to pass along all we have discerned about the purposes to which God has called us. We also must encourage them to recognize the cruciality of understanding and serving God's redemptive program as best we have come to understand it. However, as with *Solomon's* temple, the members of rising generations must be permitted to leave their distinctive imprint upon this unfolding project, as we have been. This is not always easy; a great deal of heartache has been visited upon local churches in recent decades because of power struggles over the question of which generation's plans will be allowed to win the day.[9]

Puritans were deeply intentional in many respects but perhaps lacked intentionality in relation to their own children.

7. There is no shortage of recent publications providing evidence of this desire among the members of the Millennial generation. A few selected examples include Blakeney, *Ready for More*; Bush and Wason, *Millennials and the Mission of God*; Erlacher, *Millennials in Ministry*; and Raymo and Raymo, *Millennials and Mission*.

8. Baker and Turpin, "Living Together," 91.

9. For an exploration of this issue, see Carroll and Roof, *Bridging Divided Worlds*, and Rendle, *Multigenerational Congregation*. In recent years, several resources have been devoted to exploring the power dynamics between Boomers and Millennials in

As I noted in my introductory chapter, one key aspect of being a generative church is "letting go" of the tradition and the future; each local congregation today that endeavors to invest in rising generations must adopt this posture within the circumstances of their unique contexts.

Third, like David, we are invited to invest *resources* that will help position the next generation to make the kingdom contribution that God intends for them. As Rainer's research shows, one characteristic of dying churches is that their budgets become focused on their own interests; they essentially fail to be generative in how they appropriate their financial resources. Generative churches will pay careful attention to how their commitment to empower rising generations is reflected in their budgets. If they have the means to do so, they might subsidize the cost of summer camp, support youth who participate in mission trips, provide scholarship aid to theological students, or develop an internship program for young leaders. But congregations have many other non-financial resources at their disposal that they can devote to supporting what God is forming in the next generation: time, attention, affirmation, and encouragement. Leaders might even choose to invest some of the power that they possess within the church for the sake of empowering younger people.[10]

As with David, the willingness of generative congregations to invest their resources for the benefit of rising generations is rooted in a steadfast confidence in God's provision. Because they know that the perpetuation of God's "building project" into the next generation is a crucial part of God's plan, they are emboldened by a trust that God will provide what is needed to help position younger people to take their place and fulfill their purpose within God's kingdom.

Finally, much like David, generative churches will view their efforts within an intergenerational context of relationship with God and participation in what God is doing. As Eugene Peterson expresses, "If we are going to learn a life of holiness in the mess of history, we are going to have to prepare for something intergenerational and think in centuries."[11]

This long-range perspective—which Peterson describes as "deep time"—is captured poignantly in a scene from the first episode of the Italian-British television drama series, *Medici: Masters of Florence*. This series, which is set nearly six hundred years ago, focuses upon one of the most prominent families of medieval Florence. During one scene, the father of

---

the church; see, e.g., Sider and Lowe, *Future of Our Faith*.

10. This is the core argument in Powell et al.'s second chapter in *Growing Young*, "Unlock Keychain Leadership" (50–87).

11. Peterson, *Contemplative Pastor*, 47.

the family, Giovanni de' Medici, and his son, Cosimo, are seen traveling on a journey through the countryside together. As their conversation unfolds, the topic turns to their city's cathedral, which at this point has sat in a domeless state of incompleteness for many years.

Giovanni initiates the conversation, desiring to test his son's thinking. "Why would the people of our city build a cathedral so enormous there was no way they could complete it?"

Cosimo replies with obvious disdain for what he perceives to be a source of embarrassment for the city he loves. "It was folly. Their ambition exceeded their ability," he exclaims.

"They knew it was impossible. The cathedral is too grand, too glorious," Giovanni fires back, determined to challenge his son's thinking.

Cosimo reacts to this with incredulity. "If they knew it could not be completed, why build it?"

Giovanni responds gently, "Because they had dreams, Cosimo, that God would produce future generations clever enough to realize those dreams."[12]

These thoughts bear great similarity to the vision that has been expressed throughout this volume: a confident hope that God is raising up future generations through whom the divine dream for humanity and all of creation will be continued. It is my prayer that every church will find itself captivated and compelled by such dreams, as well. May these prophetic words from David in Psalm 22:30–31 become our reality:

> Posterity will serve him;
> future generations will be told about the Lord.
> They will proclaim his righteousness,
> declaring to a people yet unborn:
> He has done it!

Bibliography

Blakeney, Sara. *Ready for More: How Millennials Like You Are Destined to Change the Church.* Grand Rapids: Credo, 2015.

Bush, Andrew F., and Carolyn C. Wason. *Millennials and the Mission of God: A Prophetic Dialogue.* Eugene, OR: Wipf & Stock, 2017.

Carroll, Jackson W., and Wade Clark Roof. *Bridging Divided Worlds: Generational Cultures in Congregations.* San Francisco: Jossey-Bass, 2002.

12. "Original Sin," episode 1 of *Medici: Masters of Florence*, directed by Christian Duguay and Sergio Mimica-Gezzan, written by Frank Spotnitz and Nicholas Meyer (Netflix, December 9, 2016).

Erlacher, Jolene Cassellius. *Millennials in Ministry*. Valley Forge, PA: Judson, 2014.

Grinenko, Dori Baker, and Katherine Turpin. "Living Together: When Radical Welcome Reaches Out to an Interfaith World." In *Greenhouses of Hope: Congregations Growing Young Leaders Who Will Change the World*, edited by Dori Grinenko Baker, 83–105. Herndon, VA: Alban Institute, 2010.

Payne, J. Barton. "1, 2 Chronicles." In *The Expositor's Bible Commentary*, vol. 4, edited by Frank E. Gaebelein, 303–562. Grand Rapids: Zondervan, 1988.

Peterson, Eugene. *The Contemplative Pastor: Returning to the Art of Spiritual Direction*. Grand Rapids: Eerdmans, 1989.

Powell, Kara, et al. *Growing Young: 6 Essential Strategies to Help Young People Discover and Love Your Church*. Grand Rapids: Baker, 2016.

Raymo, Jim, and Judy Raymo. *Millennials and Mission: A Generation Faces a Global Challenge*. Pasadena, CA: William Carey Library, 2014.

Rendle, Gil. *The Multigenerational Congregation: Meeting the Leadership Challenge*. Bethesda, MD: Alban Institute, 2002.

Sider, Ronald J., and Ben Lowe. *The Future of Our Faith: An Intergenerational Conversation on Critical Issues Facing the Church*. Grand Rapids: Brazos, 2016.

Strauss, William, and Neil Howe. *Generations: The History of America's Future, 1584 to 2069*. New York: Quill, 1991.

Van Gelder, Craig. *The Essence of the Church: A Community Created by the Spirit*. Grand Rapids: Baker, 2000.

Wilcock, Michael. *The Message of Chronicles*. Bible Speaks Today. Downers Grove: InterVarsity, 1987.